ESPECIALLY for MORMONS

VOLUME FIVE

Stan and Sharon Miller
Sherm and Peggy Fugal

Kellirae Arts
Provo, Utah

10th Printing, 1998

© Copyright 1987

KELLIRAE ARTS

P.O. BOX 300

PROVO, UTAH 84603

DEDICATION TO THE BOY SCOUTS OF AMERICA

In 1980, because of a new high council appointment, I was thrust headlong into adult leadership in the Boy Scouts of America. It's not an assignment I wanted or sought, and I didn't understand a thing about it. But I had it, and I determined to make the best of it.

My first assignment was to visit a certain unit in our stake to see whether it was functioning properly. I was lost.

How I got from there to here is a long story, but today I have experienced a real "conversion" to this great program. I now know why the Church has adopted Boy Scouting as the official activity program of the Aaronic Priesthood in the United States, Canada, and several other parts of the world.

Like most programs, however, Scouting is usually under-funded. Providing meaningful outdoor programs for boys takes money. There are camps to build, equip, and staff; leaders to support; advancements to achieve; local units to operate; and, most importantly, boys to love. And it all takes money.

A large part of the operating money for a local troop should come from the efforts of the boys themselves. But they can't do it all. And the boys contribute very little toward the function of their support organizations on the district and council levels.

With this in mind, earnings from this volume of Especially for Mormons will be shared with the Boy Scouts of America, with special instructions that the money be used directly for the benefit of the boys: a new canoe for the Scout camp, a shelter for a campsite, a Dutch oven for the troop, and so on.

Today's boys are tomorrow's Melchizedek Priesthood leaders. Scouting, operating properly as an arm of the priesthood, will have great effect on the future of the kingdom of God. This is money well spent.

ACKNOWLEDGEMENTS

In this, as in previous volumes, as permissions have been secured every effort has been made to acknowledge the contributor of each entry. Deep appreciation is expressed to each person whose writings appear herein. We are sure each shares our desire to have his writings reach and inspire as many people as possible.

With this volume, as well as those previously published, many have helped, suggested, and encouraged. Thanks are especially due to Beverly Martin, Barbara Werrett Nielsen, Frankie Barlow and many others who helped in gathering the materials contained within these pages. Credit should also be given to Kathryn Frandsen, Lori Johnson and Grant White for editing, indexing and typesetting.

But the biggest debt of appreciation is due to each of you who read and use these writings. It is for you that this book is created.

Stan and Sharon Miller
Sherm and Peggy Fugal

MODERN-DAY PARABLES

Recently I learned of a BYU study concerning sacrament meeting speakers. In the Church of Jesus Christ of Latter-day Saints, where all members speak and teach, there is a great variety of abilities, styles, and degrees of effectiveness. That's great--it provides all members with opportunities to share testimonies, knowledge, and experiences and to experience development and growth.

But not all sacrament meeting speakers are memorable. And, according to the BYU study, people remember principles taught in parables far better than those taught in any other way.

What is a parable? It's usually a story or poem that teaches a righteous principle. Parables are usually found in your own experiences.

The Savior taught the greatest lessons of mortality by telling about real-life experiences that everyone could understand. The wonderful thing about his stories is that they continue to teach long after he originally told them. Those stories have been told over and over, each time reinforcing the righteous principles he taught two thousand years ago.

The same thing happens in sacrament meeting and in class: when the speaker tells a story, the people listen. It's that simple. And the stories are remembered.

It was parables that prompted <u>Especially for Mormons.</u>

How?

When I was young, my family lived in a ward comprised mostly of elderly people. I remember attending a seemingly endless blur of classes and sacrament meetings taught by people who delighted in talking about their grandchildren, quoting scriptures from memory, and expounding gospel principles with enthusiasm. But I was bored.

I remember once, with all my seven-year-old wisdom, telling my mother that I didn't like sacrament meetings anymore because the speakers always said the same things. She patiently explained why I needed to keep attending, but I wasn't convinced.

Then one Sunday a miracle happened in my young life. I actually listened and enjoyed a sacrament meeting! I told my mother on the way home that it sure was a good meeting, and she asked why I liked it so much. I didn't know. But the next day at dinner, we talked about a story the speaker had told.

"That's it!" I shouted.

"That's what?" asked my dad.

"That's why I liked Church so much yesterday. The guy told lots of stories. Remember the one about. . . ."

That night I made a resolve. If I ever got a chance to speak in a meeting, I was going to tell stories so all the kids would listen. In that momentous sacrament meeting, I had been touched by a story. The Holy Ghost, for perhaps the first time, had spoken to my heart--and I liked it! I wanted more. And if stories were the avenue to the spirit, I was going to have stories.

When I was about twelve, I began collecting stories and other writings I liked. By age sixteen or seventeen, I had boxes full. It was a real hobby, as well as a challenge to get them all. I wanted every faith-promoting story ever written. Of course, that didn't happen--and it never will!--but I learned another interesting thing.

I learned that almost everyone has had at least one or two experiences that, if told properly, can spiritually reinforce some gospel principle. Relatively few of those experiences, however, are told. I thank God for those that have been shared. These volumes of Especially for Mormons are dedicated to sharing those stories--especially those that may never be published elsewhere. I have received hundreds of letters from Church members everywhere containing stories or poems or saying born from personal experience. Each of these is a modern-day parable, and this book brings them to you.

                    Stan and Sharon Miller
                    Sherm and Peggy Fugal

CONTENTS

AMERICA

THE MEANING OF THE PLEDGE OF ALLEGIANCE

When you pledge allegiance to your flag, you promise loyalty and devotion to your nation. Each word has a deep meaning:

"I pledge allegiance" (I promise to be true) "to the flag" (to the sign of our country) "of the United States of America" (a country made up of fifty states, each with certain rights of its own) "and to the Republic" (a country where the people elect others to make laws for them) "for which it stands" (the flag means the country), "one nation under God" (a country whose people believe in a supreme being), "indivisible" (the country cannot be split into parts), "with liberty and justice" (with freedom and fairness) "for all" (for each person in this country, both you and me).

*****

WHY I LOVE HER

You ask me why I love her? Well, give me time and I'll explain!
Have you seen a Kansas sunset or an Arizona rain?
Have you drifted on a bayou down Louisiana way?
Have you seen the cold fog drifting over San Francisco Bay?

Have you heard a bobwhite calling in the Carolina pines?
Or heard the whistle of a diesel at the Appalacia mines?
Does the call of the Niagra thrill you when you hear her waters roar?
Do you look with awe and wonder at her Massachusetts shore
Where men who braved a hard new world first stepped on Plymouth Rock?
And do you think about them when you stroll a New York City dock?

Have you seen a snowflake drifting in the Rockies way up high?
Have you seen the sun come blazing from a bright Nevada sky?
Do you hail to the Columbia as she rushed out to the sea?
Or bow your head at Gettysburg. . .at our struggle to be free?

Have you seen the mighty Tetons? Have you watched an eagle soar?
Have you seen the Mississippi roll along Missouri's shore?
Have you felt a chill at Michigan, when on a winter's day
Her waters rage along the shore in thunderous display?

Does the word "aloha" make you warm? Do you stare in disbelief
When you see the surf come roaring in at Waimea Reef?
From Alaska's cold to the Everglades, from the Rio Grande to Maine,
My heart cries out, my pulse runs fast, at the might of her domain.

You ask me why I love her? I've a million reasons why!
My beautiful America. . .beneath God's wide, wide sky!

*****

WHO MADE OUR FLAG?

Who made this banner that floats on high?
Who made this flag against the sky?
Who tore it from the tyrant's yoke?
Who bore it through the fire and smoke?
Who raised it to a lofty height?
Whom did it clothe in dark of night?
Who fought for it, and died for it?
Who are dying now to believe in it?
We will tell you.
We will tell you.
Betsy.
Betsy Ross. You know her, too.
Not Betsy Ross alone, but hundreds of--
Annas, Carolees, Jennys, and Sues,
Lindsays, Sherrys, and Amandas, too.
Michaels and Davids and Chris's and Johns,
Phillips, Brandons, Jareds, and Toms.
All these boys and girls, from every street and slum,
From every town and home.
Italian, German, French, and Swede,
Russian, Polish, Turk, and Greek.
Protestant, Mormon, Catholic, 'tis said,
White, yellow, black, and red.
And many more too long to tell,
But all of you do know them well.
All these Americans helped to sew
A tiny stitch in the flag we know.
Its stars and stripes belong to all;
Exclude just one, and the flag will fall.
But we won't think to soil it so;
We will keep it still aglow
With freedom in its every bar
And tolerance in every star.
We thank you, then, oh men of old
Who made this flag that we now hold.

*****

THE STAR-SPANGLED BANNER

O say, can you see by the dawn's early light
  What so proudly we hail'd at the twilight's last gleaming,
Whose broad stripes and bright stars, through the perilous fight,
O'er the ramparts we watch'd, were so gallantly streaming?
  And the rocket's red glare, the bombs bursting in air,
  Gave proof through the night that our flag was still there.

O say, does that star-spangled banner yet wave
O'er the land of the free and the home of the brave?

On the shore dimly seen through the mists of the deep,
  Where the foe's haughty host in dread silence reposes,

What is that which the breeze, o'er the towering steep,
As it fitfully blows, half conceals, half discloses?
   Now it catches the gleam of the morning's first beam,
   In full glory reflected now shines on the stream.
'Tis the star-spangled banner--O long may it wave
O'er the land of the free and the home of the brave.

O thus be it e'er when free men shall stand
   Between their lov'd homes and the war's desolation!
Blest with vict'ry and peace may the heav'n-rescued land
   Praise the Pow'r that hath made and preserved us a nation!
   Then conquer we must when our cause it is just,
   And this be our motto--"In God is our trust."
And the star-spangled banner in triumph shall wave
O'er the land of the free and the home of the brave.

--Francis Scott Key

*****

BIRTH OF OUR NATIONAL ANTHEM

No anthem ever written has a more historic, inspiring, and patriotic setting than "The Star-Spangled Banner," which was composed in 1814 when the United States and England were at war. After the British redcoats had burned Washington, the enemy moved on Baltimore, where the soldiers were to attack by land while a powerful British fleet formed for action off Fort McHenry, at the water gates of the city. All during the night of September 13-14, the entire fleet concentrated its fire on the fort, from whose flagpole flew the Star-Spangled Banner.

Francis Scott Key, from the District of Columbia, was held as a captive on one of the British warships. As the battle raged throughout the night, in silence and darkness he paced the deck of the ship, wondering whether the flag he had seen when the fight began was still flying over the fort. It was for him a harrowing night.

At last came the break of day. With strained, eager eyes, through the early-morning mist, he saw that the flag was still there. In patriotic exultation Francis Scott Key, writing on an envelope he had found in his pocket, poured out of his soul the inspiring words of "The Star-Spangled Banner," which later were set to music. Thus the song went forth to sing itself into the hearts of the living generation and of generations to come.

*****

THE FLAG

Having heard that Mrs. Nellie Stocks of Marysvale had received as a gift the flag that draped her son's casket before he was buried in France, he having been killed in action, we sent the lady a letter, a part of which was as follows:

"Madam, I was told they sent you a flag that draped your boy's casket before he was buried in France. I would treasure that flag as a thing almost divine. I would love and fondle its folds and hug it to my bosom as something sacred that should abide with me while life shall last. I would worship every shade and thread of it, and I would never let anything in the world come between me and it. I would keep it in a safe and secret place all to itself, and sometimes when all alone, in the brightness of midday, in the sunset's glow, in the still twilight of a summer's eve, or by the fireside's glow on a wintery night, I would tenderly and lovingly take it forth in the solitude of my chamber and drop a tear onto its folds for my hero boy. Over its shimmering silk I would dote on his memory the boy of my love whom I bore and reared. And ever in the center of that flag I would in fancy frame his picture, and forever keep him and it one and inseparable. And always I would thank Almighty God that my son had the privilege of having his life so nobly woven into the story of his country's flag. I would try to believe that his pulsing blood made the red in that holy banner; that his throbbing soul made the white of it; and that the light of his spirit enters into every star in its field of blue. And the prayer on my lips should be, 'Flag of my heart and flag of my boy, I love you! Wave till the world is free!'"

*****

FREEDOM

On May 25, 1787, fifty-five delegates from the various states met in Philadelphia to discuss the drawing up of a Constitution to take the place of the Articles of Confederation. George Washington presided, and, after a long struggle and many compromises, the resultant document was referred to the several states on September 27. By June 21, 1788, the required nine out of the thirteen states had ratified it, and the new federal government was in effect by President Washington's inauguration at New York on April 30, 1789.

The Preamble

"We, the people of the United States, in order to form a more perfect Union, establish justice, insure domestic tranquility, provide for the common defense, promote the general welfare, and secure the blessings of liberty to ourselves and our posterity, do ordain and establish this Constitution for the United States of America."

Then follow the seven articles of the Constitution, which were finally ratified by all thirteen states.

What are we doing to perpetuate this precious God-inspired document that guarantees our freedom? It is possible that we may lose it.

"Behold, this is a choice land, and whatsoever nation shall possess it shall be free from bondage, and from captivity, and from all other nations under heaven, **if they will but serve the God of the land, who is Jesus Christ,** who hath been manifested by the things which we have written." (Ether 2:12.)

4

Notice the condition which accompanies that prophecy. Both the Jaredites and the Nephites were destroyed because they did not abide by it.

In 1770 Richard Hill bought a huge tract of land between Taneytown and Frederick, Maryland. He dug what proved to be a very choice well which was known far and wide as Richard's Well. He bequeathed a portion of that farm, including the well, to my great-grandfather, James Hill, a revolutionary officer under George Washington. The road between Philadelphia and Washington, D.C., passed right by that farm. George Washington, on his trips between Washington and Philadelphia, used to stop to refresh himself at Richard's Well and to visit with his friends, James Hill and his gracious wife, Ruth McKinney Hill. They often talked about Washington's great concern regarding things the Constitution provided. Apparently, Washington was aware of the dangers to these freedoms which the Constitution of the United States made possible.

"We are in the midst of continuing international crisis. The outlook for world peace and security is dark indeed. The gravity of the world situation is increasing almost daily. The United Nations seems unable to settle the troubles of the world. In truth, we are faced with the hard fact that the United Nations seems to have largely failed in its purpose. Yes, the days ahead are sobering and challenging.

"We live today in an age of peril. It is an age in which we are threatened with the loss not only of wealth and material prosperity, but of something far more precious--our freedom itself. The very thing that distinguishes man from the beasts--his freedom to act, freedom to choose--is threatened as never before by a total and atheistic philosophy of life known as communism."

May all who read this unite in keeping all of God's commandments and in continuous prayer to him for preservation of our freedom.

--George R. Hill

*****

THE FAITH THAT MADE US FREE

Place: The City of New York, British Army Headquarters
Date: September 22, 1776

It is not yet the end of September, but the nights are exceedingly cold here in the open fields on the northern part of New York Island. I have had my orderly build a small fire in front of my tent to give me a little warmth before I go to bed. As I sit before it writing, I look up and see the campfires of the American army on the heights of Harlem, little more than two miles away. For a month now we have been drubbing them unmercifully every time we fight them. Everyone in our army is sure that the war will be over in a month or two. I thought so, too, until this morning. Now I am not so sure. A man named Nathan Hale has changed my mind.

He was captain in the American army. Two weeks ago we drove them out of New York, chasing them across the open fields so disgracefully that one of our officers had his bugler sound the "view halloo"--the hunting call that means fox in sight. After that, their general, Washington, realized that they were doomed unless they had better information about where we planned to attack.

Washington called in the commander of his ranger battalion and told him to recruit a spy from his officers. The rangers were supposed to be the most daring, most enterprising men in the American army. But not a single officer volunteered. One of them told the colonel, "I am willing to go and fight them, but as for going among them and being taken and hung up like a dog, I will not do it." An understandable reaction--a spy's work is the most thankless, the most despised job in war. If he is caught, he dies an ignominious death. If he succeeds, he can take no credit for his exploits.

Yet Hale, when he saw his brother officers hesitate, volunteered. Friends tried to dissuade him. But he was immovable. He had been in the army a year and he felt he had yet to render his country any real service. So he disguised himself as a loyalist Dutch schoolmaster and entered our lines in mid-September.

He traveled throughout Long Island making careful records about the men and fortifications we had there, and then crossed to New York Island, where he did the same thing. He was a diligent spy and had accumulated a mass of valuable information, which he concealed in his shoes. He was caught attempting to pass through our lines, and was led under guard to headquarters. There, General Howe questioned him. Hale made no attempt to deny his mission or conceal his identity. He admitted he was a spy. Under orders from his commander-in-chief, he knew his fate.

The general is a phlegmatic man, seldom given to much emotion. But Hale's manly bearing, the calm resolution with which he comported himself, obviously affected him. There was regret in his voice as he told the young American--Hale was only twenty-one--that the stern rules of war would not allow him to exercise the compassion he felt. Hale was handed over to the provost marshal, who confined him in the greenhouse of the mansion which the general was using for his headquarters.

This morning he was marched here, to the artillery park, which the provost had selected as his place of execution. The marshal, a mean-tempered man named Cunningham, was called away on other business, and Hale was left with his guard to endure a cruel wait. My heart went out to him, and I invited him to take a seat in my marquee.

He was amazingly calm. He asked me for writing materials, with which I gladly supplied him. With an untrembling hand he wrote two letters, one to his brother and another to his colonel, telling them what had happened. He sealed the letters and handed them to me, asking me politely to make sure they reached his intended correspondents. I told him I would do my best, but would have to pass them through the hands of the provost marshal first.

We sat in silence for a moment. Then I asked him how he came to join the rebellion. He told me he had hesitated for several months. He had had an excellent post as a schoolmaster in New London, Connecticut. But he decided that his country's cause would not permit him to be selfish. He spoke at length about the deep sense of gratitude to God which his father, a deeply religious man, had inculcated in all of his nine sons. He described his wonderfully happy boyhood on his father's Connecticut farm and the satisfying years he spent at Yale.

For some years at Yale, he said, he considered devoting his life to the ministry, hoping to persuade others to feel the same grateful sense of God's abundance he did. But another brother was already a notable preacher, and Hale decided he could serve his country equally well as a schoolteacher, planting the seeds of knowledge in young people.

He felt that he had been successful to some extent as a teacher. Many of his pupils corresponded with him during the year he had spent in the army. Looking back on his short life, he could honestly say he had no regrets about anything he had done, even this last role as a spy.

I found myself vexed--no, more than vexed--troubled by the serene certainty with which he spoke those words. "No regrets?" I asked. "None? Not even when you think of all the pupils you will never teach, of the years you spent at study, preparing yourself for a long and useful life? If you had remained neutral, as many of your countrymen have, you would still be able to look forward to a long, happy life."

"I cannot see how such a life would be happy if it was spent in self-reproach, in tortures of conscience," he replied. "My brother Enoch is up there," he continued, gesturing toward the heights of Harlem. "He's in the army at this moment. If he suffered my fate--or the fate of a soldier in battle--while I sat snug in New London? No, Captain Montresor, I had no other choice."

"But you cannot hope to win this war. Isn't that apparent by now? Wasn't that part of the reason you hesitated?"

"I only hesitated because I wanted to make sure in my own mind that my country's cause was a just one," he replied. "Once that was clear, once I saw that our liberties were truly threatened, my hesitation was over."

"To fight a war you cannot win!" I cried.

"We will see about that, Captain Montresor. The war is not over yet. You have defeated some Americans, but not all of them. The very act of bringing this great army here will, I predict, arouse tens of thousands more Americans to the fact that their liberties are endangered. They will act out of the same depth of feeling, the same conviction that God has not given us this country in vain. It is a trust which we must protect and cherish, no matter what the expense or the sacrifice."

"No regrets, not one," I murmured. I was almost petulant by then, but I was still deeply troubled by my failure to turn this young man's mind away from rebellion.

Striding toward us came the provost marshal, death on his lean, set face. Captain Hale saw him as I spoke. He stood and held out his hand. "Thank you for your kindness, Captain Montresor," he said. I grasped his hand, temporarily overwhelmed. How petty my arguments about rebellion suddenly seemed! "I'm sorry. In a better world, we would have been friends."

"I am going to a better world," he said softly. "I hope I shall meet you there."

Back straight, shoulders set, he walked out of my marquee. The guards shouldered their muskets and surrounded him. The drummer began to beat the death march. I was so agitated I retreated back inside my tent.

Later in the day, after Hale's body had been cut down and buried, I discovered the letters he had written. I took them to the provost marshal, who growled angrily when he saw them. "I don't think we should deliver them," he said.

"Why not?" I asked.

"I don't think anyone should know that the rebels have men who can die with such firmness."

I nodded. I was not about to challenge his considerable authority. But as I turned to go, I could not help asking, "Did Hale say anything before he died?"

"Oh, a pretty little speech," the marshal said. "He said he had been asked if he had any regrets. He had thought about it and found but one-- that this was the only life he had to lose for his country."

--Told by Captain John Montresor,
British Army
Reprinted from Guideposts Magazine

CHARACTER

We are always in the forge or on the anvil. By trials, God is shaping us for higher things.

--Henry Ward Beecher

*****

Poise is defined as the art of raising the eyebrows instead of the roof.

*****

Ability will enable a man to get to the top, but character is the only thing that will keep him there.

*****

The high-minded man must care more for the truth than for what people think.

--Aristotle

*****

The wind of anger blows out the lamp of intelligence.

*****

To err is human--but when the eraser wears out before the pencil does, you are overdoing it.

*****

No matter what you do, someone always knew you would.

*****

If you are patient in one moment of anger, you will escape a hundred days of sorrow.

--Chinese Proverb

*****

There are two things we should learn to forget: the good we have done to others, and the evil they have done to us.

*****

It is considered a good thing to look wise, especially when not overburdened with information.

--J. Golden Kimball

Unless the way we live draws us closer to Heavenly Father and to our fellow men, there will be an enormous emptiness in our lives.

--Spencer W. Kimball

*****

It is trial that proves one thing weak and another strong. A house built on the sand is in fair weather just as good as if built on a rock. A cobweb is as good as the mightiest cable when there is no strain upon it.

*****

To one who said, "I do not believe there is an honest man in the world," another replied, "It is impossible that one man should know all the world, but quite possible that one may know himself."

--Millennial Star

*****

Why were the Saints saints? Because they were cheerful when it was difficult to be cheerful; patient when it was difficult to be patient; and because they pushed on when they wanted to stand still, kept silent when they wanted to talk, and were agreeable when they wanted to be disagreeable. That was all. It was quite simple, and it always will be.

*****

Be small enough to walk with the lowly and not feel superior. Many will agree with this, but few will follow it. Those few will carry the light of everlasting sunshine on their countenances, and man and God will walk with them.

*****

It is not what men eat, but what they digest that makes them strong. It is not what we gain, but what we save that makes us rich. It is not what we read, but what we remember that makes us learn. And it is not what we preach, but what we practice that makes us Christians.

--Francis Bacon

*****

No one is any higher or lower on the scale of righteousness than are his thoughts. They are, therefore, the standard of his morality, the gauge by which his worth to the world is measured. He can, in his mental home, entertain angels or devils, as he sees fit.

--Dallas News

*****

Character is like chiseling a statue: one has to knock off huge hunks of selfishness, which requires self-discipline. Only then does character begin to emerge.

--Fulton J. Sheen

*****

Talk of divinity in man! See how he cowers and sneaks, how vaguely all the day he fears, not being immortal nor divine, but the slave and prisoner of his own opinion of himself. Public opinion is a weak tyrant compared to our own private opinion. What a man thinks of himself, that it is which determines his fate.

--Henry David Thoreau

*****

Behind the light that floods the room with brightness is a powerhouse that generates the current. Without the current, the filament in the bulb would not glow.
Behind every personality is a powerhouse of right thinking and worthwhile purpose. If you would spread light in the world, which has all too much darkness, see to it that your ideas and your ideals are the kind that glow.

*****

The. . .commandments are not rules to obey as a personal favor to God. They are the fundamental principles without which mankind cannot live together. They make of those who keep them faithfully strong, wholesome, confident, dedicated men and women. This is because the commandments come from the same divine hand that fashioned our human nature.

--Cecil B. DeMille

*****

To bear up under loss, to fight the bitterness of defeat and the weakness of grief, to be victor over anger, to smile when tears are close, to resist evil men and base instincts, to hate hatred and love love, to go on when it would seem good to die, to seek after the glory and the dream, to look up with unquenchable fath in something evermore about to be--that is what any man can do, and so be great.

--Zane Grey

*****

All the water in the world
However hard it tried
Can never sink the smallest ship
Unless it gets inside.

All the evil in the world
The blackest kind of sin
Can never hurt you the least bit
Unless you let it in.

*****

I can reveal the way I feel
By the things I say and do.
By changing the things I say and do,
I can change my feelings, too.

--Jennie Lou Vance

*****

WHAT KIND OF A MAN AM I?

What kind of a man am I
When I'm all alone,
Gone away on business,
Many miles from home?

When there is an evening free
And no demands at all,
Am I one who will behave,
And go home standing tall?

Lord, I can make a show of faith
And righteousness at home,
But the kind of man I really am
Is when I am alone.

Oh, may I have that strength and power
To be kind and good at home--
A genuinely Christian man
In public, and alone.

--Jay M. Richardson

*****

I took a piece of plastic clay
And idly fashioned it one day,
And as my fingers pressed it still
It moved and yielded to my will.

I came again when days were past;
The bit of clay was hard at last.
The form I shaped it still it bore,
And I could change the form no more.

I took a piece of living clay
And gently formed it day by day,
And molded with my power and art
The young child's soft and yielding heart.

I came again when years were gone
And it was a man I looked upon.
He still that early impression wore,
And I could change him never more.

--Author Unknown

*****

OUR NEEDS

A little more of patience
With the faults of other folks,
A little more of charity
When a worldly act provokes,
A little more devotion
To the ones whom we should love,
A little more reliance
On the God who rules above,
A little more forbearance
With the cross we have to bear,
A little better learning
By all that is right and fair,
A little more of giving
Of the things we have to give--
Would make this world a better place
For you and me to live.

A little less of prejudice,
A little less of hate,
A little less of ridicule
About our good and great,
A little less of vanity,
A little less of show,
A little less of telling
All the scandal that we know,
A little less complaining
O'er the ills we have to bear,
A little less of wickedness,
A little less of sin--
Would make this world a pleasant spot
To be abiding in.

--Charles E. Warner

*****

The story is told of a boy who was a total abstainer and who was about to be apprenticed to a trade. The foreman of the place offered him a glass of beer, but the lad refused, saying he never drank such stuff. Somewhat irritated, the foreman said angrily, "We have no teetotalers in this place!"

"You'll have one if you have me," said the lad. More irritated than ever, the foreman cried, "Look here, boy, you must have this beer inside or outside!"

"Well," answered the little fellow, "you can please yourself, sir. I came here this morning with a clean jacket and a clean character. You can soil my jacket if you like, but you cannot soil my character."

--David O. McKay

*****

President George Albert Smith was known far and wide for his keen interest in his fellow man. Those who knew him believed he would cross a continent to do someone a favor.

Nor did his concern for the proper character traits include just his wide circle of friends. It included, as he so often expressed it, "all our father's children."

On one occasion while his automobile was parked on a street in downtown Salt Lake City, someone stole his auto robe. That night he recorded the incident in his diary, along with the comment, "If I thought the man who took it really needed it, I would have presented it to him, and he would not have been a thief."

*****

SELF-CONTROL

Seneca wrote, "To master oneself is the greatest master."

Aristotle said, "I count him braver who overcomes his desires than him who conquers his enemies, for the hardest victory is the victory over self." And Browning penned, "When the fight begins within himself, a man's worth something."

"The virtue of all achievement is victory over self," wrote A. J. Cronin. And Edgar A. Guest expressed such thoughts in this verse:

"I have to live with myself, and so
I want to be fit for myself to know;
I want to be able, as days go by,
Always to look myself straight in the eye.
I don't want to stand with the setting sun
And hate myself for the things I've done."

Oh, if our young people could learn this basic lesson: to always keep good company, to never be found with those who tend to lower our standards. Let every youth select associates who will keep him on tiptoe, trying to reach the heights.

--Spencer W. Kimball

*****

The human heart is not like a box that will hold just so much, and no more. The heart may be very small--so small as only to embrance one's self in its thoughts and desires--this makes a very mean, selfish person. The heart may be enlarged to embrace a town--this makes a good townsman. Or it may take in one's whole nation--this makes a patriot. Or it may take in all mankind--this makes a philanthropist. Or it may embrace the whole universe and the great Creator of it--this makes one God-like. All the way, its happiness will be in proportion to its enlargement.

--Horace Mann
From "Letter to Young Americans"

*****

A ONCE-TOLD STORY

The story is told that once a young boy was extended an invitation to visit his uncle, who was a lumberjack in the northwest. For months the boy had looked forward with anticipation to this trip as an exciting adventure.

Finally, the time for his journey to the vast timber empire came. His uncle met him at the depot, and as the two pursued their way to the lumber camp, the boy was impressed by the enormous size of the trees on every land. There was a gigantic tree that he observed standing all alone on the top of a small hill. The boy, full of awe, called out excitedly, "Uncle George, look at that big tree! It will make a lot of good lumber, won't it?"

Uncle George shook his head, then replied, "No, son, that tree will not make a lot of good lumber. It might make a lot of lumber, but not a lot of good lumber. When a tree grows off by itself, too many branches grow on it. Those branches produce knots when the tree is cut into lumber. The best lumber comes from trees that grow together in groves. The trees also grow taller and straighter when they grow together."

*****

THE PINE TREES TALK

By a quiet lake in the moonlight, I paused and listened, and this is what the pine trees said to me:

"We have grown tall, because we have grown straight; we have grown big, because we have reached toward the stars. We have learned that the

15

way to increase our height is to keep growing; we have grown strong because we have rooted deep in the good earth. We have been patient, for we have learned that it takes time to grow a great tree; we have faced life bravely as it came, sunshine or storm, snow or rain. We have filled our sphere with the sweet aroma of our needles, and have given shade to those who come our way; we have known the joy of service by sheltering with our branches the nests of birds. We have been still and listened to God, and we have seen his face in the dawning of each new day."

--Wilferd A. Peterson

*****

THE GREAT STONE FACE

In the mountains of New England there lived a little boy named Ernest. He loved to sit at the cottage door with his mother at the close of day and watch the sun set behind the western mountains. The rugged cliffs seemed to have been chiseled by the master into the shape of a human face. So natural were the features that as Ernest gazed, they seemed to smile down upon him in a kindly way.

The people who lived in this mountain valley had been told by the Indians many years earlier that some day a child would be born there who would grow to be a noble and great man, and whose face would resemble the face on the mountain. Little Ernest wondered if he should live to see this man.

As the years went on and Ernest grew to manhood, the Great Stone Face became more and more a part of his life. After the day's work was done, he would look with hope at the face, and it never failed to give him encouragement and comfort. He could not do an unkind act or think an ignoble thought while the Great Stone Face was looking down on him.

Then it was told in the town that Gathergold, a merchant who had gone to the city many years earlier and won a fortune, was to return to the place of his birth. Many people said he was the man who had been foretold so long ago. But when Ernest looked at his harsh, scheming countenance, from which the children shrank in fear, he sadly shook his head. This was not the man.

Then a great soldier who had become known for his bravery as General Blood and Thunder returned to the valley. Again, the people said, "This is he who was foretold." But his stern countenance, bespeaking a man of iron will, lacked the understanding and sympathy of the Great Stone Face.

Years passed. A great statesman, who had lived in the valley as a boy, returned and was heralded as "Old Stony Phiz." His face was more nearly like that on the mountain than the others had been, but it lacked the courage and frankness which shone from the one of stone. Ernest began to wonder if he should live long enough to see the fulfillment of the old prediction.

Ernest was an old man, his hair silver with age. His neighbors had grown to love him and to seek his wise counsel. Even people from outside the valley heard of him and came to hear his words. One day a great poet visited him. As Ernest talked with him, he wondered if at last this was not the man of the Great Stone Face. But, no, the face on the mountain had a depth of character not shown by this man.

The last rays of the setting sun fell upon Ernest's calm face, lighting it with a radiance so beautiful that the poet stared in wonder. His features, so noble and kindly, were surely the same as those of the Great Stone Face. Ernest himself was the long-awaited man.

*****

GEORGE WASHINGTON AND THE COLT

Whatever the facts may be, with this story or George Washington or with the story of the cherry tree, the story is full of truth. The boyish bravado, the sudden determination to conquer the untamed animal, the struggle and final courageous facing of his mother--whom he respected, feared, and, at the same time, loved and trusted--are true to type. Moreover, this story shows the type of boy that is the strongest boy today, and it embodies both physical and spiritual courage.

George Washington's mother had some fine horses, and the finest of all was a young colt. No one had ever ridden it, and it was allowed to gallop about the pasture, doing no work until it should grow to its full size. The colt was to be the best horse on the farm.

One day George and some other boys were playing down in the pasture. They were catching the horses and riding them. They all rode well, but George rode best of all. He was very proud of his riding. "I can ride any horse on the farm," he boasted. "No horse can throw me."

"You can't ride that colt," one of the boys said, pointing to the prized horse.

"Of course I can ride him," George answered, "but my mother allows no one to get on his back."

"How could you hurt him?" they jeered. "He is almost full grown, and you are not heavy. The only reason you won't try is because you know you can't ride him."

George's face flushed angrily, and as the colt galloped past him, he sprang out and caught him by the mane. Then he swung up on his back. They colt was frightened, and rushed around the field, kicking and jumping. George clamped his knees tight to the colt and clung to him. The colt at last reared in the air and fell over backward. George jumped clear of him as he fell, and then stood, waiting for the colt to get up. The colt didn't move. George began to feel frightened. He went over to the horse and tried to make him stand up, but he could not. The colt was dead; he had burst a blood vessel.

17

As George stood looking down at the colt, he began to think of how sorry his mother would be that he had disobeyed her. "She'll never trust me again, either," George thought, miserably. "I should have known better than to be so foolish. I was afraid to have the boys laugh at me. How can I tell my mother?"

The more he thought of it, the harder it seemed. At last, he turned and walked away toward the woods. "I can't tell her," he thought. But suddenly he lifted his head and said, "Nonsense! I'm not a coward! I can tell my mother anything!"

He quickly walked to the house. When he came into his mother's room, she looked up from her sewing and smiled at him. "Where have you been, George?" she asked.

"Down in the pasture, mother," he answered.

"Did you see our young colt? I think we must begin training him soon."

George did not answer for a moment. His mother looked at him and said, "What's the matter, my son?"

"Mother," he said, "the colt is dead."

"Dead?" Mrs. Washington exclaimed. "Why, I saw him just this morning, and he was not sick then."

"It was my fault, mother," George said. Then he told her all that had happened.

Mrs. Washington listened without saying a word. When George had finished, she walked to the window and stood looking out until she had controlled her indignation and disappointment. Then she came over to George.

"My son," she said, "I'm glad you came and told me. Remember, you can always tell your mother anything. You were foolish to mind what the boys said. Never let the remarks of anyone affect you. Do the thing you know to be right, but if you do make a mistake, be brave enough to admit it."

*****

UPON A MOUNTAIN CALLED COURAGE

Some folks say that the day of heroes has passed. Some people say that youth of today don't have the courage young people used to have, but I saw courage displayed just the other day that shined so brightly that it caused my heart to beat faster and my throat to tighten. I felt like rising to my feet and shouting, "Hurray!"

This courage was not shown in the roaring flames of a burning building, nor during a plunge into the icy floodwaters of a roaring river.   It was not displayed during a reckless dash in front of a speeding auto to save a toddling child, nor was it the physical courage to thwart a threatening bully.

It happened instead in a rather common place, for that seems to be where most heroic deeds happen.   It happened in a stake priesthood meeting on a hot July afternoon.   The chapel was filled to overflowing, and the partition doors leading into the cultural hall had been opened to accommodate the many who were in attendance.   A special spirit seemed to be with us that day as our beloved stake president presided over us and conducted the affairs of the stake.

One lad, who appeared to be about the age of a priest, sat in a rather conspicuous place on the stand near the stake presidency.   I had correctly guessed that he was a part of the program, and I sympathized with his contained nervousness prior to being called upon.

Soon the president announced him as the next speaker.   He arose quietly and walked the short distance to the stand.   His outward composure was one of calmness, but my vantage point near the front of the room permitted me to see the quivering hands that told of the fear he had to conquer.   His few notes were held in his hand, hidden behind the pulpit.

Taking a deep breath, he began to speak.   It was quickly obvious that he had spent much time in preparation. An occasional glance at his notes was all that was required. I began to relax a little in my apprehension for him, but about then I noticed that his speech was beginning to get faster and faster.   Words were coming so fast that they were being repeated unnecessarily.   In the middle of the next sentence, he began to stammer.   This increased his nervousness, and finally his stammering rendered him completely speechless.

A sympathetic silence filled the room.   I longed to reassure him or indicate in some way my sympathy and understanding, but, like the others, I waited.   I waited for him to surrender and perhaps try again another day.   It was then that it happened!   I could see him waging an inward battle as he stood there before us.   Finally, almost as if announcing the winner, he squared his shoulders and girded himself to the task, uttering, as nearly as I can recall, these words: "Brethren, I ask for an interest in your faith and prayers, that I might have sureness of speech."

It was as if I had seen a miracle!   He began again to speak--slowly, deliberately, but with sureness and conviction.   His young voice rang out in a message that thrilled my soul.   It is not his words I remember, but, stamped indelibly on my memory is the message of himself.

Somehow, it will never be the same again when I am called upon to perform a task that may seem difficult.   Perhaps I can take a few steps up the same trail blazed by this brave young man, for he had climbed the mount of courage and stood unflinching upon its precipice!

His speech was soon completed. He gathered his notes and turned away from the stand, and for a moment I saw more than a young man in a white shirt. I saw a knight in shining armor with a sword at his side and a token of victory in his hand. The words of a song surged into my mind so strongly that they seemed to be crying out to be heard: "Behold! A royal army, with banner, sword, and shield, is marching forth to conquer, on life's great battlefield; its ranks are filled with soldiers, united, bold, and strong, who follow their commander, and sing their joyful song! Victory! Victory! . . ."

And victory <u>will</u> be their song if the ranks are filled with young men like this.

--Wayne Lynn

CHASTITY

As fire is discovered by its own light, so is virtue by its own excellence.

*****

If you can't find anything else to do, go home. Limit your "parking," no matter where it might be. Say goodnight, and mean it. Set a decently reasonable hour, and stick to it. When the hour is late, the body might be so full of fatigue that poisons that clear thinking will fade out very rapidly. Most mistakes of youth--if not all--are made after midnight.

*****

Remain in places or with people where you are known and familiar. Then you won't forget your ideals and standards. In strange places you might lose your sense of direction, become confused, and do things you would not do in familiar surroundings.

*****

There are some things that never become old-fashioned. The sweetness of a baby is one. The virtue and chastity of manhood is another. Youth is the time to lay the foundation for our homes. I know there are those who tell you that suppression is wrong, but I assure you that self-mastery, not indulgence, is the virtue that contributes to the virility of manhood and to the beauty of womanhood.

*****

FROM MOTHER TO SON

Dear Stephen:

Happy birthday! This is a blessed day to me and so--apart from the gifts and celebrations--I want to write you a special little note. I hope that you will want to keep it for a while and read it over a time or two. I am so grateful for you, Steve. You're full of pranks, but you've never given me cause for real anxiety in all of your seventeen years. I've known right from the beginning that you were honest and sincere--that you were generous and kind and loyal and clean. What more could a mother ask?

In a year or two you will probably be called on a mission. Every day of our lives can be a mission if we make it so. I am conscious that this year or two ahead are here now for us to build courage and faith needed for the future. Good fun and sports and study are important, but most of all now I would like you to remember that life is basically spiritual, and that each of us has the privilege of walking through it with our Heavenly Father, along the way clearly marked by our elder brother and savior, Jesus Christ. This privilege is ours if we are humble, obedient, and clean.

That is one reason why your father and I have always stressed chastity in talking with you children. Satan has great power in the world today, and so, almost side by side with those who strive for righteousness, will be found those who are both deceived and deceiving. . ."designing men" who try to make evil seem good. I am not afraid that you will be fooled by them if you will study diligently and prayerfully and put your trust in God.

The law of chastity has been stated clearly and forcefully in every generation by the prophets of God. Ponder their statements in your heart. Keep your mind clean. Remember that once lost, chastity can never be fully restored. This is one of the reasons why unchastity is such a grievous sin. Remember that your spirit came from God, to whom it will someday return. You hold the priesthood of God, for which someday you must give an accounting. Both spirit and priesthood must be housed in a clean, pure body if you would enjoy eternal life. Unchastity wrecks all three--spirit, priesthood, and body.

Watch the little things that lead to the big things. Choose carefully the girls you date and the boys with whom you pal. Give and merit respect. Bestow reverence on life at its source. Remember who you are. Render each day humble obedience to righteousness, and you need never fear life or death.

Stay clean, my son. It is the beginning and almost the whole of everything that is lovely and happy and worthwhile in this life or in eternity. It is the dearest wish of my heart. Pray for it constantly as I pray for you.

Lovingly,
Mother

*****

TO DAUGHTER FROM DAD

Dear Gayle:

Time for our weekly chat again, and as I sit here wondering what you are doing there at school, I remember the priceless moments you and I have shared talking together. You won't recall, but this delightful woman-to-man, dad-to-daughter tradition had its beginning here in this chair. You sidled up to my knee, peered around my paper, and asked, "Daddy, what's in the temple?" I searched for the words that I prayed would nurture your love for the house of the Lord. I have many times since
purposely talked with you of the temple. And now I answer finally your question of twelve years ago.

The blessings of eternal life and exaltation are in the temple. The unspeakable joys of eternal glories are fleetingly glimpsed. There we contract with the Lord that for the blessing of being raised to his presence, we will live lives of impeccable purity, service, and sacrifice. It was there at the altar of the Lord I held your mother's hand in mine while the priesthood of God made us eternally one. It is there that he who is worthy of you will hold your hand in his.

Many hazards will try your devotion to the gospel and jeopardize your right to go to the temple. The most insidious, the most fearful of all is the hazard of moral uncleanliness. Remember that you belong only to him into whose eternal keeping you place your heart, and into whose hand you place your own in the temple of God. Resist with all your being any infringement of the law of chastity. Call upon your Heavenly Father in earnest prayer to protect you from the undying grief that will stem from moral weakness.

While you were home during Christmas vacation, the house was alive with your spirit. The night Bob Morgan came to take you to the dance, I watched you sweep down the stairs in that beautiful white dress to meet him. You took my breath away. As you paused there on the landing for my appraisal, I thought, "She's like a dream of heaven." I fleetingly remembered the times your mother and I had plead with the Lord during your childhood illnesses to let you live to be such a vision of loveliness. You have lived to be the fulfillment of all your mother and I have worked for-- prayed for. We have been true to you. Be true to yourself.

Goodnight, sweetheart,
Dad

*****

I'M SIXTEEN--FUN'S AHEAD!

Sweet sixteen--it's wonderful! I've waited just ages for this very special year. Now it's arrived, and I'm thrilled about all the fun that's ahead.

I'm thinking especially about dating. I want to have a lot of fun on all the exciting dates that are ahead--school dances, church parties, movies, firesides. Whether I pair off with a special date or go along with the crowd, I want them to be happy, fun occasions--something I'll always remember.

We girls talk about dating a lot, and we've decided it's important to go only with the right kind of boys. I've been thinking more about that lately, and I've decided there are several things I expect from the boy I date.

I like boys who are clean--clean in mind and in body. I like boys who are honest and who love their homes. I like a fellow to respect the priesthood he holds, one who is not ashamed to stand up and say he is a Latter-day Saint.

I want to date fellows with whom you can have fun, but this fun must always be on a high plane. Give me always the boy with high ideals and good moral character. When I become serious with a boy, I want him to have the same ideals I have and to be as clean morally as I am. I want to be respected to the degree that my boyfriend will not start anything that will make either of us sorry. Because of this, I feel that "parking" is a definite evil, especially if you seem to like the person a great deal. You would do things while parked on the side of the highway or in one of the customary parking spots that you would not dream of doing in your own driveway where you would probably be under the eye of your parents or neighbors. In short, I guess I want the boys I date to be reared as I have been.

Yes, I'm sixteen--fun's ahead. The right kind of fun!

*****

WHAT I LIKE IN A GIRL

Frankly, I like a girl who knows how to have good, clean fun! It is a good feeling to know that you can have fun and still be in accord with our Heavenly Father's teachings.

I like a girl I can respect. The girl I eventually become serious with must not be a "second-hand" girl. She must be chaste.

I like a girl who is understanding--one who shows a real concern in what I am and what I do. That will make me always try to be at my best. To make an effort to really understand one's friends, one's parents and family, and one's sweetheart is to exercise the principle of love for mankind that Christ taught.

I appreciate in a girl an attitude of humility in the right things. Humbleness is a part of self-development, and I like a girl who continues to grow and develop in the spiritual and mental fields and who makes use of her talents through service in our Church.

I like a girl who has poise. She doesn't have to be beautiful, but I like her to be clean and well-groomed and to stand tall. A smile is also a must for that special girl.

All these things I like in a girl. Then, too, I guess I like a girl who likes me!

*****

A LETTER TO MY DAUGHTER'S FRIEND

Dear Ned:

You are a fine young man who takes my daughter out quite regularly, and both she and I like you a great deal. Our feelings for you are very different, naturally. She thinks of you as a good friend, and one with whom she has fun, interesting evenings. You call for her, and she dresses in her most attractive clothing and joins you merrily to depart for a show, a dance, or perhaps a party. I stay home and think about you, and my feelings about you are those of "partnership." I am entrusting you with the most precious thing I own. Perhaps that sounds sentimental, but it's true. For years I guarded the tiny person she used to be--fed her the right food, put her to bed for a long night's rest, watched her teeth and temperature and general health, and for what?

I tried to watch her mental health, and the health of the spirit within her as well. I tried to teach her to be fair, honest, and strong, to regard herself as valuable, as something not to be neglected or thrown away carelessly. I don't know how well I succeeded. You'll know far better than I. She'll tell you things she won't tell me--just as I said things to her father that I couldn't have said to my mother. She is something like a gardenia to me--a flower overwhelmingly white and sweet. I'm letting you borrow that flower for a while.

All I ask of you is that you keep it in cool, fresh, clean air, that it might come back to me fresh and sweet and white. If you have ever seen a gardenia brown and shriveled around the edges of the petals, you'll know what I mean. Take care of her for me--I'm trusting you, lad.

Her Mother

*****

WHY I WANT TO GO TO THE TEMPLE

God has given his children on earth many blessings, but the crowning blessing of all is the privilege of going to the temple.

An inscription on the Alberta Temple reads as follows:

Hearts must be pure to come within these walls
Where spreads a feast unknown to festive halls.
Freely partake, for freely God hath given,
And taste the holy joys that tell of heaven.
Here learn of Him who triumphed o'er the grave

And unto men the keys, the kingdom gave;
Joined here by powers that past and present bind,
The living and the dead perfection find.
                    --Orson F. Whitney

As long as I can remember, I have had a desire to go to the temple. Something deep inside me has always warmed and thrilled at the thought of it.

When the time comes for me to choose my companion, I want it said of my "Sir Galahad" that "his strength is as the strength of ten because his heart is pure." I want to kneel with him at the altar in the house of the Lord and be sealed for time and for all eternity. Then all the children we may have through the miracle of birth will be ours forever. My lifelong desire of eternal happiness may then be complete, if we, as partners, live up to the covenants we have made.

Marriage is a serious bond. I want to have the assurance that my home will be built on the rock and not torn apart by every storm that threatens. My children will have the security of being wanted, and will have the blessing of the deep love and tender care of both parents.

--An Eighteen-Year-Old Girl

*****

DISILLUSIONED

I am a disillusioned young man.

Last night I was out with the girl I love--the girl I want to marry, and she allowed me certain intimacies no girl should allow anyone but her husband.

It was my fault. I thought I wanted them. I begged and coaxed, and she gave in because she loves me and wanted to please me and make me happy.

It hasn't made me happy. I am miserable. I realize now that I didn't really want her to give in to me. I hoped she was strong enough to keep saying no.

I wanted a girl I was sure was sweet and clean. I wanted a girl who could keep saying no to me--whom she loves--so I could know positively she would say no to any other boy, too. She is a sweet, good girl, and I am going to marry her--but I will never feel quite the same about her.

From now on, I will be very stern with myself--I am afraid she would let me go all the way if I asked. Then I would hate both of us.

I do want her for my wife, but I want to wait for a husband's privileges until we are married.

I guess women were made with a desire to give and give to make their men happy.

I wish they could realize that sometimes they make us happiest by a good, firm, unyielding "NO."

*****

SOME THOUGHTS ON KEEPING STANDARDS HIGH WHEN DATING

If you want to keep your standards high while dating, rehearse these dozen questions in your mind:

1. Would you want your own children to do the same things you do?

2. Boys, would you like some other boy to treat your sister like you treat girls?

3.   Where should you "draw the line"? Where would you like the person you are to marry to have drawn the line during his or her high school dating days?

4.   Does the one you are to marry have a right to know what kind of life you have led? Suppose you decide to live carelessly for a while, then shape up and marry a wonderful person. When the topic of marriage comes up, that person asks how morally clean you have kept yourself. If you haven't kept your standards high, how will you explain yourself? (Stop right now, and think about exactly how you would say it.)

5.   Make up your mind **before** the situations arise which moral standards you will keep on a date; then, regardless of what temptations arise, your decision is made. You are in control.

6.   Who has a better chance to build a marriage based on trust, loyalty, and happiness--those who keep themselves morally clean, or those who refuse to wait until marriage to display affection?

7.   Review often your goals of marriage, home, and future--and decide what you must and must not do to attain them.

8.   Can you spend your dollar a penny at a time? How much of your dollar is left when you have spent all but the last few pennies? Can you spend virtue in the same way?

9.   Is it true that "no one will know"? You know. Your Father in Heaven knows. The other person involved knows. The devil knows.

10.   No one goes to hell in one jump.

11.   It is a long road back.

12.   When a young man or a young lady starts to shop for a mate, where will you be found--all sparkling clean in the showroom, or a little grimy in the used car lot?

*****

HOW TO SAY **NO** DISCREETLY AND EFFECTIVELY

"Thanks, but no thanks!" That's a phrase so often easier read than said--depending, of course, on the taunts of the crowd and the strength of your willpower in a moment of temptation.

Whether it's an invitation to take a beer "just this once," park on a lonely lane, or break the Sabbath day, a teen must say no gracefully--but still make it stick. The sooner you learn this trick, the better you can use it!

The time to decide anything is not at the moment of crisis, really. You may succeed only in raising a gulp in your throat when a good, firm refusal is just what's needed.

A **no** in any other language may be just as meaningful. But learning to say it in more words than one is a trick you would do well to master. A wise phrase lightly uttered can ease the tension of teasing. A ready answer can steal further temptation. A bit of wit can shift the mood, and your point has been gained without insult or offense.

A holier-than-thou approach not only is unbecoming and uncalled for, but usually adds fuel to a crackling blaze--making the crowd more determined than ever to break down smug defenses.

Your basic reasons for refusal should be well grounded. You should know **why** you don't want to smoke, drink, park, go steady, go slumming, or cheat.

Your refusal should be based on a firm personal conviction arrived at by study, an understanding of gospel principles, observance of the lives of others, self-analysis, and prayer for guidance.

In other words, don't lean your case on "my mother says I can't" or "my Church says no!" Know for yourself. Answer for yourself, and the results will be far better. And don't listen to the foolish suggestion that everyone is doing it. The fact is that not everyone is doing it. In fact, no one with good sense is doing it!

When you get in a spot, try these answers out:

The question: Will you go steady?

Some answers: I'm too young to be buried alive! . . .You deserve a better fate than this. . . .Think it over carefully in the harsh light of day. . . .Do we have any witnesses for an agreement of this kind? . . .Could we make it "steadily"? . . .I like you too much to tie you down. . . .Would we have a joint checking account?

The question: How about a beer (or cigarette)?

Some answers: I'm in training for the Russian ballet. . . .I like raw oysters better. . . .May I have a soda pop instead? . . I can get the same effect inhaling exhaust. . . .Do you want me to get sick right here? . . .Better not--I'd break out in a rash.

The question: Let's head for a lonely lane, hmmmm?

Some answers: Am I **that** dull? . . .What's the matter--are you too tired to drive? . . .You must have me confused with someone else. . . .I turn into a pumpkin at midnight. . . .Let's think of something more original. . . .I've seen the place, and the view is ghastly. . . .I never go there with boys in blue (or whatever color) ties. . . .Did you ever hear the one about (tell your favorite joke). . . .If it's time to park, it's past my bedtime.

*****

THE MOMENT

How long can a boy and a girl simply say, "I love you"?

Without really meaning to, I had fallen into a beautiful and innocent young love. For the first time in my life, I began to feel and give of myself unselfishly. And the boy I had come to love returned twofold any happiness that I may have given him. I guess that is the wonderful thing about true affection.

Through our moments together, our relationship continued to grow into one of deep understanding and mutual respect and trust. Each day that I wore his ring on my finger only added to the love I felt in my heart.

But a feeling of such complete devotion has a funny way of playing tricks on a person. And when you are only seventeen, a year becomes a long time to have been telling a guy, "I love you." So as we shared these deep feelings for each other, we explored the thrills of kisses and carresses together.

I think we always knew that a moment of final decision was inevitable, yet we pushed such serious thoughts to the back of our minds, telling ourselves, "It won't happen to us this time."

But tomorrow always arrives, and our time also came. After months of nights filled with dark roads and searching kisses, we encountered a brick wall that had only one door. We now had a choice to make. It would be so easy to go through that door with the excuse that we were doing it for love, yet we knew we would pay a dear price--our innocence.

Maybe the complete unselfishness I thought we had felt was not so complete after all, for on that night there was something in each of us that made us stop. We knew we would be losing something that could never be replaced, and we just could not bring ourselves to make the sacrifice. Whatever the reason, we didn't open the door that night. But we realized that we could be terribly tempted--and we knew that many nights of temptation lay before us.

We had to find some way of either changing or justifying the thing we were doing. We became aware of one fact--our awful misconception that love and sex are synonymous was on the verge of destroying us. We had begun to forget how to laugh and be happy just that we were together. Tears no longer eased the shame. Words became hollow and meaningless sounds. We needed a solution. Where could we turn?

It is a little ironic that the solution was so simple and was with us all the time. It came along with one of the greatest moments in my relationship with the boy I love. He held me and said, "Let's pray." Only two small words, but they lifted the burden from our shoulders and put it in the hands of someone far, far stronger: the God who had given us these emotions and desires would now guide us in their use.

We found that the road back is not an easy one. Sometimes we stumble and fall, but there is always a firm and gentle hand to pick us up and urge us on our way. We know now that a small part of us died that night, but at the same time a new seed of faith was planted and began to grow.

Perhaps someday, if it is his will, the God who gave us the courage to turn back and keep that beautiful love we held will give us his blessings to return to that door, open it, and really begin our lives together. Until that day, my friend and I have an obligation to keep. We have promised to care for and nourish our young love until the day when it blooms in full--in glory.

--Shirley Tatro

*****

BOYS ALWAYS TELL

One evening a few weeks ago I had just finished addressing the parent/teacher association in one of our San Francisco high schools when I was pulled into a corner by an anxious woman.

"You look worried, Mrs. Howard," I said. "Was it something I said in my remarks?"

"Yes and no," she answered, "but I've been doing some thinking. I'm up against a stone wall with Marjorie. She has a blind spot on this petting business. I've pleaded with her on moral grounds, I've tried to talk like a sister, and she has been given the Dutch uncle approach by her father. She says she's smart enough to keep her fingers from getting burned. She's so terribly proud. . . .I wish you'd talk to her sometime."

"I will," I said, "on one condition--I don't pull any punches." She agreed gladly, and a few days later I went to her home for dinner. Marjorie, a nice, bright girl, suspected why I was there, even though I had known the family for several years. When we were alone later in the evening she said, "All right, Mrs. Sullivan, now you can give me the lecture on petting."

"Not at all, Marjorie. I think you're a fool."

That startled her a little, and I could almost see her defenses stiffen. "What do you mean by that?" she asked resentfully. "You're a fool," I repeated calmly, "because boys always tell." Marjorie looked at me for a moment, and then grinned.

"Well," she said, "that's a new approach."

"You know Patty Blane, don't you?" I went on, ignoring her jauntiness. Marjorie nodded. "Last Saturday night she sat in the back seat of a car at the beach with Eddie Smith for two hours. Last Wednesday she was petting with another boy in the Roof Garden at the Forest Hotel. The week before--"

"Oh. . .I see," Marjorie interrupted angrily. "The police spy squad is out again!"

"No, Marjorie," I said slowly. "The boys talked themselves. They always talk. Eddie tells Bill, Bill tells Jack, and you girls are just verbal footballs for their boasting."

She was thoughtful for a moment, but she wasn't going to be sold so readily. "Maybe they do talk," she said uneasily, "but it's only about girls like Jackie Brown. She necks with everybody."

"How do you know?"

"Well. . .uh. . .because everybody says so," she said, weakly.

"That's just it, Marjorie. I knew Jackie Brown when she first went to your school. She was just as pretty and just as nice as you are. And then some boy talked about her, and she got a lot of dates. The boys talked, one after another. They've done such a good job, she's been talked right out of school. And pretty soon," I continued, "they'll be talking about what you did at Ted Johnson's party last week."

"They can't! No one saw me!" she blurted. Then, as the significance of my remark dawned on her, Marjorie suddenly burst into tears and ran up to her room. It was drastic treatment, perhaps, but I had touched a vulnerable spot, and she would remember the sting of it for a long time. But since the first time a parents' group asked me to talk frankly to their daughters about petting, I have drummed at their pride with that one thought: "Boys always tell." I've found that boys from sixteen to sixty can't resist the urge of bragging. And finally, because I have seen some tragic results of wagging tongues, I have accepted invitations to talk against petting.

In my relationship with girls, both in and out of the juvenile court, I have discovered that many yielded to rash impulses the first time only after the boys promised, "You're the only one I've been with," or "We'll keep this our own little secret," or "I won't tell anybody." In 98 percent of the cases, the girls learned to their shame that the boys have told.

I'd rather have a girl dance all night than take an hour's automobile drive on a dark road. For I know that when petting starts, gossip is only a step behind, and enough idle talk will leave a scar that doesn't heal without heartaches. I've learned, too, that when girls get into a jam, most boys claim, "Well, you can't prove I'm the one," or "I wasn't the only one who went with her." And the harsh truth is that you can't prove it in seven cases out of ten.

Why do boys always tell? It's quite simple. It's human nature to boast. It gives the boys a sense of conquest, and they put girls in the same class with their other accomplishments. Just keep that in mind, girls, the next time you're tempted to pet--or worse. Boys always tell!

--Kathryn Sullivan

CHRIST

In 1956 a guide in the Holy Land led the late Elder Adam S. Bennion to the tomb which belonged to Joseph of Arimathaea in the days when Jesus lived, and in which Jesus was entombed after his crucifixion. As the guide stood there, he said, "There are many tombs of great men to be found all over the earth, but this one is different from any of the others: this one is empty!"

--Harold B. Lee

*****

THY WILL BE DONE

If all the sunsets would be fused
In one celestial scroll,
Or all the love on earth were poured
Into one golden bowl,

If all the tears congealed into
One iridescent pearl,
While all the restless winds rushed on
In never-ending whirl. . .

The beauty and triumphant power
Of all would not compare
With Jesus of Gethsemane,
With his one yielded prayer.

--Elberta Leisure

*****

WHEN THE LILIES BLOOM

Our Savior has risen from his darkened tomb. . .
the sun shines again, and the lilies bloom.
The birds are winging through the shimmering trees,
bursting forth with sweet melodies.
The warm breezes whispering over sea and earth
fill our souls with joyous mirth.
A scented fragrance spreads far and wide
of the beautiful flowers we thought had died.
Their tiny heads bobbing out of earth
ring out clearly a brand new birth!
Yes, it's springtime. . .what a glorious time of year,
for our Savior has risen. . .this message is clear.
He has risen from his darkened tomb.
The sun shines again, and the lilies bloom.

--Reeta B. Turner

*****

In the cathedral at Tubeck, Germany, was near the turn of the century the following inscription:

<u>Thus Speaketh Christ Our Lord To Us:</u>

Ye call me Master,
    And obey me not;
Ye call me light,
    And seek me not;
Ye call me life,
    And desire me not;
Ye call me wise,
    And follow me not;
Ye call me fair,
    And love me not;
Ye call me rich,
    And ask me not;
Ye call me eternal,
    And seek me not;
Ye call me gracious,
    And trust me not;
Ye call me noble,
    And serve me not;
Ye call me mighty,
    And honor me not;
Ye call me just,
    And fear me not;
If I condemn you,
    Blame me not.

*****

ALL THIS I KNOW

I have not seen the stable where
    they say his life began;
Nor Nazareth, the city where
    he grew from child to man;

    Yet surer than the eye can see,
    My heart knows certainly that he
    Was there--and lived for me.

I've never seen the winding Jordan
    flow from Herman's slope;
Nor Galilee, the beautiful, where
    'oft he taught and spoke;

    Yet in my heart there is no doubt,
    That in those lands he moved about
    With men; but as the Son of God.

Jerusalem, the city of our Lord,
    I've never seen;
Nor Bethany, where 'oft he found
    retreat with friends serene;

    Yet in my soul is bedded deep
    This truth (that I shall ever keep)--
    He is the shepherd of God's sheep.

I have not seen the garden where
    he prayed in final hours;
Nor Calvary, where he was nailed
    and pierced by evil powers;

    And yet unhesitatingly
    I feel and know he set me free;
    Yes, even more, he died for me.

All this I know.

                    --Alma E. Gygi

                    *****

THE ARTIST'S SECRET

There was an artist once, and he painted a picture. Other artists had colors more rich and rare, and painted more notable pictures. He painted his with one color, a wonderful red glow; and the people said, "We like the picture. . .we like the glow."

The other artists came and said, "Where does he get his color from?" They asked him; he smiled, and said, "I cannot tell you," and he worked on, his head bent low.

One went to the Far East and bought costly pigments; he made a rare color and painted, but after a time, the picture faded. Another read in the old books, and made a color rich and rare, but when he had put it on the picture, it was dead.

But the artist painted on. Always the work got redder and redder, and the artist grew whiter and whiter. At last one day they found him dead before his picture, and they took him up to bury him. The other men looked about in all the pots and crucibles, but they found nothing they had not.

And when they undressed him to put his grave clothing on him, they found above his left breast the mark of a wound. It was an old wound that must have been there all his life, for it was old and hardened--but death, which seals up all things, had drawn the edges together and closed it up.

And they buried him, and still the people said, "Where did he find his color?"

And it came to pass that, after a while, the artist was forgotten--but the work lived on.

--Olive Schriner

*****

OF FOOLISH VENTURES

Something was wrong with my dog, Spotty. I could tell by the way he was acting. Instead of his usual bounding, barking, tail-wagging greeting, he slipped quietly like a shadow around the corner of the building.

Sensing his need for my attention, I, too, slipped around the building to learn the reason for his strange behavior. A quick glance told the story. Spotty's face was bristling with white pointed silvers that gave him the look of a grizzled old prospector covered with whiskers. He whimpered pleadingly, and rubbed his nose toward the ground, pawing at his face and lips, trying to remove the cause of his pain. A porcupine had driven a multitude of sharp quills deep into his tender nose and quivering flesh.

He saw me now, and looked up toward me with pleading eyes as if to say, "I know I have been foolish. I should have known better, but won't you please help me?" He made another futile pass at the cruel barbs protruding from his bloodied face, which merely added to his pain and further proved the hopelessness of his situation.

I walked over to my nearby car, removed a pair of pliers from the glove compartment, and walked back toward him. "This is going to hurt, old fella," I said softly as I carefully pillowed his pain-ridden head in my lap. He looked back at me with limpid eyes as if to say, "I understand."

As I began making the painful extractions, I talked to him quietly. I suppose I was talking to myself as much as I was to him. "What would you do without me now, old fella? You are in a rather hopeless situation, aren't you? How would you ever get these quills out by yourself?" He looked directly at me, and I felt he understood. I wondered what would have happened to him had I not come to his aid. I could imagine those painful barbs finding their way deeper and deeper into fevered flesh. In my mind I could see his face festering and swelling as the pain became so unrelenting that old Spotty would do most anything to escape from it.

"How like old Spotty we are," I thought to myself. "How many times do we find ourselves in foolish circumstances from which we cannot escape?"

My thoughts carried me to a man kneeling in a garden alone. Upon him was placed the burden of all the sins of the world. The weight of this debt brought pain and anguish beyond our understanding--pain of such magnitude that he, the Son of God, sweat blood from every pore.

35

I thought of my own life--of foolish ventures that brought me sorrow, but because of this man kneeling alone in the garden, I could be spared. Jesus had done that for me which I could not do for myself. My pain could be removed, my tortured spirit healed. I could look up once again with hope and promise.

I could feel old Spotty tremble with pain each time I touched him, but he made no protest. Finally, the last quill was removed from his sad face. I stroked his fevered head gently and felt the warm softness of his fur beneath my fingertips. With a painful effort he lifted his head and turned with gratitude to lick my hand.

--Wayne B. Lynn

*****

RULERS AT THE TIME OF CHRIST

Herod the Great, who ruled all of Palestine, made provision in his will that after his death this land was to be divided among his three sons, Archelaus, Antipas, and Philip. His will, however, had to be approved by Caesar Augustus, who resided in Rome. Therefore, upon the death of Herod, the sons all rushed to Rome to claim their inheritance. While they were away, some of the more determined Jews rose in rebellion throughout Palestine, especially in Judea, making it very difficult for Archelaus--who had received that land as his inheritance--to subdue the riots when he returned. Roman armies, acting without mercy, were used to quell the opposition. With the quelling came an additional hatred of Rome.

Archelaus ruled without mercy. Herod had willed to his son the title of "king," but Augustus Caesar had held back the title until Archelaus could prove himself worthy of it. Therefore, in an effort to impress Rome, Archelaus added greatly to the taxation of the people and increased his building program. Archelaus's ambition finally proved to be his greatest weakness, and he was removed after ten years because of misrule. His punishment was banishment to the country known today as France.

Feeling that a local person capable of handling troublesome Judea could not be found, Rome next sent Roman rulers to reign in Samaria and Judea, the former inheritance of Archelaus. The fifth of these rulers (called procurators) was Pontius Pilate, who ruled during the last part of the life of Jesus. Following the example of the other procurators, he resided in the Samaritan seacoast town of Caesarea.

Pilate also drew the hatred of the Jews. He aroused their anger by taking into Jerusalem military insignia bearing the image of Caesar. The Jews rose in rebellion, feeling this to be a violation of God's commandment, "Thou shalt not make unto thee any graven image," and Pilate was forced to remove these insignia. Later, he further antagonized the Jews by taking money from their temple treasury to build a water pipe into Jerusalem. In the resulting revolt, many Jews lost their lives. Shortly after the death of Jesus, Pilate was removed from office for misrule and for the slaughter he ordered in Samaria. He was forced in disgrace to take his own life.

In the land of Judea, Jesus was more restricted than in any other area, since Judea was the center of Judaism. During his life Jesus received the greatest opposition from the leaders of the Jewish church and nation who resided in Jerusalem.

Antipas was made ruler of Galilee and Perea after the death of Herod the Great. He outlasted Pilate as a ruler by three years, but was also finally banished because of his ambition and misrule. Antipas often resided at the fortress of Machaerus, which bordered on the land of the Mabatean territory. He married a Mabatean princess, but later sent her home in order to enter into an adulterous marriage with Herodias, the wife of his brother. From this point on, the Mabateans warred with Herod Antipas, causing him untold trouble.

Later, John the Baptist began preaching against the adulterous life of Antipas. Because of this, John was imprisoned and, by order of Antipas, was put to death. Antipas's conscience was plagued by this act to such an extent that he later developed a fear of Christ, thinking he was John returned from the grave.

Herodias, the wife of Antipas, finally caused his downfall. She goaded him to the point that he demanded the title of king. Rome was not willing to bestow upon him the kingship, however. They refused his demand, banished him, and gave his territory to another.

Philip ruled the area northeast of the Sea of Galilee. Since most of his subjects were gentiles, he was far more popular with his people. Philip seems to have been the best of the Herods, and in his territory Jesus often found protection and seclusion.

Philip entered into an extensive building program, just as his brothers did. Two of his main cities became important in the life of Christ. Near the headwaters of the Jordan River he built a city called Caesarea; to distinguish this, his capital city, from the city of the procurators in Samaria, he added his own name--making the full designation Caesarea Philippi. Here Simon Peter was later to bear testimony to the messiahship of Jesus. Another city, Bethsaida (by Galilee), became a constant refuge for Jesus in time of trouble.

Philip died three years before Antipas was banished, and his property was annexed by Rome to Syria.

*****

"COME UNTO ME"

Three times I met this Jesus of Nazareth. Each time I felt strange and confused in his presence. Each time he gently spoke three simple words: "Come unto me." Yet each time, gentle and tender as he was, it seemed almost terrifying. How can I explain how my heart fought desperately to follow him even to the grave, and yet was held back by some force stronger even than the intensity of my love for him? Some would question that I did love Jesus, scoffing at my avowal of devotion, saying, "Then why didn't you follow him?" Why didn't I follow him? How many times have I tormented my soul with that question? How I have pleaded with my heart to send the answer! And yet I did not know then, and I do not know now. Why did I not follow Jesus?

The first time I met him I was traveling to a neighboring town with several of my comrades. As we approached him and three of his disciples, I knew even from a distance that his man was different. My steps faltered, and I stood transfixed as he approached. My comrades, who had heard the ugly rumors about this king, began laughing and jeering at him. One was even so bold as to spit before his feet. But he walked on as if he saw only me. If my thoughts and feelings were reflected in my eyes, it is no wonder that he gave full attention to me. I was scared, and yet calm and immovable, and I was only vaguely aware of my friends beginning to shout at me for not joining in with their railing and ridicule. He stopped before me, and as I looked into his eyes, it was like looking into all of eternity. I felt my heart whisper, "If you have never loved before, and if you never love again, here is one to whom you should give your dearest and deepest love." I felt a surge of love for him such as I have never felt before--warm and sweet and pure. I'm sure he felt this, too, for with kindness in his eyes, he smiled so tenderly and said, "Come unto me." At that moment one of my friends came up and slapped me on the shoulder and said, laughingly, "Oh, no! Don't tell me you're falling for the magic spell of this mighty king!" Suddenly I realized how foolish I must look to my comrades; almost unconsciously, and with a slight laugh, I replied, "Me? Of course not! What do you take me for, a common peasant?" We all laughed, and then I turned to join my friends, but not suddenly enough to miss seeing his eyes change from love to pain. That momentary glance pierced me more deeply than any sword, but still I walked off with my friends, laughing at the common carpenter who had proclaimed himself a king.

The second time I met him I was alone. It was early evening, and I was drawing water from my well when he walked up beside me and gently laid his hand on my arm. I did not need to look to know it was him; now I could look into those eyes again! I avoided his gaze and hurried with my task so I could leave more quickly. And yet, once again, I felt tranfixed. My eyes involuntarily were soon enveloped by his own, and all I could see in them was forgiveness--forgiveness and that ever-present sea of love, wider and deeper than the oceans of the world. And once again he spoke but three words--the three words that cut into my soul and made my heart gush with tears: "Come unto me." I spilt the water and ran from the well before reason could stop me. Oh, how can I explain the torture of that brief moment? I longed to go with him! I wanted desperately to run back and give him my heart, the heart he already had too firm a hold on. But I didn't. I didn't even look back. I couldn't. I dropped to the ground and tried to drown his words with my tears, but I couldn't do that, either. Why didn't I follow him? Why didn't I follow him?

I only saw him once more. It was the last night. I was only visiting Jerusalem and had been there but one day, but I wished at that moment I had been a thousand miles from that horrible city. As soon as I heard of the trial, my heart sickened; soon I heard the shouts of the crowd become boisterous and rude and hateful as they marched him up to the Hill of

Calvary. I knew I couldn't join the crucifiers, yet neither could I join the mourners who stood beside him. I knew I couldn't stay a moment longer in the city. I ran until I could run no farther, and then threw myself on the ground and wept until there were no more tears. How long I was there I do not know. I only remember that suddenly I felt myself walking back to Calvary. I didn't want to return, but I was going. I walked, slowly and thoughtfully, never stopping until I was standing beneath his feet as he hung, dying. It was dark, and no one else was there. I stood several minutes before I raised my eyes to look into his face. And when I did, strangely enough, it seemed the same as before-- radiant with power, glowing with love. Even as he hung there, the life seeping out of him with every passing moment, I knew they could not kill him--not any more than they could kill the love I still felt in my heart. And then, once again, I heard those words. This time he could barely whisper them, and yet to me they sounded like the rushing of winds: "Come unto me." At that I could stand no more! I fell to my knees, and my heart broke. I had no more tears to give, but I at last answered his three simple words: "Yes, my Savior, I will come."

The next day the Roman soldiers found the body of a man at the foot of Jesus's cross; thinking it was only a common peasant friend, they kicked it out of the way to lower the body of Jesus. No one could identify the man, nor could they find a reason for his death. In his hand he was clutching a small piece of paper that contained his final message to mankind, scratched in weak handwriting: "I did not lack the love--I only lacked the courage." And so they dug a hasty grave, and buried one who died of a broken heart.

--Sandy Wilcox

SIXTY HOURS THAT CHANGED THE WORLD

Without doubt, the most important short span of time in the history of the world was approximately sixty drama-packed hours that occurred nearly two thousand years ago.

Into this short period were crowded the world-shaking events that occurred from the time Jesus sat with his disciples at the last supper until he appeared to Mary, one of his beloved followers, as a resurrected being.

Jesus had spent the previous two days at Bethany with his family and friends, those he loved best. He knew, and he had tried many times to make his disciples understand, that to fulfill his Father's divine plan for the atonement of all, he must suffer and die on the cross. Yet, those he loved and who so loved him could not--or would not--understand.

As they prepared for this last supper on Thursday night, they still expected he would proclaim his power and in some perhaps miraculous way establish himself as their king and Savior. Hadn't he, just a few days earlier, demonstrated this power by chasing the thieves and money-changers out of the temple and by scattering his enemies before him? Surely, he was speaking in parables when he had told them repeatedly that before he could be their leader and savior he must suffer and die.

At the last supper there was optimism and even some merriment. Jesus, too, resigned to his fate and having bade farewell to his closest friends and those of his household at Bethany, appeared confident and encouraging.

Let not your heart be troubled; ye believe in God, believe also in me. . . . .Peace I leave with you, my peace I give unto you. . . . .As the Father hath loved me, so have I loved you: continue in my love. . . . .These things have I spoken unto you, that my joy might remain in you, and that your joy might be
full. . . . .love one another, as I have loved you. . . . .

Greater love hath no man than this, that a man lay down his life for his friends. (John 14:1, 27; 15:9, 11-13.)

After the supper, late in the evening, Jesus with all of his disciples (except Judas) went to the beautiful Garden of Gethsemane--a place frequented by the Savior and his friends. Taking Peter, James, and John with him and leaving the others at the gate, Jesus went in under the beautiful olive trees and prayed mightily to his father, ". . .O my Father, if it be possible, let this cup pass from me: nevertheless not as I will, but as thou wilt." (Matthew 26:39.)

Almost immediately thereafter, Judas, leading his motley crowd of priests, elders, and the riffraff of Christ's enemies among the people, came with swords and staves and bound him and took him before the high priests and the governor for condemnation.

Although neither Herod nor Pilate could find any wrong in the man, they scourged him and condemned him to crucifixion to please the people. The wiley Pontius Pilate, however, always carefully thinking of his own well-being, publicly washed his hands of the whole affair so that, as the Jews requested, his blood would be upon them and upon their children.

That Friday evening, after the Lord had proclaimed his work "finished" and had given up the ghost, one of his disciples, Joseph of Arimathaea, obtained permission to remove the body and to put it in his new-hewn tomb in his own beautiful garden.

It was here, at Joseph's tomb, early on the second morning following, that the glorious events of the resurrection took place. The previous afternoon there had been earthquakes accompanied by darkness at midday, and the veil of the temple had been torn from top to bottom. Even the captain of the Roman soldiers had exclaimed, "Truly this man was the Son of God."
(Mark 15:39.)

Then, on that glorious Sunday morning, came these words from an angel whose countenance was like lightning: ". . .Fear not ye: for I know that ye seek Jesus, which was crucified. He is not here: for he is risen, as he said. Come, see the place where the Lord lay." (Matthew 28:5, 6.) And then came that marvelous first appearance to the beloved and chosen Mary Magdalene. Thinking he was the gardener, Mary had sorrowfully inquired, ". . .Sir, if thou have borne him hence, tell me where thou hast laid him, and I will take him away."

Then Jesus said to her, "Mary." In rapt astonishment, the devoted Mary responded, "Rabboni," or "Master!" (John 20:15, 16.)

Thus, in less than sixty short hours, transpired the greatest living drama of all time.

These were the divine events which, through the sacrifice of the Son of God himself, ushered in the atonement and the resurrection.

For, as Jesus had told his beloved Martha, ". . .I am the resurrection, and the life: he that believeth in me, though he were dead, yet shall he live; And whosoever liveth and believeth in me shall never die. . . ." (John 11:25, 26).

--O. Preston Robinson

CHRISTMAS

A MOTHER'S CHRISTMAS WISH

Come dear family, gather 'round our Christmas tree;
Let us spend a little time in love and harmony.
Tomorrow we will celebrate the birth of Christ our Lord,
But I've a wish this year to see it's meaning's not ignored.

The gifts are neatly set about with names and tags and bows.
And Christmas goodies are in sight, the stockings are in rows.
But as I look into your faces, what I wish to see. . .
Is a love for Christ our Savior, not "What's Santa bringing me?"

Each time one of you were born and laid here in my arm,
I thought about the Christ child in the manger safe and warm.
I thought of how his life began, and all the things he taught.
I thought of how he died for us--that death could conquer not.

I wonder how his face would look, if these gifts to him we gave--
A shirt, a train, a story book. . .which of these would he save?
I think he'd rather see us give kindness to each other,
To say our thanks and give our love to him, our oldest brother.

So, as the colored Christmas lights are blinking in your heads,
I hope to find you each with love, kneeling at your beds,
And giving him a birthday wish that will be sure to please:
Just vow to love your fellow man, and promise from your knees.

Then in the morning when you pass your Christmas gifts around,
Give the gift of love and joy. . .let true peace here be found.
For Jesus will be here to join, he's told us so, you see. . .
"If you do it unto the least of these. . .you do it unto me."

--Suzanne Dean

*****

NO GREATER LIGHT

There was no family doctor,
There was no midwife there--
Just a loving husband,
A donkey, and a mare.

There was no bed with linens,
And no comfort for this wife;
No help at all was given
For the bringing forth of life.

But, in the quiet hours
As her time was growing nigh,
She met the pain of labor
With faith in God on high.

And, soon fulfilled the promise
That a Savior would be born
Within a lowly stable
Before the break of morn.

The Savior breathed the breath
Of life, and it all began,
For here was born the Prince of Peace--
At last, the Son of Man.

There was no special clothing,
Nor cradle for the king;
Swaddling clothes to wrap him in
Was all that they could bring.

Yet, here within the stable
As the animals watched on,
The light of God shone all around
And warmed them until dawn.

The legionnaires of Caesar
That occupied the inn
Had no idea how very near
The miracle they'd been.

That night there were a very few
Who really understood--
Just those who prayed for answers,
Whose hearts were kind and good.

They knew he would be coming
To bring light to the earth,
And long had watched to see the star
That signified his birth.

And high above the stable
It shone as if to say
The world would long remember
This morn as Christmas day.

And even though there were so few
To celebrate that night,
There's been no sweeter miracle--
There's been no greater light!

--Suzanne Dean

*****

WHAT IS CHRISTMAS?

Faith and hope and love, which cannot be bought or sold or bartered, but only given away, are the wellsprings--firm and deep--of Christmas celebrations. These are the gifts without price, the ornaments incapable of imitation, discovered only within oneself, and are, therefore, unique. They are not always easy to come by, but they are in unlimited supply-- ever in the province of all.

This Christmas, mend a quarrel. Seek out a forgotten friend. Dismiss suspicion, and replace it with trust. Write a love letter. Share some treasure. Give a soft answer. Encourage youth. Manifest your loyalty in word and deed. Keep a promise. Listen. Apologize if you are wrong. Try to understand. Flout envy. Examine your demands on others. Think first of someone else. Appreciate. Be kind. Be gentle. Laugh a little. Laugh a little more. Deserve confidence. Take up arms against malice. Express your gratitude. Go to church. Welcome a stranger. Gladden the heart of a child. Take pleasure in the beauty and wonder of this earth. These are inklings of a vast category. . .a mere scratching of the surface.

They are simple things. You have heard them all before, but their influence has never been measured.

*****

THE FADED BLUE BLANKET

The most frightened shepherd that night was little Ladius, just ten. He cowered behind his three older brothers when the blinding star lit the hillside. When the angel appeared, he hid behind a huge rock.

Yet after Ladius heard the glad news, fear left him, and he limped back to his brothers, who were planning to set out for Bethlehem.

"Who will tend the sheep?" asked Samuel, the oldest at sixteen. Ladius, leaning against his shepherd's crook to support a crippled foot, volunteered, "I'd only slow you down. Let me stay with the sheep." He wet his lip as he talked. The brothers weakly protested at first, then made plans to go.

"We must each take a gift," said Samuel. One brother chose his flint to start a fire for the Christ child. Another picked meadow lilies to make a garland for the king. Samuel decided on his most precious possession--his gold ring.

"Here--take my blanket to him," said Ladius. It was badly worn, a faded blue with patches.

"No, Ladius," said Samuel, tenderly. "The blanket is too tattered to give even a beggar--let alone a king. Besides, you will need it tonight."

The brothers departed, leaving Ladius alone by the fire. He laid his head upon the blanket and buried his face in his hands. Tears forced

44

their way between his fingers, but soon the hush of night soothed the boy's heartbreak. **The world in silent stillness lay.** . . . .

"Are you coming, Ladius?" called a voice. Standing nearby was the same angel who had brought the news. "You wanted to see the child, didn't you?"

"Yes," nodded Ladius, "but I must stay here."

"My name is Gabriel," said the angel. "Your sheep will be watched. Take my hand, and bring your blanket. The child may need it."

Suddenly, Ladius was outside a stable. Kneeling by a manger were his brothers. Ladius started to call out, but the angel lifted a finger to his lips.

"Give me the blanket," Gabriel whispered. The angel took it and quietly covered the baby. But the blanket was no longer faded. Now it glistened like dew in the brilliance of a new day. Returning, Gabriel squeezed Ladius's hand: "Your gift was best, because you gave all that you had. . . ."

"Wake up, Ladius, wake up!" The boy rubbed his eyes and tried to shield them from the glaring sun. Hovering over him was Samuel.

"Did you find him?" asked Ladius.

"Yes," replied Samuel, "but first tell me why you were sleeping without your blanket."

Ladius looked about with wonder. The faded blue blanket was nowhere to be found--then, or thereafter.

-Follow the star -reach our savior-

--Fred Bauer

*****

REPAINTING THE ANGEL

The statuette of an angel holding the hand of a little boy had been placed on a neglected back shelf in an antique shop. It was covered with soot and dust, lost amidst the clutter of jars, dishes, and ornaments.

A man browsing through the shop discovered the figurine and took it in his hands. He had an inspiration: he would rescue it from oblivion, restore it, and give it a place of honor among his Christmas decorations.

At home, in his basement workshop, the man covered the angel and the child with glistening white paint. Then he painted the wings of the angel and the hair of the little boy with sparkling gold. Each brush stroke worked magic. The old, grime-covered statuette vanished, and a shining, new one appeared. The statuette was transformed before his eyes into a thing of radiant beauty.

As the man painted, he thought: Isn't this what happens to people at Christmas? They come to the end of the year dust-covered from the struggle. And then Christmas inspires them to repaint the better angels of their nature with love and joy and peace!

The art of repainting the angel! This is man's lifelong task: never to stay down in the dust and the dirt, but, heroically, to rise again after each fall--to create a new life.

Repainting the angel! A man need never lose his ideals, dreams, and purposes. He can always make them gleam again with the glory of renewed hope.

Repainting the angel! There is a hidden goodness within every man, and he has the power to bring it forth.

Repainting the angel! Each high thought a man thinks works magic. It helps to transform him and renew his spirit. Just as gold paint will change a statuette, golden thoughts will change a man.

--Wilferd Peterson

*****

THE ETERNAL SEASONS

At Christmas time the world pauses to remember the birth of Jesus Christ. And though the voice of the Lord himself in latter-day revelation has declared the date to be April 6, we as Saints continue to commemorate it at its traditional time in December. Why? Some say we keep Christmas in December to eliminate a stumbling block to new converts who have been reared with the tradition; others maintain that it matters not what day we celebrate the Savior's birth. Yet, there is a another element present--an element that renders logical and meaningful its celebration at the onset of winter; indeed, a symbolism that exalts the beauty and very purpose of Christmas.

Christmas falls only a few days after the beginning of winter; Easter comes soon after the commencement of spring. Between these two events lies winter, a time of probation. Thus was the advent of Christ. He entered mortality on earth, a symbolic winter in comparison to the glory of the eternal burnings from whence he came. He walked the ice and snow of the flesh and surmounted the chilling blasts of the temptor. Yet never did he lose his footing; never did he cry out against the bite of the flesh. He overcame all things at Gethsemane and Calvary--the equinox of life. Then, in the dawn of spring, he rose triumphantly from the tomb into the resurrection, as likewise the world in reverential response puts on its coat of life anew in preparation for summer.

So it is with us, the spiritual brothers and sisters of Jesus, the sons and daughters of God. We also were in the beginning with God. We dwelt with him as sons and daughters of glory in the summer of our eternities. We progressed and developed. Then came the autumn of our premortal destinies--the fall, when the winds began to blow, the trails grew steeper, and a third of the leaves of Heaven--who could not endure--fell from the branches of life to form rotting subterfuge below. We entered the winter; we inherited the blizzards and the sub-zero trials of today.

But, like our older brother, we, too, may overcome all things and see the spring. Then we will find that the rotting leaves at our feet have only decayed until they, through their presence, have enriched our entire existence--that we might be strong, able to stand firmly throughout the night, prepared to reap the blessings of a warmer season. We may rise and stand in the morning of a spring--resurrection, Millenium, family reunion--as we flower and bud, preparing for the summer ahead. At spring's end the storms rage--Satanic fury unleashed--but if our roots are deeply planted, these also will be for our good.

When at last we find ourselves in the fulness of summer, a voice will whisper, "You're not a stranger here. You were here another summer. But now there is a difference. Then you were only a child of the sun; now you are a priest or priestess, a king or queen to the most high God, to rule and reign forever and ever. Now you are ready to give rise to eternal lives, children who will walk the paths of autumn and winter and spring--paths familiar to you, for you walked them before. You see, this is one eternal round."

Thus, we celebrate the birth of our Redeemer. It is a time of birth, of beginning. He began a path through the snows of life, a path without which our very spirits would be frozen in the ice of eternity. His is a warming fire--a refiner's fire--in days of cold. The days are coldest and darkest at the start of the winter months. The world had not seen darker days than those before our Savior entered the winter of his existence. Yet he was the light, a light that shone in darkness. As surely as the days begin to be longer and brighter at Christmas time each year, so did the light of his influence begin to increase in the world. It is still growing, and will go on until it attains unto the perfect light--even the light of summer.

*****

A CHRISTMAS STORY

T'was the season, and as Ann shuffled her list of "Things to do Wednesday," "Things to do Thursday," and "Things that should have been done yesterday," she wondered, "'Tis the season for what? For tired feet, volumes of extra work, and myriads of things to remember!"

She knew she had lost control of her "season" when she found herself the night before screaming down to the children in the living room, "And don't touch those packages, or I'll blister your bottoms til you look like a Solarcaine ad!" It had sounded so funny to nine-year-old Cindy, but she hadn't dared to laugh after taking one look at her mother's face.

Ann returned for the nineteenth time to her cookie-making. "I hate to make cookies at nine o'clock at night!" she thought, miserably, as she tried to erase thoughts of her comfortable bed from her mind. Bart had come in from school and announced that he needed twenty-four cookies for kindergarten. She had made a mental note. But mental notes don't taste very good, so after the children were all fed and bathed and their daddy (lucky man) had escaped to a meeting, Ann had tackled the cookies--and had told herself that if she really "got into it," she would enjoy it.

She had not enjoyed it. Just as she was about to drop the dough onto the cookie sheet, Angela had announced that she, too, would sure like to take cookies to her preschool Christmas party, and Ann had suddenly remembered the note asking mothers to help with the refreshments. She sighed, and removed all the ingredients once more from the cupboards so she could double the batch. At the precise moment that she slid the last tray of cookies into the oven, first-grader Jed had announced that he was supposed to take two dozen cookies to school in the morning. "That was the moment," Ann thought, clenching her teeth, "the precise moment that I lost the Christmas spirit!"

On the counter in Ann's kitchen were another unread newspaper, two issues of the Church News (she felt it a sin of omission not to read at least the back page), a pair of shoelaces that had to be threaded into Rhett's shoes before he outgrew them, and four Christmas cards that had arrived that day (the very day she had finished mailing out her Christmas cards). She jotted down on her list of "Things to do on Wednesday" to mail out four more Christmas cards.

Why is it, she mused, that just as you finish mailing out Christmas cards, you get a handful in the mail--all from people you forgot to send cards to? The same thing happens on neighborhood treats, she remembered--you no sooner bake a Christmas pie for all the neighbors than three more families have the audacity to move in to the neighborhood!

Ann's life seemed mirrored in the pile of "Things To Do" she had growing on her counter. There was the list of fourteen new Primary children, all of whom she personally needed to welcome to Primary. And that reminded her of the sixty-two miniature nativity scenes she had cut out, but not yet assembled, for her Primary children.

"Birthdays should be outlawed in December!" she grumbled, wrapping a gift for her six-year-old's friend's party. "But," she mused with a tired smile, "I guess that would eliminate two of my children, and that's not such a good idea."

She had a play to finish writing for the Warner family party, a half-decorated Christmas broom for her aging grandmother, and twenty-four separate doll clothes cut out for her daughters' four dolls. (And Rhett had just asked her to make his Gremlin a pair of levis. "I must look like Betsy Ross!" she had wailed.)

The days sped by, and Ann's pile of "Things To Do" grew on her counter at a frightening rate. "I wish Fisher-Price toys proliferated like this mess on my counter!" she had cried out in a moment of utter frustration. Nine-year-old Cindy left the room, hiding a giggle behind her hand.

Finally, there came a day, very close to Christmas, that the pile on the counter began to disappear. Ann had finished up all the millions of details that seemed to sap her of her Christmas spirit. The birthday parties had been attended, and each child had left happy--present under arm, confident that they had mattered enough for their mother to supply the gift, brush the hair, throw the gum away, and get them there, somehow, on time. The party announcements could be thrown away!

The message from the Relief Society president about the Hansen family had been attended to--Ann had taken over a casserole and a box of toys. She threw the message away. She threw away the tickets to the ball game she and her husband had missed because of the caroling party they had attended instead. They had caroled at the old folks' home on Spencer Street. A note she had written in red magic marker and hung on the kitchen counter for months--WRITE YOUR MISSIONARIES!--was thrown in the bathroom garbage on her way out to the mailbox with their Happy New Year cards. "Better late than never," she thought, glad to have finally accomplished that task.

Little by little, task by task, Ann had waded through her "Things To Do" pile on the kitchen counter--and it was now three a.m. on Christmas morning. She had tossed and turned for two hours, too tired to sleep, and had finally decided to investigate the strange light emitting from the living room. As she came down the hall, she realized the light came from the Christmas tree.

"Utah Power and Light Company thanks you once again, children," she mumbled, bending to pull the plug on the glowing balls of red and green. But just then she decided she might as well sit and enjoy the tree rather than toss and turn in bed. She noticed the power switch to the stereo had also been left on, and she decided to treat herself, at long last, to some of her favorite Christmas songs. She chose Handel's "Messiah." As the sweet words "for unto us a child is born, unto us a child is given" reached the corners of her tender heart, great tears welled up in her eyes.

"I'm afraid I haven't taken much time to think about the real meaning of Christmas," she mumbled apologetically. But then, a thousand images crowded into her mind. She saw her little children with presents tucked under their arms, happily skipping to their neighbors' birthday parties. She saw her grandmother's smile as she received the broom Ann had made-- and she remembered the aged fingers happily placing the broom on the front door to welcome her holiday guests, perhaps for her last Christmas. . . .

Ann smiled as she remembered the amateurish production of her family play, and the giggles of the wise men and the awkward announcement of the three-year-old innkeeper, saying, "There is no room in this inn." And she remembered how her father-in-law had put his arm around her waist and thanked her for taking the time to write them a play.

She remembered how proud her children had been to take her cookies to school--baked, under duress, at nine p.m. She thought with anticipation how each of her little girls would love those soft, fluffy new doll clothes when they opened their gifts in just a few short hours--and she was glad, so glad, she had taken the time to make them. She re-read a Christmas card, sent from a friend who had long ago lost her address: "Dear Ann and Kenneth, Thank you so much for writing to us! We think of you often. Isn't Christmas a wonderful time of year!" She thought of all her neighbors, whom she rarely saw in the wintertime, and how they had welcomed her as she came bearing pies; she remembered the warmth of their friendship, and the feeling that welled up inside of her because she had taken the time to reach out.

She let her mind wander to the far-off countries where each missionary in her ward labored--and where each would, in the next few weeks, receive her cheerful New Year's cards. She hoped that when her own sons served missions, others would take the time to cheer them, too.

She lingered on the remembered faces of those dear elderly people she and her husband had caroled to on Spencer Street. One woman had clasped her hand and whispered, "You remind me so of my daughter. It's been like having her back for a time, just to watch you sing." Her mind raced back to the Hansen home, and how she and her next-door neighbor had cleaned up the house, delivered the casserole, and distributed the toys to the excited children. "I wish I had bought them better toys," she sighed.

The music enveloped her, and she pushed her head back, far into the cushion of the couch. "I don't think I have ever just relaxed on this couch," she thought, as her eyes surveyed the pleasant room that was hers to clean, entertain in, have family home evening in, but never relax in. Then her eyes rested on a homemade envelope, addressed to "The Best Mommy in the World." Inside was a coupon in third-grade cursive writing: "Good for one day of tending the baby, so you won't have to be so busy. Love, Cindy."

Her record on the stereo had reached the "Hallelujah Chorus," and with tears dropping from joyful eyes, Ann held the coupon to her cheek and thought of the sixty-two nativity scenes she had made for each Primary child. The love and contentment of the Spirit of Christ entered her heart.

"Oh, Lord," she said aloud. "I was afraid I had lost the spirit of Christmas. But I didn't lose it. It was there all the time, in the pile of things to do on my kitchen counter. It was there all the time! I just didn't have time to notice it until now."

--Barbara Werrett Nielsen

*****

DEATH

Death is one of those inexplicable items of life that robs, and in the robbing gives something in return.

*****

Silently into the night I go,
    Into the starry night of heavenly blue;
What matter where the road may lead. . .
    If I but come again at last to you!

                        --Clara Edwards

*****

THE ROSE STILL GROWS BEYOND THE WALL

Near shady wall a rose once grew,
    Budded and blossomed in God's free light,
Watered and fed by morning dew,
    Shedding its sweetness day and night.

As it grew and blossomed fair and tall,
    Slowly rising to loftier height,
It came to a crevice in the wall,
    Through which there shone a beam of light.

Onward it crept with added strength,
    With never a thought of fear or pride
It followed the light through the crevice-length,
    And unfolded itself on the other side.

The light, the dew, the broadening view
    Were found the same as they were before,
And it lost itself in beauties anew,
    Breathing its fragrance more and more.

Shall claim of death cause us to grieve,
    And make our courage faint or fall?
Nay, let us faith and hope receive--
    The rose still grows beyond the wall. . .

Scattering fragrance far and wide,
    Just as it did in days of yore,
Just as it did on the other side,
    Just as it will forevermore.

                        --A. L. Frink

*****

A PRAYER

O Father, help me understand
   And know the reason why
The boy that thou didst give to me
   So early had to die;
Why one whose life had been so pure,
   Who never knew deceit,
Should droop and wither like a flower
   Crushed under ruthless feet.
O Father, help me understand
   Thy purposes divine,
In letting death, with ruthless hand,
   Tear his dear heart from mine.
O let me see the veil beyond,
   Where dwells his spirit pure,
And know he's happy where he's gone;
   O let me feel secure.

Forgive the surging doubts that rise
   Within my aching heart,
And take the dimness from mine eyes,
   Let darkness all depart.
Let light and knowledge come to me
   From heaven, thy home on high,
O help me put my trust in thee:
   O Father, tell me why.
Perhaps I sin in asking this,
   More faith should I have in thee;
But, o, I miss his loving kiss,
   He was so dear to me.
Just let me know that I sometime
   Shall find him once again,
And clasp again his form to mine,
   I ask in Jesus' name.

THE ANSWER

Grieve not, my son, for time shall be
   When death shall be no more.
Thy loved one I'll return to thee,
      To cherish evermore.
'Twas in the plan that man should die,
   And slumber in the grave,
But rise again, as even I,
   For this my life I gave.
For mortal life is but a part
   Of God's eternity,
In which the souls of men embark
   To find felicity.
What men call death is but a step
   From low to higher plane,
And all who in the dust have slept
   Through me shall live again.

Then grieve not for the one that's gone,
    Nor let your heart despair;
For God in wisdom called your son,
    To work for him up there.
The prison gates are open wide
    For those who died in sin,
And through repentance them to guide
    Again to worship him.
Let this, then, be your answer why,
    And let your heart rejoice,
For unto God they do not die,
    Who answer to his voice:
But walk with him in realms of love,
        Where all the righteous be.
Be comforted, for there above,
    Thy boy will welcome thee.

--Rey L. Pratt

*****

A SCIENTIST ON ETERNAL LIFE

In our modern world, many people seem to feel that science has somehow made such "religious ideas" untimely or old-fashioned.

But I think science has a real surprise for the skeptics. Science, for instance, tells us that nothing in nature, not even the tiniest particle, can disappear without a trace.

Think about that for a moment. Once you do, your thoughts about life will never be the same.

Science has found that nothing can disappear without a trace. Nature does not know extinction. All it knows is transformation!

Now, if God applies this fundamental principle to the most minute and insignificant parts of his universe, doesn't it make sense to assume that he applies it also to the masterpiece of his creation--the human soul? I think it does. And everything science has taught me--and continues to teach me--strengthens my belief in the continuity of our spiritual existence after death. Nothing disappears without a trace.

--Dr. Wernher Von Braun

*****

EXPLAINING DEATH TO CHILDREN

And now let me tell you what she did--the finest lesson I have ever heard being taught to children. She planned what will come to be known in her family as a great holy hour. She took the children upstairs, all in a room together. This was on Saturday, seven days after the father had been taken to the hospital. This was the day that, according to their family plans, the father and mother always took the children somewhere for recreational and educational purposes and to solidify their family life.

There, this well-poised woman got a blackboard and placed the names of all the children on the board. She then conducted a class, as had often been done in their home on family nights. She told them that their Father in Heaven had a very important mission for someone to perform-- that it was of unusual importance, and that he had been looking all over the world for someone to choose for such a mission. Whom would they suggest he call?

One of the youngest children immediately said, "Daddy," and in that sacred hour all the others applauded by clapping their hands. In their childish feeling and unsophisticated faith, they were willing that their father be spared for any mission the Lord wanted.

She then told them that their opinion of their father had been shared by their Heavenly Father. In this way, they were told of their father's death.

Death to them was made a glorious and sacred event. It was pictured as a glorious end. Beverly, who right to the last thought that her husband would be healed, had triumphed over her own feelings and resigned herself in peace and tranquility to the will of our Heavenly Father. In this glorious way, death to the children was made a living symbol of further opportunity and service for their father, and the beginning of a new and glorious venture for them.

> --Told at the funeral service of
> Beverly Cutler's husband

*****

DETERMINATION

You cannot run away from weakness; you must sometime fight it out or perish; and if that be so, why not now, and where you stand?

--Robert Louis Stevenson

*****

If it is to be, it is up to me.

--E. Wilford Edmar

*****

The clouds may drop down titles and estates; wealth may seek us; but wisdom must be sought.

--Edward Young

*****

PATRIOT'S OATH

I am only one--
　　But I am one.

I cannot do everything,
　　But I can do something.

And what I can do,
　　That I ought to do;

And what I ought to do,
　　By the grace of God
　　I will do.

--Edward Everett Hale

*****

WILLPOWER

Everywhere I go
The story is the same.
Someone's always complaining
About this dad-gum diet game.

One person wants to lose,
Another wants to gain.
Why, this constant battle-of-the-bulge
Is driving me insane!

Determination

It's pretty hard to figure
How lucky some people are,
To never have to worry about
Keeping their figures up to par.

The story of my life has been
Thinking diet all day through.
It's enough to drive you crazy
And wonder what to do!

All I want is my slim figure,
Can someone help me get it back?
Guess no one else can help me
Except the willpower, which I lack!

--Glenna Bigelow

*****

BE COMMITTED

What happens to men who refuse to be stopped once they decide where they are going?

Cripple him, and you have Sir Walter Scott. Put him in prison, and you have John Bunyan. Bury him in the snow at Valley Forge, and you have George Washington. Have him born in poverty, and you have Abraham Lincoln. If you give him a speech impediment, lock him in jail, and put him out of office almost in disgrace, and you have Winston Churchill. Persecute him from town to town, state to state, and finally murder him, and you have Joseph Smith.

*****

WHO IS A FAILURE?

From time to time, all of us are called on to listen to tales of woe in which men recount the ill fortune of their ventures. Sometimes these ventures have deserved failure, because they were badly conceived or carelessly managed. Often, however, the result is a disheartening return for men who planned well and worked diligently. To renew the courage of these men, and his own when needed, one executive keeps at hand the biography of a "failure." It reads this way:

Failed at business	'31
Defeated for legislature	'32
Again failed in business	'33
Elected to legislature	'34
Defeated for Speaker	'38
Defeated for Elector	'40
Defeated for Congress	'42
Defeated for Congress	'46
Elected to Congress	'48
Defeated for Senate	'55

Defeated for Vice-President '56
Defeated for Senate   '58

Here, indeed, is a record that might cause any man to lose faith in himself and hope for his ideals. Fortunately, the man who compiled it lost neither faith nor hope. He tried again. He was Abraham Lincoln, elected in 1860 to serve as president of the United States.

*****

COURAGE

Are you having difficulty? Have you lost hope? Take courage from a man who overcame all these feelings, and succeeded.

Death took the life of his mother when he was just nine years of age. When Abraham Lincoln was but a young man, he ran for the legislature in Illinois, but was badly defeated.

He entered business with a partner who proved to be worthless. After the business failed, he spent seventeen years of his life working to pay the debts that his dishonest partner had left him.

He became engaged to Ann Rutledge, a beautiful girl from New Salem, his first and only true love--and she died. He proposed to Mary Owens a year or two later, and was rejected.

After a courtship and one broken engagement with another, Mary Todd, he finally married but was never completely happy in his marriage.

Of Lincoln's four children, all but one died when they were young.

He ran for Congress and was badly defeated. He tried to get an appointment to the United States Land Office, but was unsuccessful.

He was badly defeated when he became a candidate for the United States Senate. In 1858, he was defeated by Stephen A. Douglas. His associate, Stanton--as well as many others, whom he regarded as friends--publicly ridiculed him.

Through all these losses and disappointments, Abraham Lincoln remained cheerful and carried on with a quiet determination. He later became the president of the United States, and is today respected among all peoples.

*****

FIGHTING OFF DISCOURAGEMENT

Many times as time passes, we get a discouraged, sometimes referred to as "down in the dumps" feeling. As members of the Church of Jesus Christ, I think it is our duty to help people defeat this negative feeling and to rediscover the great happiness and reassurance that comes from the gospel. I feel that one short story has helped me many times when things weren't going well:

A man came walking down life's street. Satan said to the little devil, with a bitter face, "Go get him for me."

Quickly the imp crossed the street, silently and lightly hopped to the man's shoulder, and whispered in his ear, "You are discouraged."

"No," said the man. "I am not discouraged."

"You are discouraged."

This time, the man replied, "I do not think I am."

More loudly and decidedly the little imp said again, "I tell you, you are discouraged."

The man dropped his head and replied, "Well, I suppose I am." At that, the imp hopped back to Satan and reported, "I got him. He is discouraged!"

Another man came walking down life's street. Again old Satan said, "Get him for me."

The proud little demon of discouragement repeated his tactics. The first time he told the man he was discouraged, the man replied emphatically, "No, I am not!" The second time, the man replied, "I tell you, I am _not_ discouraged!" The third time, he said, "I am not discouraged. You lie."

The man walked down the street, his head held high, going toward the light. The imp of discouragement returned to his master crestfallen. "I couldn't get him. Three times I told him he was discouraged. The third time he called me a liar, and that discouraged _me_!"

*****

A CREED FOR THE DISCOURAGED

I believe that God created me to be happy, to enjoy the blessings of life, to be useful to my fellow beings, and to be an honor to my country.

I believe that the trials that beset me today are but the fiery tests by which my character is strengthened, ennobled, and made worthy to enjoy the higher things of life, which I believe are in store for me.

I believe that my soul is too grand to be crushed by defeat; I will rise above it.

I believe that I am the architect of my own fate; therefore:

I will be master--not slave--of circumstances and surroundings.

I will not yield to discouragements; I will trample them underfoot and make them serve as steppingstones to success. I will conquer my obstacles and turn them into opportunities.

My failures of today will help to guide me on to victory on the morrow.

The morrow will bring new strength, new hopes, new opportunities, and new beginnings. I will be ready to meet it with brave heart, calm mind, and undaunted spirit.

In all things I will do my best, and leave the rest to the infinite.

I will not waste my mental energies by useless worry. I will learn to dominate my restless thoughts and look on the bright side of things.

I will face the world bravely; I will not be a coward. I will assert my God-given birthright and be a man. For I am immortal, and nothing can overcome me.

--Virginia Opal Myers

*****

THE HEROISM OF SERGEANT IRWIN

The first great American B-29 airplane strike against the enemy of World War II flown from a land base was led by an airplane named "City of Los Angeles." Aboard this aircraft were twelve men--eleven regular crewmen and a colonel, flying as commanding officer. They were to reach a place appointed for meeting sixty to seventy-five miles off the enemy's mainland, then assume regular fighting formation and fly in on the target--a large number of gasoline tanks.

They reached the appointed place on time, and Colonel Sprouse ordered the dropping of the phosphorous bomb, which was supposed to let off its yellow fumes when it hit the ground as a marker for the dropping of regular bombs. Sergeant "Red" Irwin skidded this dangerous bomb down the airplane shute as ordered. The act was loaded with death. The flap at the end of the bomb shute had somehow gotten stuck. When the bomb struck it, it exploded ahead of time and burst back into the interior of the airplane, right into the face and chest of Sergeant Irwin.

Dropping to the floor, it began to swiftly burn its way through the thin metal flooring separating it from the incendiary bomb stored in the bomb bay below. In moments, the "City of Los Angeles" and its crew would be blown to bits far out over the ocean in enemy territory.

Sergeant Irwin, terribly wounded, got to his knees, picked up the bomb in his bare hands, cradled it in his arms, and staggered up the passageway. Crashing into the navigator's table, he had to stop and unlatch it with fingers that left burn marks on the hardwood. By now, the airplane was filled with eye-stinging smoke, blinding the pilot, and was wallowing less than three hundred feet above the water. Irwin staggered into the pilot's compartment, shouting, "Window! Window!" He could not see that it was already open, and his fumbling fingers left burn marks on the metal. He threw the bomb out of the window and collapsed to the deck.

Determination

Colonel Sprouse ordered the "City of Los Angeles" back to base in the slim hope that Irwin's life might be saved. Two hours later, they reached Iwo Jima, a small island in the Pacific. Irwin's flesh was still smoking with embedded phosphorous when he was removed from the plane by comrades who had to hide their faces from his awful wounds.

Sergeant Irwin lived to receive the Medal of Honor, his nation's highest honor for extreme bravery, and he survived nearly fifty plastic surgeries that helped restore him to a somewhat normal life. He lived to marry and to become a father. With him, there lived eleven other men, who, but for his almost unbelievable courage, would be dead. Eleven men, spared to their lives, work, and families through the decision and courageous act of one man!

ESPECIALLY FOR MORMONS

Too often we expect the <u>programs</u> of the Church to save us. Brother John Covey, who was a mission president in Australia, had to go to the island of Sabu in the Philippines. The people there were so poor that they could not afford any of the lesson manuals of the Church. They used the scriptures. They were keeping the commandments of the Lord, and they were doing everything they could to have personal revelation in their lives.

Brother Covey returned to Salt Lake, and reported to President Spencer W. Kimball. President Kimball asked, "How are the people in Sabu? How are they getting along? Are they living the gospel?"

Brother Covey replied that there was not enough money for lesson manuals.

"That is not what I asked you!" President Kimball replied. "How are they getting along?"

"Oh, they are getting along very well."

"What are they using?"

"They are using the scriptures in all their meetings to teach all of the lessons."

Thoughtfully, President Kimball exclaimed, "Oh, that more members of the Church did not have enough money to buy lesson manuals!"

*****

A MOTHER'S CALLING

Tonight I have a meeting.
All day I must prepare,
For I've a special calling.
Each week I must be there.

Our dinner won't be fancy,
And the house won't look too great.
But I'll rush out at six o'clock,
For I must not be late.

Because the Lord has asked me
This time with him to share,
To teach his children of him
And of the need for prayer.

He's promised me that on these nights
When I must be away
That he will bless my family
And with them he will stay.

So tonight while I am serving him
As I know I must,
I know my family's cared for.
His promise I will trust.

Then I can go and teach my class
Without another care.
Because while I'm away from home
Heavenly Father will be there.

--Suzanne Dean

*****

"IF"
For Latter-day Saints

If you can love the sinner all the while you
    loath the sin;
If you can cheer and comfort others, when your
    heart is broken within;
Fight temptations thrust upon you when your
    wants are at their peak;
Be praised for your achievements, yet be humble
    and stay meek;
If you can see jobs go to others without thinking
    "That's not fair!"
But instead be helpful and constant with
    your prayer;
If you can live your own religion but on others
    never slur,
Can keep your thoughts and visions clear when a
    tear has caused a blur;
If you can be the kind of neighbor that the Lord
    has told us to,
When all around you scorn and laugh at things
    most dear to you;
If you can learn and teach others without an air
    of "know-it-all";
If you can bend your knees when need be and at
    other times stand tall;
If you can keep the Word of Wisdom, be clean in thought,
    word, and deeds,
Yet not be so good you wouldn't help another
    in his need--
If you can do all this, my friend, without
    restraint,
Then the world will know you as a true
    Latter-day Saint!

*****

MORONI, THE SOLITARY SCRIBE

Quiet is the earth. The waning sun
Lights the opening avenues of night
And the wistful winds drift through the tree
Like Spirit wanderers.
Sloping gently from Cumorah's Hill
The landscape, torn with ditches deep,
Darkens as the sun departs.

The stillness is a shroud:
No voice of husbandman, no mother's lullaby,
No song of children greets the ear:
No sound save the whispering of winds
And the call of birds
Seeking a resting place.

In a cavern, manmade for refuge,
In Cumorah's southward side, a log is blazing.
The flames cast furtive lights about the strange retreat
Revealing a stone of bulk and smoothness,
And seated there a figure lost in thought
And writing with a deftness born of tutored hand.
He pauses, yet his eyes turn from his task toward
The leaping flames. These luminate a face
Of sorrow fathomless, noble of profile, yet furrowed
By some mighty tragedy. His eyes flash as they pierce
The half-darkness of the cave, then soften as they
Turn aloft for Light.

Who is this man of grief, secreted and alone,
This man of princely brow?
Alas, 'tis he, sole remnant of his race--
Moroni, the solitary scribe;
Moroni, the prophet, patriot, patriot's son,
Moroni, the consecrated one,
Girt with the armor of the Lord,
The God of Lehi, Nephi, Alma, and his noble sire;
This is Moroni, hidden from the prowling Lamanites
Who seek his life. Their hosts have triumphed
On the battlefield, and Nephite legions,
Men of all degrees, bowmen, spearmen, swordsmen,
Captains, all, now lie uncounted where they died
Their wives, fair daughters of the once-proud Zarahemla,
Are cold in death, ravished by the foe, their children
Falling, too, before the sword,
Innocents, yet victims of this culminating curse.

Erase the scene, O God of Heaven.
This fearful harvest of a nation's guilt!
Let it be lost in full forgetfulness,
And yet this cannot be:
The past must needs be bared to guide the children
Of the present day who, if they ape the foolish dead,

Must reap in turn the fruits of sin.
History--what is it, pray?
A monument of truth, enduring, tall,
Austere it stands, the testament of time:
Its base set in the rock of changeless law,
Its shaft the vivid pattern of the race,
Its pinnacle the fadeless star of Bethlehem.

So from the pen of this sad scribe
The chapters grow, writ in plates of gold;
The hours advance, and in the still sky
The wan, white moon moves silent in its course.
Midnight passes, the scribe still writes;
The first rose flush of dawn
Arches the eastern sky and with the falling
Of the dew the task is done.

Burns low the fire, the embers die,
The sun climbs higher in the sky;
Forth from the cavern steals the weary scribe
Bearing the precious plates.
He scans the broad world, then hastens
To a sturdy cavity of stone,
Wherein are placed the plates of gold,
The sword of Laban and the shield,
The Thummin of the Seers, the gift of God,
There to repose until God's voice
Shall call them forth.

Fear is lifted from the prophet's countenance;
He kneels in prayer, then draws
His robe about him and with hasty step
He leaves Cumorah by a hidden path.
Now the solitary scribe is lost to view--
Lost in the forest's unfrequented depths,
There till the summons home shall come,
He roams the melancholy earth alone with God.

--C.Frank Steele

*****

So often we forget the realness of the spirit world that surrounds us.
We forget to honor the salvation of our ancestors. Many of us have even
been warned that these people wait for us to do their work, and that
through our efforts they will be blessed to receive the gospel we share
and love so much here in our physical life.

This understanding was brought strongly to my attention in a dream. I
had been working a little on our records, but had still not sent in the
papers after three years. But one night I learned the consequences. I
was babysitting across the street from my home when, as I looked out the
window, I saw a large, old black car drive up, and its occupants inquire
at our door. After talking with my mother, a small procession of people

headed toward the door of the house where I was babysitting. They knocked and entered, and as each one politely but coolly greeted me, I identified each. First my grandfather, then his wife, then my great-grandfather, then his wife, then each of his children. They stayed a short, uncomfortable while, and then left.

I was deeply hurt that they hadn't sincerely taken me into themselves. I loved each one, but I could feel that they intensely disliked me--for it was I who had rejected them. I had not completed the way for them to share the eternal happiness that work would have brought.

I know now that when I meet them again, I will need their love, and to have it, I must do their work!

*****

THE TEN DEMANDMENTS OF A PROGRESSIVE LATTER-DAY SAINT

1. Demand of yourself a straight and narrow course, neither sidestepping nor stopping along the way. The man of decision cannot be stopped, and the man of indecision cannot get started.

2. Demand of yourself no excuses, neither offering alibies, nor blaming the other fellow. Develop those great qualities within yourself with which you have been endowed.

3. Demand of yourself tolerance. Our most profitable business in life is that of personal growth, and letting others grow, too.

4. Demand of yourself a disposition that is not easily offended. It is best to be a person of action, not of reaction to every opposition or misunderstanding.

5. Demand of yourself a day's work for a day's pay. Be a body who is busy, not a busybody.

6. Demand of yourself thrift, and stay out of debt. You owe so much to yourself that you can't afford to owe others.

7. Demand of yourself honest praise for others. Real people need no sugar-coated hosannas, only appreciation for work well done.

8. Demand of yourself a curiosity to gain knowledge, remembering that when you do obtain knowledge, it is only a cup from an ocean of knowledge. Thus we gain humility.

9. Demand of yourself self-control. Those who lead others must first learn to lead themselves.

10. Demand of yourself profit from your failures. Defeat is a destructive force only when you accept it as failure. It will be a turning point in your life if you use it as a stepping stone.

*****

STEWARDSHIP

In June 1965 in his Hotel Utah apartment, President David O. McKay spoke to a group of brethren in the Physical Facilities Department of the Church. While explaining to them the importance of the work they were engaged in, he paused and told them the following:

Let me assure you, brethren, that someday you will have a personal priesthood interview with the Savior himself. If you are interested, I will tell you the order in which he will ask you to account for your earthly responsibilities.

First, he will request an accountability report about your relationship with your wife. Have you actively been engaged in making her happy, ensuring that her needs as an individual have been met?

Second, he will want an accountability report about each of your children. He will not want this report to reflect family stewardship, but he will request information about your individual relationship with each and every child.

Third, he will want to know what you personally have done with the talents you were given in the preexistence.

Fourth, he will want a summary of your activity in your Church assignments. He will not necessarily be interested in what assignments you have had--for in his eyes the home teacher and the mission president are probably equals--but he will request a summary of how you have been of service to your fellow men in your Church assignments.

Fifth, he will have no interest in how you earned your living--but he will want to know whether you have been honest in all your dealings.

Sixth, he will ask for an accountability on what you have done to contribute in a positive manner to your community, state, country, and the world.

--From the notes of Fred A. Baker

*****

THE EAGER STEWARD

A loud knock awoke a servant early one morning. Upon opening the door of his humble cottage, he was surprised to find his master awaiting him.

"I am taking a journey. Would you like to join me?" asked the master.

"Most certainly," replied the servant. "Will we be gone long?"

"Only a few days."

The way was new to the servant, and he saw many interesting and beautiful things. But none so beautiful as the sight he beheld when they reached their destination.

As they came over the brow of a hill, stretched out below them was the most luxuriant valley the servant had ever seen. Flowing through the fields, deep and green with grass and foliage, was a sparkling stream that the master said teemed with fish. Cattle and other animals were grazing. Bees were buzzing as they gathered nectar from the profusion of flowers. Across the valley, the slopes of a mountain were covered with trees, and the master said precious ore and stones were under the surface.

"How would you like to move your family here and live in this valley?" asked the master. "You could till these fertile fields, build a mill on the stream, cut the trees, and mine the minerals."

"Oh, there is nothing I would like more," replied the servant. "But, if I worked all the rest of my life, I wouldn't have enough money to pay for even a portion of this beautiful valley."

"This valley is not for sale," said the master. "I propose only to share it with you."

"That would be splendid," said the servant eagerly. "I could farm the land, build factories, raise cattle, gather the honey, and 50 percent of all I raised or produced I would gladly pay you for the privilege of living here and using these rich resources."

"But I don't require 50 percent," was the master's astonishing response. "For your use of everything in this valley, I require only 10 percent of your annual increase."

"Gladly I will pay you a tenth of all I produce. You are most generous." And gratitude filled the eyes of the servant as he spoke to his master. "To what point shall I deliver each year your tenth of the field and of the flock and of the factory?"

"I do not wish to take delivery. I wish to leave my tenth with you."

"Leave your tenth?" The servant was now dumbfounded.

"Yes, leave it with you to be used as I designate--for the relief of the widows, the fatherless, the sick, and the needy in the valley; and to build houses in which to worship, that you may ever remember to live a good life; to be obedient to all the instructions I leave with you, and to be helpful and generous to others. One more thing I would require of you--that you instruct your children, and they their children, for all succeeding generations, that the rent for this valley is 10 percent."

The servant faithfully promised not only to pay the 10 percent during his lifetime, but to teach each of his children to do likewise, and they their children after them. And for generations the greater part of the servant's descendants kept their promise, and the rent was used for the purposes the master had designated.

But as time progressed, the people in the valley became careless, and then forgetful. Some saw no need to foster the activities for which the rent had been used. Others continued a part of the activities, but raised the necessary funds in other ways--a tenth seemed far too much.

One day the master visited the valley and reminded the residents of his instructions. He told them that if they would return unto him that he would return unto them. But many, untaught, did not even know what he was talking about. "Wherein shall we return?" they asked.

"Will a man rob his master? Yet you have robbed me."

"Wherein have we robbed thee?" asked the occupants of the valley, some innocently, some knowingly.

"In the 10 percent rent you were to pay me. If you choose not to pay, then you are using the land and the resources unlawfully, and you will be deprived of the promises I have made. But if you will repent, and bring your rent to the storehouse I have designated, you can prove to your own satisfaction that I will bless you beyond your capacity to receive."

The master _is_ coming.

--Richard W. Maycock

*****

AUTHORITY: KEY TO ACTION

The call came on Wednesday. "We are having a special priesthood restoration program Sunday, and we would like you to give a ten-minute talk on the priesthood and what it means in your life." I accepted the assignment, and mulled it over several times in the next few days.

By Saturday evening I had determined pretty much what I wanted to say. I would define priesthood and discuss our obligations as priesthood bearers. And yet something was not right. My discussion was too general, too unfeeling. It was a repetition of rote phrases. Priesthood seemed far too personal, even intimate, to be dismissed with the general statements I had in mind. It would take a definition in highly personal terms to describe such a sacred concept. I clearly needed a new approach.

In an effort to order my thoughts, I climbed into my car and drove out the boulevard away from the city. The lateness of the hour left the streets almost empty. Without having determined any particular destination, I was soon driving through a dark and silent canyon east of the city. The solitude was broken only by an occasional car heading back down the canyon. The only other light came from the glow of a half moon, which broke through the trees at places where the canyon floor widened out briefly before closing in again. Perhaps in this setting I could search out what priesthood really means in my life.

My search produced a flood of long-forgotten incidents. All seemed to relate the same message. Priesthood is people; it is best understood through the lives of people. Priesthood is a little group of high priests in a little Utah town walking as a quorum behind the casket of my grandfather, paying honor to one of their number who had been faithful. Priesthood is my father, returning from his mission at a time when the missionary ranks had been sharply depleted by war and difficult times. The Church had made an urgent request that each priesthood quorum send out at least one missionary as quickly as possible. In my father's quorum there was no one else able to go. And so he accepted a second call, and within a few weeks of returning from his first mission, he was on his way to a second. Perhaps there is some priesthood meaning in my mother's decision that if my father was worth waiting for through one mission, he was worth waiting for through two.

Priesthood is what happens when a boy of six or seven wakes up in the night with a severe earache. His signs of discomfort soon awaken the entire family. His father calls in a fellow priesthood holder, and they place their hands on the boy's head and give him a blessing. In a matter of minutes all is quiet; the earache has subsided, and the family returns to bed.

Priesthood is a newly retired neighbor who, with his wife, is called on a mission. Their field of labor is an unaccustomed climate in an area with sharply different social conditions. They become discouraged and occasionally wonder what is being accomplished by their efforts; but they will stay and do their task, because their faith in the Lord is strong.

Priesthood is a prominent educator, confiding that much of his career has been shaped by one sentence in his patriarchal blessing, given while he was still a boy.

Priesthood is a young man on his way to the mission field.

Priesthood is the overwhelming sense of awe at his calling engulfing a missionary as he travels from a tiny branch to a district conference. A devout woman in poor health has just queried, "But what will we do if we need the priesthood while you're gone?"

Priesthood is sitting in the Tabernacle with eight thousand other men, leaning forward to catch an occasional word from the speaker at the rostrum, because he is the prophet of God.

As I drive along I think of a middle-aged man in a psychiatric ward at the hospital. The two elders assigned to administer have spent several hours going from floor to floor. It is late before they gain admittance to the patient's section. He has not yet gone to bed; he is lightly dozing in a chair in his room. "I was afraid you wouldn't come," he says as we enter the room. "I left the door open and stayed up just in case."

After a blessing is given, there is little that can be expressed by words. The man embraces the elders and cries softly. In a shattered and crumbling world, there is still the priesthood.

Priesthood is a fine professional man who has been vocal in his criticism. His associates have frequently heard his complaints. But on this occasion he asks the elders to administer to his wife, who has been stricken seriously ill.

Priesthood is a letter received at the personnel section of a large military base. A bishop from a tiny Idaho community has written on behalf of a soldier from his ward. The boy's father has just died, and the boy is needed at home to help bring in the hay. The letter is poorly written. But one person reads the letter with deep pride, knowing that it represents a good man who has accepted an awesome responsibility. The bishop is using all his talents in the service of the Lord as long as the Lord may request them.

By now the canyon ride is almost completed. Soon the lights of the valley to the west will explode into view. The words of a popular song cross my mind almost imperceptibly: "Love isn't love 'til you give it away." Maybe that is the definition I'm searching for. Priesthood is really inoperative unless it is used in someone else's behalf. It is a gift of God, given to insensitive, imperfect, and doubting men for their own perfection. But it is a gift to be shared. Like love, it must be given away. One honors his priesthood by using it for the uplifting of others. It suddenly seems so clear. Priesthood is really service.

The lights of the city now sparkle like a jewel. The streets are strangely deserted now. I snap from my reverie and head for home. When the dawn comes, I will have my talk.

--Reed P. Wahlquist

ENDURANCE

THE LONG PULL

It's the steady, constant driving
To the goal for which you're striving,
Not the speed with which you travel
That will make the victory sure.
It's the everlasting gaining,
Without whimper or complaining
At the burdens you are bearing
Or the woes you must endure.

It's the holding to a purpose
And the never giving in;
It's the cutting down the distance
By the little that you win.
It's the iron will to do it
And the steady sticking to it.
So whatever your task, go to it--
And life's purpose you will win.

--Anonymous

*****

THE RACE

"Quit!" "Give up, you're beaten!" they shout at me and plead,
"There's just too much against you now, this time you can't   succeed."
And as I started to hang my head in front of failure's face,
My downward fall is broken by the memory of a race.
And hope refills my weakened will as I recall that scene,
For just the thought of that short race rejuvenates my being.
A children's race, young boys, young men; now I remember well.
Excitement, sure, but also fear; it wasn't hard to tell.
They all lined up so full of hope. Each thought to win that race
Or tie for first, or if not that, at least take second place.
And fathers watched from off the side, each cheering for his son,
And each boy hoped to show his dad that he would be the one.
The whistle blew and off they sped, as if they were on fire
To win, to be the hero there, was each young boy's desire.
And one boy in particular, his dad was in the crowd,
Was running near the lead and thought, "My dad will be so proud."
But as he speeded down the field, across the shallow dip,
The little boy who thought to win lost his step and slipped.
Trying hard to catch himself, his arm flew out to brace,
And 'mid the laughter of the crowd, he fell flat on his face.
So, down he fell, and with him, hope. He couldn't win it now.

Endurance

Embarrassed, sad, he only wished he'd disappear somehow.
But, as he fell, his dad stood up and showed his anxious face,
Which to the boy so clearly said, "Get up and win the race!"
He quickly rose, no damage done, behind a bit, that's all.
And ran with all his mind and might to make up for the fall.
So anxious to restore himself, to catch up and to win,
His mind went faster than his legs. He slipped and fell again.
He wished he had quit before with only one disgrace.
"I'm hopeless as a runner now, I shouldn't try to race."
But, in the laughing crowd he searched and found his father's face.
That steady look that said again, "Get up and win the race!"
So, he jumped up to try again, ten yards behind the last;
"If I'm to gain those yards," he thought, "I've got to run real fast!"
Exceeding everything he had, he regained eight or ten,
But trying so hard to catch the lead, he slipped and fell again.
Defeat! He lay there silently, a tear dropped from his eye.
"There's no sense running any more. Three strikes, I'm out. . .
    why try?"
The will to rise had disappeared, all hope had fled away.
So far behind, so error-prone, closer all the way.
"I've lost, so what's the use?" he thought, "I'll live with my
    disgrace."
But then he thought about his dad, who soon he'd have to face.
"Get up," an echo sounded low, "Get up and take your place.
You weren't meant for failure here; get up and win the race."
With borrowed will, "Get up," it said, "You haven't lost at all,
For winning is no more than this--to rise each time you fall."
So up he rose to win once more. And with a new commit,
He resolved that win or lose, at least he wouldn't quit.
So far behind the others now, the most he'd ever been.
Still, he gave it all he had, and ran as though to win.
Three times he'd fallen, stumbling, three times he rose again.
Too far behind to hope to win, he still ran to the end.
They cheered the winning runner, as he crossed the line, first place,
Head high and proud and happy; no falling, no disgrace.
But, when the fallen crossed the finish line, last place,
The crowd gave him the greater cheer for finishing the race.
And even though he came in last, with head bowed low, unproud,
You would have thought he'd won the race, to listen to the crowd.
And to his dad, he sadly said, "I didn't do so well."
"To me you won," his father said, "you rose each time you fell."
And now when things seem dark and hard and difficult to face,
The memory of that little boy helps me in my race.
For all of life is like that race, with ups and downs and all,
And all you have to do to win is rise each time you fall.
"Quit!" "Give up, you're beaten!" They still shout in my face,
But another voice within me says, "Get up and win that race!"

                        --D. H. Groberg

                        *****

A few years ago, along about the first of May, I was out planting a little garden with my youngest boy, who was then just finishing his first year in school. He said, "Dad, what are you going to do Friday?"

"I don't know, son--why?"

"I want you to come to school with me," he explained. "It's our field day, and we are going to run races. Dad, I'm going to be in one of those races, and I want you to come and watch me."

"All right," I said, "I can make it."

"I won't win the race, Dad. But I want you to come anyway." With his head down, he was rather quiet for a minute. Then he said, "Dad, I'll probably come in last; I can't run very fast. But I want you to come and watch me run."

I thank my Heavenly Father for the lesson taught me by my little seven-year-old boy. I don't know how many boys want their dads to see them come in last in a race or in any athletic event. I don't know how many dads want to go and see their boy come in last. We say, "Oh, I want to go to the ball game. That's _my_ boy who made all of the baskets! That's _my_ boy who made all of the touchdowns. That's _me_ out there!" I am wondering how many of us want to go to see our boy come in _last_.

Well, Friday came. The little boy was all excited. He said, "Dad, this is the day. This is it! This is the big day we have been waiting for! I have to be there at four o'clock." By a quarter to four we all started out toward school. On the way he was still thinking about his great race. He said, "Dad, you know, even if I come in last, I'm going to get a prize anyway. Our teacher told us she didn't think it was fair that only the winner should get a prize." Again I thanked my Heavenly Father for teachers like Miss Ferre of the Oquirrh School in the Granite School District, who can teach my boy how to fail.

We arrived at school; I sat on the bleachers, of course, with the parents, and the children chased each other around a ring and threw a ball up in the air. Finally, Miss Ferre blew her whistle for those little first-graders. The boys lined up on one side, and the girls lined up on the other. She blew her whistle, and the girls raced down to one end. She then gave each one of them an all-day sucker.

Then it was the boys' turn. She blew her whistle again. They started in that broken line, and ran down to the other end. I watched one little boy--his legs going so fast, mostly up and down rather than forward-- moving as fast as he could. I watched until he came within about ten feet of the goal line. He couldn't contain himself anymore. He turned his head around and looked--was Dad still watching?--and he stumbled and fell. The rest of the boys went across the finish line. Then I saw that one little fellow on his hands and knees, down in the dirt, crawl across the goal line. I saw Miss Ferre reach down, take hold of his hand, and lift him up. A smile broke out across his face, and he received his all-day sucker. He came to the bleachers where I was sitting. He looked at me and said, "Dad, did you see me run?"

73

Oh, if I should live to see him the greatest runner of all time, and Olympic champion of the world, I would never be more humbly grateful than I was that afternoon when I saw him come across the goal line--the last one, down in the dirt on his hands and knees.

You know, that is probably the way I will go out of this old life--oh, missed by a few relatives and a small circle of friends. But if I have run the race of life the best I could, if I have walked along that old path the best I could, even though I cross the goal line on my hands and knees, down in the dirt, I will have a good teacher over there who will say, "Well done, my good and faithful servant. Enter into the presence of thy Lord. Remember, I told you when I was down upon earth, the race is not to the swift nor the battle to the strong, but to him who endureth to the end."

--Ray F. Smith

*****

I KNEW COURAGE

The hot pain in my chest burned in sharp contrast to the cold fear that iced my heart. Here, in the vast, lonesome, black, interminable night, I lay trying to make myself face the possibility that I had cancer.

As days and fearsome, sleepless nights of pain followed, I found myself constantly thinking about what it would be like to die. But it was another drama, a year earlier, that made this thought more poignant. It wasn't until now that a true realization of the depth and breadth of Greg's courage came to me.

Greg was a big, handsome, clean-cut seventeen-year-old, and a fine runner. When he had announced, five years earlier, his decision to follow a family tradition of competing in the mile run, my heart sank. He was poorly coordinated, and I could foresee nothing but heartbreak for him. His life had been full enough of this already, I felt. He had always had to do things the hard way; events conspired against him, making everything he desired an uphill struggle. Instead of quitting, however, he always seemed more determined to work even harder than before.

With his running, Greg trained the year around instead of the usual practice of training only during track season. He severely denied himself every food or activity that he felt would impair his running. He spent summers working for his grandfather on his cattle ranch. After spending a full, hard day in the hayfields, he would care for a large vegetable garden, which he had insisted on planting, and then go for long runs in the nearby foothills.

Everyone pleaded with him to stop demanding so much of himself, worried about the rigorous schedule he set for himself, but to no avail.

He was a perfectionist, and had decided this would give him the strength and stamina he needed in running.

When he returned from the ranch to start school, he didn't look well, and he always seemed tired. Since he had had rheumatic fever as a child, we watched his heart closely. To allay our worry, we had him undergo a cardiogram and a complete physical examination. But all tests indicated he was well. We knew he had driven himself too hard all summer, and supposed this accounted for his looking and feeling tired.

Cross-country racing began, and Greg went on driving himself unmercifully. After school each day he would come home, change into old clothes, and sit on the kitchen hearth to chat for a few minutes about how the day had gone while he laced up his heavy hiking boots. He ran daily in the mountains, wearing those heavy boots to build his strength and stamina. He joked about how good it seemed in competitive racing to run in track shoes after having run in heavy boots. There was more to running in the mountains; he loved nature, and depended on that time alone to replenish his soul while training his body.

One October afternoon Greg looked unusually tired and commented on the soreness in his left thigh. He wondered what he had done to injure it. But it wasn't unusual for him to have stiff muscles--runners seem to have plenty of them, so I was used to it. But what _was_ unusual was that he allowed me to dissuade him from running that day.

Not many days later, a race important to the school was scheduled. Though he admitted wishing he didn't have to further strain his sore leg, he insisted on participating. During the race, his leg completely failed, and he was in agony. When we took him to the doctor, Greg told how his leg had given way during the race. The doctor said he could feel a torn muscle, and told him it would continue to be painful--it would take a long time to heal, and it probably meant that Greg couldn't run again. He had to walk with crutches.

As always, Greg reacted with determination that he would find a way through and build back his leg so he could someday run again.

The doctor had told him to come back for a checkup. At school, someone kicked the crutch as he was going down stairs, and he fell the full flight. The pain was intense, but Greg thought it would just be a matter of being careful and giving the muscle time to heal again, so he didn't go back to the doctor. He steeled himself to suffer it through, but each day he looked worse and he lost considerable weight. The suffering that spoke from his eyes and his wasted body told us how really excrutiating his pain was.

When we finally returned to the doctor, we discovered that Greg's "torn muscle" was osteogenic sarcoma (cancer that originates in the bone). His left leg was amputated near the hip.

Greg faced the rebuilding of a shattered life and shattered dreams. How does one convincingly tell a seventeen-year-old in December that there is a satisfying life left for him--a boy who in August had had his first date and danced his first dance; who was just learning to drive a car; who had just tasted his first success in sports and was a leading contender for the mile championship; who at long last could see life going his way after so many heartbreaking struggles?

Since it was necessary to amputate high, Greg was left with less than a four-inch stump--not much with which to fit a prosthesis. His legs were long, creating a difficult problem in manipulating an artificial limb.

It was some time before he found a way to get into the driver's seat of the car. Then a new problem loomed: because of the short stump, his artificial limb would lose its suction when he sat squarely. So he sat on one hip, throwing his spine out of alignment. The resulting pain left him ill. He constantly feared the prosthesis would come loose when he was away from home.

The doctors advised that Greg go back to school and be among people as soon as possible, but Greg was determined not to return until he could walk well.

Does anyone ever stop to think how complex the simple procedure of walking is? Together we studied how one walks. I walked across the room, and he followed, trying to imitate a natural leg swing with his artificial limb. Hour after hour, day after day he practiced, stopped only by sheer exhaustion.

Finally came the deadline we had set for his starting school: the beginning of spring term. He knew everyone was watching. Besides psychological obstacles, he faced new physical hazards, such as school ramps and stairs.

Greg resented being treated less independently than before the amputation. He didn't want special concessions, even though he desperately needed them. No one will ever know, I'm sure, the mental torment one in such a position endures. I believe the physical pain is minor in comparison.

Having to be driven everywhere he went, passing the track team out for practice as he left school each afternoon, and not being able to run in his beloved mountains were a few of the thorns that sorely pricked him.

I glimpsed the extent of his frustration and his complete mastery of it one day when he had prevailed upon me to drive him up by his mountain haunts. The snow was deep there, but without his prosthesis he insisted on making his way up the hillside on one leg and his crutches. He reminded me of a great and noble bird with broken wings, still trying to fly. I wanted to run up the hillside screaming, "Why? Why?" But when he came back to the car, he calmly brushed the snow from his leg and said, "Shall we go, Mother?" When we arrived home, he shoveled the snow from the driveway and sidewalk.

Greg made the adjustments, just as he had conquered all other obstacles in his life. No one had thought he could possibly do so well.

Not content with this, he set about to out-swim and out-wrestle his friends.

At the time of his amputation, we were told that his was a particularly insidious type of cancer that attacks the lungs and is fatal in three out of four cases. But one always thinks he will be the exception.

Greg wasn't. When he went for his three-month x-ray checkup, the doctors discovered cancer in both his lungs. From the beginning, Greg had known his full hazard. Now he knew there was no possibility for cure, as it was not possible to perform surgery, and any treatment could merely hold the cancer at bay, if that.

Until that point I had been able to build up his morale, but I could find nothing more to say. It was an insult to his honesty and forthrightness to say there was hope, when we both knew there was none. I felt abject desolation.

Greg said little during the ten-mile ride home from the doctor's office. When we arrived home, Greg's best friend was there helping his small brother fly a kite in the March wind. By this time, the little brother had tired of the sport and run off, leaving the kite. Greg liked to see everything in perfect order, so he picked up the kite and let out the string, and it began to soar. Soon he sent for more twine. By this time, the kite was only a speck, and we were all breathless at the dizzying height to which it had flown.

Greg turned to me and said, "A new high, Mother." I knew he wasn't talking just about the kite.

The weekend that followed was one of complete depression. By Sunday night when the rest of the family had retired and Greg was alone with me and his father, our feeble efforts at cheerful talk finally bogged down in speechless grief and dejection. Finally Greg said, "I can't go on like this. I have to go on planning to live. There is always time for dying, but there isn't always time for living."

And Greg did go on "planning to live." He had an exercise set with which to rebuild his muscles; to the last, however feebly, he exercised his one leg and arms.

Unlike Greg, I was given a reprieve. My chest pain proved to have been emotionally induced. But in the interim, I was brought to a realization of Greg's true courage. His was not the fright-incited courage of battle heroics; rather, it was calm, calculated, raw courage.

Yes, I saw courage. I saw it in Greg, who kept a calm face when I told him, an outstanding runner, that he had to lose his leg. I saw it when he defiantly climbed a mountain, hip-deep in snow, with only one leg. I saw it in his face, again calm, as the doctor told him he had only a few months before he would die of lung cancer. I saw it when he came home and, in the face of a death warrant, flew a kite to real and symbolic new heights.

I saw <u>courage,</u> as Greg lived nobly up to the final moment in hundreds of mundane words and ways, undaunted by the terrible pain and fear I know were his to bear.

He dictated to me a final entry to his journal, which is its own testimony:

Life has been good to me. Although I have had many disappointments, I have had many, many satisfactions. One of the worst kinds of torture I remember is the mental torture. . .the monotony of staying in the same place. Saturday, August 1, my soul was wrought up. It was extremely difficult for me to get a breath, and I hurt every time I tried. Now a feeling of peace has come over me, and I feel as though every night is Sunday night. [Sunday night was a special family night to us.] My prayers have been answered many times, and I am grateful to the Lord for his many blessings. Somehow, the mere physical sports, which I valued so highly before, seem as nothing compared to the tasks that I will soon embark upon. I bid the reader farewell, wishing the Lord's blessings upon him. I have no feeling of bitterness, no malice of any kind, for I know in my heart that this is the Lord's will. I know truly that the Lord does live. And I know that only through obeying his commandments can we be happy on earth.

Yes, I knew <u>courage.</u>

--Jean Hart

EXAMPLE

Setting a good example is better than giving advice. Good example is a language all can understand, and an argument none can deny.

*****

In the course of the Armenian atrocities, a young woman and her brother were pursued down the street by a Turkish soldier. They were cornered against a wall, and the brother was slain before his sister's eyes. She dodged down an alley, leaped a wall, and escaped.

Later, being a nurse, she was forced by the Turkish authorities to work in the military hospital. Into her ward one day was brought the same Turkish soldier who had slain her brother. He was very ill. A slight inattention would ensure his death. The young woman, now safe in America, confesses to the bitter struggle that took place in her mind. The old Adam cried "vengeance," and the new Christ cried, "love." And, equal to the man's good and to her own, the better side of her conquered, and she nursed him as carefully as any other patient in the ward.

The recognition had been mutual, and one day--unable to restrain his curiosity--the Turk asked his nurse why she had not let him die. When she replied, "I am a follower of him who said, 'Love your enemies and do them good,'" he was silent for a long time. At last he spoke: "I never knew that there was such a religion. If that is your religion, tell me more about it, for I want it."

--Harry Emerson Fosdick

*****

"I would think he must be suffering, anybody who's like that; we ought to feel sorry for him," said April Aaron of the man who sent her to a hospital for three weeks following a brutal San Francisco knife attack.

April Aaron is a devout Mormon, twenty-two years of age. She is a secretary who's as pretty as her name, but her face has just one blemish--the right eye is missing. April lost it to the "wildly slashing knife of a purse snatcher" near San Francisco's Golden Gate Park while en route to a Church dance. She also suffered deep slashes on her left arm and right leg as a result of the struggle with her assailant after she tripped and fell in her efforts to elude him, just one block from the Mormon meetinghouse.

"I ran for a block and a half before he caught me. You can't run very fast on high heels," April said with a smile. Slashes on her leg were so severe doctors feared for a time it would need amputation. The sharp edge of the weapon could damage neither April's vivaciousness nor her compassion, however: "I wish that somebody could do something for him to help him. He should have some treatment. Who knows what leads a person to do a thing like this? If they don't find him, he's likely to do it again."

Example

April Aaron has won the hearts of the people in the San Francisco Bay area with her courage and good spirit in the face of tragedy. Her room at St. Francis Hospital was filled with flowers throughout her stay, and attendants could not recall when anyone received more cards and expressions of good wishes.

FAITH

A belief is not something you carry around, but a conviction is something that carries you around. How strong are your convictions?

--Anonymous

*****

WHERE IS MY FAITH?

Where is my faith. . .

When something I've lost doesn't get found
In spite of my prayers and pleas?
When the money is not forthcoming
That my son in the mission field needs?

When someone I love is allowed to endure
The suffering of sorrow and pain?
And fasting and prayer and everyone's faith
Doesn't result in our much-needed rain?

Where is the help that I hear all about
When I sit in a testimony meeting?
Has the Lord decided that I don't really need
All the things I think that I'm needing?

Do I have the faith to love and to trust
In my Father's wisdom and care?
And know that he'll never ask me to endure
More than he knows I can bear?

--Susan Hiatt Biggs

*****
A THIN VEIL

Sometimes,
Dear Lord,
I feel your touch--
Your gentle,
Guiding hand
On my shoulder,
Softly placed
To show
You understand.

Sometimes,
When I speak
To you
In hours
Of reverent prayer,
I lift my eyes

Faith

To see your face--
So sure
You will be there.

Those special
Moments
When I ask
The questions
Of my heart,
I hear your
Answers
With my ears
And know
How great
Thou art.

When I reach out
To take your hand,
Although
The veil is there,
Your presence
Is so very real
I feel you
Everywhere.

The veil
Must be
Very thin
That renders
Mortals blind,
For when
In conference
With you, Lord,
I reach you
With my mind.

--Suzanne Dean

*****

THE PRINCIPLE

First,
In obedience,
I take the book
And wade through
Ancient dialect.

Turning pages
One by one
To face the quest--
Obedient, yes--
Without conviction.

82

But, bits of truth
Leap from scripture
To spark
Silenced knowledge
Within my soul.

Then,
In eager faith,
I drink the words--
Their message clear,
I begin to see

All the
Great principle
Obedience
Can yield
To me.

--Suzanne Dean

*****

FAITH: THE SEED OF TRUTH

A young stonecutter arrived from the Old Country with his faith and determination as his only assets. And he walked many days seeking employment. He was told to cut stones, exactly as marked.

But there was no beauty in the design. Indeed, it hardly seemed to be a design; it was neither scroll nor leaf, only a few meaningless lines to this young man, whose very soul ached for beauty.

Nevertheless, he labored on these stones for many weeks. And then, one day as he was walking through the very center of town, admiring the stonework on the magnificent buildings, he saw a new arch of stone. It was more than that--he looked more closely, and he recognized that his own craftsmanship had cut those stones.

And as he looked, he said, "I cut those blocks, and I'm so thankful I did my work right and was faithful, for I didn't know when I cut them that they were to be an arch of anything half so beautiful."

So may we be faithful to our task. Our master makes the plan; the pattern is his. He permits us to do the work if we will, and someday we will see how beautiful the design, and know God's plan.

--<u>Millennial Star</u>

*****

More than half a century ago I was standing at a little railway station in Cardston, Canada. I was leaving on a mission to England. My precious mother stood there with me and held my hand, and this is what she said:

"Hugh, my son, when you were a little tot, you often had bad dreams--nightmares--and you would often call out to me as I slept in the next room. In your fright, you would say, 'Mother, are you there?' I always said, 'Yes, my son, I am here. Just turn over and go to sleep. Everything is all right.' My boy, five thousand miles, a continent, and an ocean will soon separate us. You are not only going to call out and have bad dreams at night, but many times in the daytime you are going to call out. Now, my son, when you are in trouble and face difficulties, when you meet temptations, and when you are confused and do not know which way to go, call out and say, 'Father, are you there?' I promise you he will always answer you, and you need not fear."

Through intervening years, countless occasions have arisen where men could not help me. I felt alone; I had nightmares with my eyes wide open. I have taken the advice of my mother. I have said, "Father, are you there?" He has not spoken to me audibly; he has not appeared to me personally; but he has always answered me. There has come into my heart a quiet peace that has enabled me to know that I could, figuratively, turn over and go to sleep.

--Hugh B. Brown

*****

WHEN THE WINDS OBEYED

It was called the most remarkable steamship/iceberg collision on record in an 1891 issue of Windsor Magazine. Somehow the badly damaged Arizona managed to make it to Port St. John, Newfoundland, and safely land all its crew and passengers after colliding with an iceberg in the wake of an angry, storm-tossed sea.

Behind this story reposes an example of faith and of the power of the priesthood, for the Lord did provide for his servants in their time of need and blessed them with his authority to carry out the mission to which he had called them. Henry Aldous Dixon held such authority, and used it during this incident.

Elder Dixon was a South African convert of 1856 and a man of great faith and humility. Elder Dixon and three other missionaries--Joseph Vickers, William H. Coray, and J. L. Jones--were aboard the Arizona bound for Great Britain. As the elders prepared for evening prayers, the ship's engines suddenly stopped, and a great crunching of crumbling timbers and sheet metal rang through the cold, clear night.

Rushing to the deck with the other passengers, the missionaries beheld an immense, blue-white mass of ice on the forecastle deck in front of the vessel's bow. The ship Arizona, traveling at full speed, had struck an iceberg. The force of the collision was so great that it completely caved in the ship's bow and piled more than twenty tons of ice on top of the deck. Both anchors were broken; the anchor chains, tested to hold twelve tons, were severed. The huge hole in the bow, thirty feet deep by twenty feet wide, extended below the water mark and along the whole length of the keel. More than four thousand gallons of water filled the front compartments, and several sailors were buried in the avalanche of ice when it settled on the forecastle decks. It took some time to dig them out.

With such a huge hole in the ship's bow, the front compartments filled with water, and the weight of twenty tons of ice on the front decks, the sea had to be calm to enable the captain and crew to get the ship to the nearest port without sinking.

The four elders frequently knelt together and prayed for the safety of the ship and passengers. But this night of tragedy was unusually special. It demanded great faith and the blessings of the Master. With righteous faith and in exercise of the holy priesthood, Elder Henry A. Dixon went alone on the deck and there rebuked the wind and the waves, praying for a calm sea.

Thirty-six hours later, the ship limped into Port St. John. The prayers of the elders had been answered; the promise that Elder Dixon had given the passengers--that no lives would be lost, the ship would safely reach port, and all would reach their destination in safety--had been fulfilled.

In the middle of the night of the accident the vessel's owner, Mr. Guion, was informed of the collision. He inquired if there were any Mormon missionaries on board. He was told that there were four. He then informed those around him that he knew that the vessel would land safely and that they were to have no further worries or fears. His steamship line had carried Mormons for forty years, and he had never lost a ship on which missionaries were passengers. Carrying Mormon missionaries was the best insurance he could buy, Mr. Guion said, and with that remark, he returned to his bed to sleep.

--Clarence D. Taylor

FAMILY

Out of the dreariness
into its cheeriness
come we in weariness
home.

--Stephen Chalmers

*****

THE OLD FAMILY ALBUM

The old family album, the pages are worn,
From turning and browsing they are tattered and torn,
For mem'ries are sweet ones, we like to repeat ones,
We live them again in the old family album.

Now picture the family, we're all having fun,
We're in this together--parents, daughters, and sons.
For pictures are share times, those family affair times,
We live them again in the old family album.

The camera is snapping while gifts we're unwrapping.
The lens is recording our group as we're boarding.
The shutter is clicking while baby is kicking,
And all to record in the old family album.

So stand all together, remember to smile.
We'll all be recorded in family group style.
The camera is ready, now everyone steady,
And we'll be a page in the old family album.

*****

QUESTIONS AND ANSWERS

Mommy, Mommy, he sings his request;
What? What? I answer my best.

How does the sun shine? Where does it go?
Why is it dark when the cold wind blows?

Questions and answers the whole day through,
Questions and answers--I think I'll turn blue!

But wait, just a moment, and look at his face,
He's questioning me with hope--also with faith.

Dear Lord, please bless me more patient to be,
Help me to answer him with sincerity.

Please help me to know this gift is not mine,
But a lease from thee for my mortal time.

Help me to cherish more each day
Each little question he sends my way.

                    --Beverly Martin

                    *****

FULL CIRCLE

It quite escapes me what she wore that night
When, gay-bedecked, she left for her first dance;
I've searched my mind rememb'ring if I might,
Aught but her fleeting smile, her hopeful glance,
Her wistful youth, so dewy-fresh and new,
How tremulous her face, how like a rose
The faint blush which from her excitement grew
And threatened to o'erspread her powdered nose;

I only know a lump grew in my throat;
I thought it would constrict my breathing, sure,
As, woodenly, I waited with her coat
And, mother-proud, watched her float across the floor
To where her partner stood, well-groomed and straight,
Waiting to take her on a daddy date.

                    --Evalyn M. Sandberg

                    *****

MEMORIES OF HOME

I think of them there in the twilight
When the night shades begin to fall,
Father and Mother in the dear, old home
That has known and sheltered us all.

The house seems quiet and lonely, now,
Since the children are grown and gone,
But the bees still hum in the orchard bloom,
And the birds sing the same sweet song.

The evening star hangs over the mountain,
The whippoorwill calls to its mate.
The rising moon makes a path of gold
On the shimmering blue of the lake.

Family

The place is flooded with memories,
Memories of each sister and brother,
Memories and love that take us back
To our old home, and Father and Mother.

--Geneva H. Williams

*****

MIRAGES

I drive home
Through the mountain curves,
Because it is shorter,
That I might embrace
My little ones sooner,
Sorry for the absence.
And it seems necessary
To hold them
The first possible
Second I can.

I see the heat waves.
I know all about mirages;
I live with them.
They change, even
Before I can
Drive home
They will have grown.
Already their babyhood
Is as unreal to me
As the pools of
Cool water
Up ahead on the
Summer sun-soaked
Highway.

I hurry,
Hoping not to miss
A moment more
Of their fleeting,
Elusive
Childhood.

--Barbara Werrett Nielsen

*****

JUST A BOY

Got to understand the lad--
   He's not eager to be bad;
If the right he always knew,
   He would be as old as you.

Were he now exceeding wise,
He'd be just about your size;
When he does things that annoy,
Don't forget, he's just a boy.

Being just a boy, he'll do
    Much you will not want him to;
He'll be careless of his ways,
    He'll have disobedient days.
Willful, wild, and headstrong, too,
He'll need guidance, kind and true;
Things of value he'll destroy,
But reflect--he's just a boy.

Could he know and understand,
    He would need no guiding hand;
But he's young and hasn't learned
    How life's corner must be turned.
Doesn't know from day to day
There is more to life than play.
More to face than selfish joy.
Don't forget--he's just a boy.

Just a boy who needs a friend,
    Patient, kindly to the end;
Needs a teacher who will show
    Him the things he wants to know.
Take him with you when you walk,
Listen when he wants to talk,
His companionship enjoy,
Don't forget--he's just a boy.

*****

UNITY

I dreamed I stood in a studio
and watched two sculptors there;
the clay they used was a young child's mind,
and they fashioned it with care.
One was a teacher, the tools he used
were books and music and art;
one a parent with a guiding hand,
and a gentle, loving heart.
Day after day the teacher toiled,
with touch that was deft and sure;
while the parent labored by his side,
and polished and smoothed it o'er.
And when at last their task was done,
they were proud of what they had wrought,
for the things they had molded into the child
could neither be sold nor bought.
And each agreed he would have failed

if he had worked alone,
for behind the parent stood the school,
and behind the teacher the home.

*****

WHEN PERSPECTIVE COMES THROUGH

Forgive me, child,
For losing sight in anxious, cluttered living,
Of your bright-eyed attempts to please.
The spilled cereal and the muddy boots, kicked aside,
Are small inconveniences
When perspective comes through.

I really don't mind putting patches on the knees
Of another pair of jeans
(I'm sure the slide to home plate was worth it).

I don't care, too much, if your bedroom looks
Like the remains from a spontaneous explosion
(Though often treated like such a crisis).

I don't mind that you don't especially listen well,
Considering what there is for you to hear;
Much of what is said to you hits hard
With disappointment and defeat.
How briefly we recognize your accomplishments,
Yet how we belabor your faults!

The truth is,
I don't mind finding your socks and combing your hair
On a slept-too-late morning.

And when you tease your sisters too often and too long,
They don't mind so very much
(Though they react with mean and hateful tones).

I sent you off to the world today,
Gulping to swallow tears that answered criticism.
"Don't be late!" I hollered. "Hurry up, get going!"
I saw your helpless, aching heart, right through
The brimming pools of blue that glanced at me
As I shoved you through the door.

"Have a good day, Mom,"
Slipped from beneath your breathlessness
As the door closed abruptly at my hand.

I really don't mind if you are late getting home
Because you found another new "short-cut,"
Or if you rush through the door with mud-covered friends.

90

And when you toss papers and coats on the closest chair
I won't mind removing them
As you look to me for some small sign of approval.
Forgive me, child,
For making you think I do mind,
For treating you like such a bother.
Going through life with you is my special privilege;
Your bright-eyed desire to please means so much,
When perspective comes through.

--Suzanne Dean

*****

THE BLANK PAGE

A child's life is a blank page. You, that child's parent, write upon it. What will the first words be?

Shut up!

Get out of my sight.

Go play.

Don't touch!

These words teach fear. They register unwantedness. They say, "I don't love you."

Let your words teach gentleness and beauty. Let them supply high moral principles, courage to meet life's disappointments, pride in a job well done. Use words that reflect your love:

Beautiful, son!

You did a great job.

Don't worry--we'll clean it up together.

I'm so proud of you!

When your child is grown, you will look at him and see the words you wrote on that blank page. Write words you will be proud of!

*****

TRAIN UP A CHILD

Train your children to be intelligent and industrious.

First, teach them the value of healthful bodies and how to preserve them in soundness and vigor.

Teach them to entertain the highest regard for virtue and chastity.

And, likewise, encourage them to develop the intellectual faculties with which they are endowed.

They should be taught regarding the earth on which they live, its properties, and the laws that govern it. They ought to be instructed concerning God, who made the earth, his designs and purposes concerning its creation, and the placing of man upon it.

They should know how to cultivate the soil in the best possible manner; they should know how to raise the best kinds of fruits native to the soil and the climate. They should be induced to raise the best kinds of stock, and to care for them properly when they come into their possession.

And whatever labor they pursue, they should be taught to do it intelligently. Every incentive, at the command of parents to induce children to labor intelligently, should be held out to them.

--John Taylor

*****

ANCESTORS

Ancestors are found along with old furniture and captive skeletons in all the best families. Ancestors consist of forefathers and foremothers, to say nothing of foreuncles and aunts, who have done something grand and noble--like being beheaded by a king or having a relative who was the governor of a colony. This enables them to be pointed to with pride by their descendents forevermore.

Being an ancestor is one of the easiest and most attractive jobs. It merely consists of being boasted about by one's descendents. Thus, many ancestors have been able to make good after they are dead. More than one ancestor has gone out of this life a poor person, only a few jumps ahead of the sheriff--but has had the good fortune, a century later, to become the ancestor of some ambitious family with plenty of money. He has become so famous in consequence that his tombstone has had to be greatly enlarged and improved.

Ancestors are one of the most valuable and satisfactory possessions. They are nontaxable, and can't be stolen. Their upkeep is practically nothing, and they do not deteriorate with age or neglect. In fact, they increase in value as they grow older. An ancestor six hundred years old is worth a mass meeting of fifty-six-year-old ancestors. Adam is the oldest ancestor; he is six thousand years old, and has a fine record. But he is a common possession, like education and liberty, so he isn't very highly valued.

Almost all rich people own and operate ancestors. But poor men have them, too. Many a man who hasn't two vests to his name and cannot hold a job for two minutes has ancestors that are the envy of his neighbors. We cannot buy ancestors, if we do not have them--but we can buy them for our children by marrying discreetly!

*****

I WANT TO BE A HUSBAND

I want to be a husband--your husband. I want to lift you from undue care and worry. I want to provide sufficient for our family needs so that life will be pleasant for you.

I want to set a proper example for you and for our children so you may always be able to say with pride and satisfaction, "This is my husband. This is our father." I realize the many times I have failed to live up to your expectations. I want you to have patience with me and be forgiving when I make mistakes. Know this, my dear: I don't want to make errors. I have committed to use my agency in doing what is right, and when I do wrong it is not from a heart that _wants_ to do wrong, but from a weakness I have not yet overcome. I hope I will always be willing to accept your helpful criticisms and suggestions, that I may improve upon my conduct.

I want to honor my priesthood in the way the Lord revealed it should be honored through the Prophet Joseph Smith. Therefore, I would like to direct my home and family by persuasion, longsuffering, gentleness, meekness, and by love unfeigned--by kindness and pure knowledge, with charity and forgiveness at all times.

I want to refrain from setting my heart too much upon the things of this world and from aspiring to the honors of men.

I want to show that I know that the rights of the priesthood are inseparably connected with the powers of heaven, and that the powers of heaven can only be controlled or handled upon the principles of righteousness.

To all with whom I labor in my profession and in the Church, I want to be an example of what the Savior taught.

And, finally, I want to be understanding, kind, and thoughtful of your every need. I want my love for you and our posterity to grow until it becomes a perfect love--a love that makes us one in all things for time and for all eternity. With God's help, I hope to become that husband and father to you and to ours.

--Alma P. Burton

*****

THE SPIRIT OF A MORMON HOME

I could not define it exactly, the thing I felt about this home. But I could feel it, and it warmed my soul. It was the way in which everyone addressed everyone else. There was no shouting--not even a raising of the voice. Sure, there were disagreements--but I can still remember the reasonable way in which those disagreements were talked out. I somehow knew that it would have been very painful to all if someone had spoken sharply because, you see, they loved each other. And how can you harm someone you love?

I remember one day when the father had to take a trip out of town over the weekend. As he left the door that morning, everyone was there to bid him goodbye, and it was right there that I learned the meaning of "goodbye." To them, as tears gathered in their eyes, it meant, literally, "God be with you until we meet again."

I always say you can tell about a home by observing the everyday events. In this home, every event was important; to them, each day was the most important day in eternity.

I can still see the scene when they all knelt down to pray. You know how some people pray--it gets to be more or less a matter of form, and has something almost mechanical about it. It is something you do because it's your duty. But not here. They all joined hands as they prayed, and it seemed to me as if angels were talking to each other. There were such sentiments of thankfulness, such pleas for wisdom, such feelings of divinity!

I suppose you could say there was a distinctive kind of spirit in this home. Yes, I'm sure there was. It was the spirit of kindness, patience, loveliness, beauty, and love itself. The thought occurred to me as I left that to these people, heaven itself would not be strange when they arrived--because they had a corner of it right here on earth.

*****

WORLD, TAKE MY SON BY THE HAND

My son starts school tomorrow.

It's all going to be strange and new to him for a while, and I wish you would sort of treat him gently. You see, up to now he's been king of the roost. He's been boss of the backyard. I have always been around to repair his wounds, and I've always been handy to soothe his feelings.

But now, things are going to be different.

This morning he's going to walk down the front steps, wave his hand, and start on his great adventure--an adventure that will probably include wars and tragedy and sorrow. To live his life in this world will require faith and love and courage--so, world, I wish you would sort of take him by his young hand and teach him the things he will have to know.

Teach him. . .but gently, if you can.

He will have to learn, I know, that all men are not just, that all men are not true. Teach him that for every scoundrel, there is a hero; that for every crooked politician, there is a dedicated leader. Teach him that for every enemy, there is a friend. Let him learn early that the bullies are the easiest people of all to lick.

Teach him the wonders of books. Give him quiet time to ponder the eternal mystery of birds in the sky, bees in the sunlight, and flowers on a green hill.

Teach him that it is far more honorable to fail than to cheat. Teach him to have faith in his own ideas, even if everyone tells him they are wrong. Try to give my son the strength not to follow the crowd when everyone else is getting on the bandwagon. Teach him to listen to all men, but to filter all he hears on a screen of truth and to take only the good that comes through.

Teach him to sell his brawn and brains to the highest bidders, but never to put a price tag on his heart and soul. Teach him to close his ears to a howling mob, and to stand and fight if he thinks he's right.

Teach him gently, world, but don't coddle him; only the test of fire makes fine steel.

This is a big order, world, but see what you can do. He is such a nice little fellow. . .he is my son.

--Author Unknown

*****

ETERNAL HOME EVENING

Family home evenings weren't originated in this generation--nor even in this dispensation. Family home evening was held by righteous families many centuries ago. I'd like to recall one particular family home evening recorded in the scriptures--even though, unfortunately, it is incomplete. The family that held this home evening was very large, but the parents were deeply concerned about each individual family member--so concerned, in fact, that they continually strived to teach their children eternal principles.

At this certain family home evening, the family had a definite problem to solve. An obstacle had presented itself, and it had to be overcome if the children were going to be able to keep progressing. After the initial business was concluded, the father explained the problem to his children, and he asked them to suggest possible solutions to the problem. It was a learning activity. The father, of course, was very wise; he knew the problem well, and had himself overcome it when he was younger. He knew the best possible solution for his family, but he wanted first to teach them the eternal lessons involved.

I'm sure many plans were suggested by different members of the family, and several must have been brilliant, though varied. After he examined the plans, the father found that one was identical to his. This was the plan of the eldest son, a tremendously outstanding man to whom the father gave the task of helping implement the plan. One other noteworthy plan had been submitted by another son, who was brilliant in his own right. This son wasn't condemned for submitting his plan, because, undoubtedly, many faulty plans had been submitted. But when he started seeking personal glory and trying to impose his will and selfishness on the entire family--and when he persuaded one-third of his brothers and sisters to rebel with him--he and his followers had to be cast out of their dwelling.

Of course, it was the great council in heaven. In many ways, it was like a big family home evening. Just as our Father in Heaven wants us to learn eternal principles in our relations with him, so should we always strive to teach and learn eternal values in that eternal setting, the family home evening.

--Stephen Black

*****

TEN CONDITIONS THAT CONTRIBUTE TO A HAPPY HOME

The dearest possession a man has is his family. In the divine assurance that family ties may transcend the boundaries of death, and may continue throughout endless ages of eternity, I find supreme consolation and inspiration. When the union of loved ones bears the seal of the Holy Priesthood, it is as eternal as love, as everlasting as spirit. Such a union is based on the doctrine of immortality and the eternal progress of man.

1. Ever keep in mind that you begin to lay the foundation of a happy home in your premarital lives. While in courtship, you should learn to be loyal and true to your future husband or wife. Keep yourselves clean and pure. Cherish the highest ideals of chastity and purity. Do not be deceived.

2. Choose your mate by judgment and inspiration, as well as by physical attraction. Intellect and breeding are vital and important in the human family.

3. Approach marriage with the lofty view it merits. Marriage is ordained of God. It is not something to be entered into lightly or to be dissolved at the first difficulty that arises.

4. Remember that the noblest purpose of marriage is procreation. Home is children's natural nursery. Happiness in the home is enhanced by having children at the fireside.

5. Let the spirit of reverence pervade the home. Have your home such that if the Savior called unexpectedly, he could be invited to stay and not feel out of his element. Pray in the home.

6. Let husband and wife never speak in loud tones to each other.

7. Learn the value of self-control. We are never sorry for the word unspoken. Lack of self-control is the greatest source of unhappiness in the home. Children should be taught self-control, self-respect, and respect for others.

8. Fasten home ties by continued companionship. Companionship fosters love. Do everything to cement love for all eternity.

9. Make accessible to children proper literature and music.

10. By example and precept, encourage participation in Church activity. This is fundamental in developing a true character. Church activity should be led, not directed, by parents.

--David O. McKay

*****

THE TREASURE

Once there was a rich man who had a treasure. He wanted to give this treasure to one of his three sons. He knew his sons very well, and waited anxiously for the perfect time to present his gift.

One night the man came to the bed chamber of his eldest son. "I have brought you this night the most precious possession I own. It is yours to keep. Guard it well. Care for it. Love it as I have loved it. But I must tell you that with this gift comes great responsibility."

The son looked at the treasure. He studied it. Then he hesitated. He had never ventured out of the kingdom. He wanted to see the beauties of the world. He felt he was too young for such a responsibility. He explained to the father that his desire for travel and adventure outweighed his desire to accept the treasure. The disappointed father left the son's bed chamber and took back the treasure.

Soon afterward the father, knowing well the capabilities and needs of his second son, met him in the garden. With great anticipation, he offered his second son the same treasure. To the man's surprise, the son looked at his wife; she said, "Your son and I feel your gift is immoral, world conditions being what they are, and it would be unwise and selfish for us to accept it.
If you knew more of the world, you would know better than to offer us such a gift. Our friends would not approve, should we accept it. We question your judgment in offering us what you call a treasure."

The bewildered father then approached his third son. "I have brought you this night a treasure--the greatest thing I can bestow upon you. I humbly bid you take it. It will bring you great joy, if you live up to your responsibilities concerning it. If you live worthily, it will be yours throughout eternity."

The son studied the treasure. "I appreciate your offer, Father," said the son, "but I dare not take it now. Perhaps at another time. I have much education to obtain before I feel ready for this gift, and, although I know you would help me meet the responsibilities that accompany this treasure, I must refuse it, for I dislike asking help from anyone--even you, Father."

So the man grew old, and his sons and their wives grew very worldly and never did value the treasure he had offered them. Before he died, he wished for someone to share his treasure with. So he left his sons and traveled far from his kingdom. Soon he came to a small cottage in the forest.

"Ah," he thought. "Surely this humble abode is in need of such joy as my treasure can give. But, oh, I wonder if they, too, will be overwhelmed and frightened at the responsibility that comes with such a gift."

Hesitantly, he knocked on the door of the humble little cottage. When the door opened, there stood a man and a woman. They were dressed modestly, and much of their clothing was in need of repair. They welcomed the man, and he took from his coat a golden-haired child with wide, innocent eyes. He said, "I offer you this night the most precious possession I own. He is yours to keep. Guard him well. Love him as I have loved him. I humbly bid you take him. When your responsibility toward him has ended, and he is old, he will be returned to me so that I may

evaluate how well you have loved and cared for him. He will bring you great joy. If you live worthily, he will be yours and mine forever."

Before he oculd explain fully the great responsibilities that accompanied his gift, the couple fell at his feet and thanked the man for the child. Then tears from the woman's eyes made darkened spots on the child's golden hair as she held him close against her tattered apron. The man's face shown with joy as he kissed the child's hand. They welcomed the child into their home, and as they welcomed him, they welcomed the Father, too.

--Barbara Werrett Nielsen

*****

THE HOME IS THE ANSWER

A stabilized home, in which religious instruction plays a major part, is the only real answer to juvenile delinquency. This is the consensus of scholars who have made a serious study of the causes and prevention of delinquency. These scholars maintain that parents and children alike must be taught how to live together as a family--their home must be "God-centered," and must be associated with a church that provides an uplifting, character-building program for youth.

The scholars list two kinds of homes: one that produces delinquency, and the other that seldom has youth problems. The poor home in which delinquency thrives is described as one in which there is no genuine love between father and mother, nor between parents and children; no regular family routine in the home; no preparation, no planning; no fixed time for meals, no set time to come in at night, nor to do homework, nor to go to bed; no discipline nor rules of conduct; no group activity; and little or no religious and moral training.

Such a home usually has in it parents who drink and who give their own children liquor at home; parents who quarrel, even in the presence of their children; who party and carouse; who are often untruthful, dishonest, careless about paying bills, give their children no training in financial matters, provide no companionship for children, and have no respect for religious matters.

J. Edgar Hoover, former head of the FBI, explained that juvenile delinquency seldom results when young people are brought up in homes in which:

1. Parents try to understand their children and find time to cultivate their friendship and love.

2. Parents of integrity face facts and live by the truth.

3. Parents live within their means and give their children examples in thrift, security, and stability.

4. Parents are industrious and teach their children that most of life's good things come only from hard work.

5. Parents have worthwhile goals in life and seek to have their children join them in their attainment.

6. Parents have common sense, a capacity for friendship, and a sense of humor.

7. Parents live in harmony with each other and do not quarrel in front of children.

8. Parents have ideals and a compelling urge to serve rather than to be served.

9. Parents are unswervingly loyal to their own children, but can express righteous indignation and chastise them when necessary.

10. Parents' decisions are controlled not by what their children desire, but by what they need.

There is no doubt in the minds of scholars that, for the most part, delinquency or freedom from it is a result of home environment. The experts say that children are not born criminals, nor pampered parasites.

They are made that way by the environment in which they live. This kind of philosophy makes more persuasive than ever the decree of the Lord in the Doctrine and Covenants:

"And again inasmuch as parents have children in Zion, or in any of her stakes which are organized, that teach them not to understand the doctrine of repentance, faith in Christ the Son of the living God, and of baptism and the gift of the Holy Ghost by the laying on of hands when eight years old, the sin be upon the head of the parents."

--Ray Taylor

*****

JELLY ON THE WOODWORK

Last night I quit my job. I walked right up to the boss, whose name is Jerry and who happens to be my husband, and I resigned. He had just come in the door, whistled his familiar whistle, and called, "Anyone home?" I had a crying baby in one arm, one in the kitchen waiting for a peanut butter sandwich (with dinner only half an hour away), and the third was sitting in front of the television set, howling because he wanted two mouse cartoons instead of the usual one. Jerry kissed me dutifully on the cheek.

It was then that I gave my notice. "I quit," I said. "I've had it! If you can find anyone who will take this job on the salary I get, she's welcome to it!"

Jerry took the toddler from my arms, gave her a hello kiss, and sent her scooting. Then he put both his arms around me tightly and kissed me in a special way--that tender kind of kiss that curls my toes and wilts my heart. "How about a movie, beautiful?" he whispered in my ear. I must say, my husband knows how to handle the help around here. I shudder to think what would happen if the office got wind of his phenomenal success and put him in charge of female personnel. I mentally tore up my letter of resignation and settled for a movie instead.

Not that I don't like my job. I really do. Even though the hours are horrible, and the pay is--well, I guess I should say the pay just isn't. It's the future of my job that holds such tremendous possibilities. And the people I work for just can't be beat. I have a dream of a husband and three shining pink babies. No one could ask for more. It's just that sometimes it seems like too much! Sometimes it all seems too overpowering for any one woman to handle. It's not the daily routine tasks; it's not the washing and the ironing and the cooking and the mending. It's life's little emergencies that keep cropping up to disrupt my schedule.

We just get over a bout with chicken pox, and suddenly the flu bug hits us. We just get the tonsils out, and somebody falls off the swing and has to have three stitches in his scalp.

It's the battle of the budget. It's one new pair of shoes after the other. And the dentist calling to tell us the x-rays revealed more cavities--and the milkman subtly asking whether I got the bill or it blew away.

It's never finding enough time to wash the windows. You know that one hall window where the baby kisses the mailman through the pane? Jerry passes it on the way out the door every morning, and more than once he has slyly suggested, "Better get with it." And I always say, "Yes, dear. I'll do it for sure." Notice I don't say <u>when.</u> What I mean is, "As soon as the baby gets off to college, I intend to do a lot of things around here."

It's that permanent jelly on the woodwork. I no sooner get it scrubbed off than it takes root again. It's the cookie crumbs on the floor and the cobwebs clinging to the ceiling. It's the mudpies that get tracked across the kitchen floor. It's our bottomless sandpile that never loses its sand despite all that accumulates in front of the television set and beside the bathtub.

And the bulging closets! Every December when Jerry takes down the Christmas decorations, I say with all good intentions, "I'll clean out that closet before I put them back." And, along about March, after we've stumbled over the boxes in the hall for three months, Jerry puts them back, and I say, "Next year, for sure."

It's missing our vacation because we had a tiny tot, and missing it the summer before because we were expecting that tiny tot. Then, the summer before that we had a tiny tot, and before that we were expecting that tiny tot. And the summer before that, more of the same, and the summer before that, still more of the same.

It's confining a squirming baby in the supermarket basket and at the same time keeping track of the two who are wandering through the store putting unwanted articles in the baskets of unsuspecting housewives. It's standing in line and sorting out my purchases from the boxes of cookies and animal crackers that my little helpers have seen fit to select.

It's kicking toys under the couch when the boss's wife comes to call. What's more, and it never fails, she always asks for the bathroom before she leaves--and what can I say? The plumbing can't be out of order <u>every</u> time she drops in.

It's a collection of assorted bruises, bumps, skinned knees, runny noses, untied shoestrings, and "I'm thirsty"s.

Do you see why I threatened to quit my job last night? It was all these things jelled together that suddenly seemed to overwhelm me. But that was last night. Tonight will be different. I discovered something today. I had some errands to do, so I took a dollar out of the milk money to pay a sitter. While I was gone, I discovered exactly what happiness is. It's the very thing I have just come home to. . .the four walls of this happy house, the three little faces smiling up at me, the

101

six sticky hands around my neck, and three little mouths talking at the same time.

It's a hard job, this business of raising a family. And, like all jobs, sometimes its demands sweep over you with such unexpected force that it becomes too much. . .too difficult for you to manage. But even during those occasional discouraging days, I know it's a tender and rewarding job. It's a job I wouldn't trade for any other in the world. . .because it's _my_ job. These happy little people are a part of me. They depend on me, and they need me.

And soon that wonderful man who chose me for his wife will be home with us. And he'll put both his arms around me tight,

and he'll kiss me special. . .that tender kind of kiss that curls my toes and wilts my heart. Because tonight I have something to tell him.

The most wonderful thing has happened to us. You see, we're going to have another baby!

--Margery Rutherford

*****

WHAT IS A FAMILY?

Take one husband, one wife, four walls, one small dog or stray cat; mix well. Add a generous portion of time, and you are almost certain to have a family. The dog or cat isn't absolutely necessary for the recipe, but somehow or other it seems to give Mother Nature the right idea.

"Well, just look at that!" she will say. "I can do better than that for them."

The family always seems to start at exactly the wrong time. When the snow is the deepest or the hour is the latest, the traffic the heaviest or the tires the flattest, the wife will whisper, "Honey, I think you'd better get the car ready." So the husband and wife become a family in an awesome, frightening, expensive, terrible hour of crisis, but Mother Nature--who is really in charge of the whole affair--just smiles and hums a tune. Families are her business, and she knows her business well: no fretting, no rush, the springtime of life for the ten billionth time. There!

"It's over!" sighs the husband.

"It's here!" thinks the wife.

"It's just begun," says Mother Nature.

The family, from Dad's point of view, could be the best collection of people in the whole world--a pretty and efficient wife, a highly intelligent son, an angel of a daughter, a well-behaved dog, and, of course, himself, very nearly handsome and with a real head for business. And how he works and slaves for them, never thinking of himself! Yet what does he usually see? A wife with pin curls, who didn't mean to forget to record the check in the checkbook; a freckled-faced mischief-maker, who didn't mean to kick the football through Mr. McGonigal's greenhouse; a jeans-clad daughter, who didn't mean to burn the dinner ("But Daddy, I was talking on the telephone!"); and a miserable mongrel, who looks so sad and sorry--sitting in the middle of what used to be Dad's straw hat--with eyes that say, "But I didn't mean to--I was just playing 'catch-the-rabbit.'" If only the rest of the family could have a little of Dad's intelligence.

Mother comes to view her family with fatalistic resignation. No matter how she slaves at cleaning, cooking, washing, polishing, mending, or ironing, Dad will never notice. To him, home is a place for loafing. Then there's Sonny--she spends her life starting him on the right path, and what does he do? Spends his tithing on jelly beans. Sister, the one she has always felt so close to, has drifted away and started using lipstick and getting phone calls from strange boys. And that four-legged monster! He's tracked up her kitchen floor again! If only the family would appreciate all that Mother does for them--day in and day out.

Sonny thinks he has a keen family. He loves everybody in it, too. Of course, it would be nice if Dad were a little smarter--you know, able to make a kite that would fly instead of diving into the telephone wires.

And tight! Getting a quarter out of Dad is harder than getting out of practicing the piano. Mom is an angel--but a strict one. Do this, run here, stop that, pick that up, put it away! Sister? Well, she's better than most girls. A pretty good sport about those old gags with worms and frogs. Well, what a dope about movie heroes and disc jockeys. She can't help it; all girls are dopey, even Melissa. Old Spot has the right idea: the heck with everything--run like crazy, and have a good time!

Sister is tenderly tolerant of her old-fashioned family. Dad is a lovable old man (he must be at least thirty-five)--a nice, fattish Daddy who is so easy to persuade with a smile and a kiss. Mother is just a dear, but so far behind the times and so impossible every once in a while. Remake that old rag of a party dress, indeed! It just can't be! I simply won't go to the party dressed like Old Mother Hubbard. Sonny? Ugh! A person who would eavesdrop on a private telephone conversation has positively no sense of proprietariness. He and his dog. If Spot could walk on two legs, I'd rather have him take me to a dance.

What does Spot think of the family? We'll never know, because he keeps it all to himself behind those big brown eyes. Most likely, he has a better and truer view of the family than any of them.

When God made the family, he must have meditated a long time. The family must have food, shelter, and clothing, so there must be a father. He will also repair doorknobs, mow lawns, and stand on stepladders.

The family must have care, affection, and guidance, so there must be a mother. She will be in charge of shopping, spanking, praising, and worrying.

The family must not be dull or tiresome, so there must be a boy to shout, jump, run, get in the way, and hang by his knees from his toes.

The next family must not be forgotten, so there must be a little girl--an angel who will love them, bewilder them, and make them so very, very proud.

So all are accounted for except poor old Spot. How did he get in the family? Most of us might say that Spot just happened along, liked the free meals, and decided to stay. But perhaps he was intended to become a member of the family. His job? Well, maybe it's to be a constant example of love and devotion.

The family is a storehouse in which the world's finest treasures are kept. Yet the only gold you'll find is laughter. The only silver is the graying hair of Dad and Mom. The family's only real diamond is on Mother's left hand--yet can it sparkle like the eyes of the children at Christmas, or shine half as bright as the candles on a birthday cake? The mines of the earth yield no sapphires or rubies so precious as a baby's smile when it sleeps or a child's prayer at bedtime: "God bless Mommy and Daddy and Brother and me."

The small pleasures, the great sorrow, the hopes, the loves, and the dreams of the world are contained within these four walls called <u>home.</u>

Though you may search the far corners of the world for your heart's desire, you'll find that if it's worth having at all, it has been right at home all the time--right at home with the family.

*****

Marie had slept fitfully all through the night. The excitement of what was going to happen today had kept her awake. It seemed that every time she closed her eyes her dreams would return to the party, to the dance, but most of all to her date with Don. The first thing she saw when she opened her eyes this morning was a new dress hanging on her closet door. Its bright colors and ribbons and the matching shoes placed neatly beneath it gave her a happy feeling of excitement. Tonight was going to be wonderful! To think that Don had selected her from among all the girls to go to this big event of the school year caused her to tingle and feel funny all over. The new dress and shoes were evidence of her hard work and of the things she had denied herself in order to buy them. All of this was for the special time she would have tonight. Marie was determined that nothing would spoil it!

Last night's scene with her father now came back in grim reality. She had tried on her new dress and shoes and had danced happily in front of the family. Even her young brother had opened his eyes wide with admiration and had reached toward her to touch the beautiful material. Marie had to dance quickly out of his way to avoid the sticky fingers that would have spoiled her new dress. Mother smiled and quickly lifted the baby away, holding him out of reach. A look of pride came across her father's face. He smiled at Marie and said, "I can hardly wait to see the look on Don's face when he comes to pick you up and finds you in that beautiful new dress."

"Oh, I forgot to tell you," Marie said, avoiding her father's eyes and looking toward the floor. "Don isn't picking me up. I'm going to meet him downtown at the drugstore." Marie could see the hurt expression come across her father's face, and she turned her head away. How could she tell him that she was ashamed of her parents--the way they dressed, and the home they lived in? How could she ever tell her father and her mother that she did not want Don to come here and see her with all her little brothers and sisters and the house she lived in? But perhaps she did not need to tell her father. Marie had the feeling that somehow he already understood, and was hurt.

"You will not meet Don downtown, Marie," her father spoke solemnly. "If Don wants to pick you up, he'll pick you up at your home."

"Oh, no, Dad!" she said, turning around to face him. "It's too far--I mean, he won't know how to find our house, and, besides, I'll be meeting some of the other kids down at the drugstore, too."

"You are ashamed of your home," her father said, sadly.

"Oh, can't you see, Dad? You know our house. You know what kind of a home Don lives in. What will he think of me when he sees me coming out of this little house? This is our first date, and I must make a good impression. Please, Dad, just this once."

"No, Marie, not this once. Not ever. Don picks you up here. He meets your family at your own home, poor as it may be, or he doesn't pick you up at all, and you don't go to the dance or the party."

Marie got up quickly and dressed for school, her mind occupied with the events that had taken place the night before. Mother was sitting at the table feeding the baby when Marie entered the kitchen. There was food all over his face, and Marie said crossly, "Must he be so messy, Mother?"

"He's just learning to eat, dear," Mother said patiently.

"Oh, Mom, can't you talk to Dad? Can't you tell him how important it is--"

Mother interrupted, "No, I won't talk to your father. Your father is right. You should not be ashamed of your home and your family. If you want a boy to respect you--"

"Respect me!" Marie interrupted. "Oh, Mother, you're so old-fashioned. You just don't understand."

"I may understand more than you think," her mother said slowly as she lifted the baby from his chair and began washing his face.

Marie left the house rather quickly; the door closed loudly behind her. She walked to school, hoping that none of her friends would see her. She wanted to be alone with her thoughts. She was almost afraid to meet Don. She knew he would be looking for her to discuss their plans for this evening. Don was such a handsome, popular boy that it frightened her a little to think about it. Don's parents were leaders in the community. His mother always wore the latest style. His father was a businessman and was always dressed in a suit with a white shirt and necktie. They lived in a beautiful home and drove a nice car. Marie had that same old feeling of discouragement when she thought of the pickup truck her parents drove. And, of course, the children--including herself--had to ride in the back. She wondered what Don would think when he learned of her circumstances. How could he want a date with someone like her? As she approached the front door of the high school, she felt a light touch at her elbow and turned quickly to look up into Don's smiling face.

"Hi, Marie," she said cheerfully. "How's my girl?"

Marie's heart pounded wildly as she found the courage to look back and smile. "Oh, I'm just great, Don, if you're talking to me."

"Sure, who else?" he laughed. "Aren't you my girl?"

"I hope so," Marie said.

"When do I pick you up tonight?" Don asked, "and I forgot to ask you where. You said something about the drugstore."

"Oh. . .well. . .that's been changed," Marie said haltingly. "I think it would be better if you picked me up at my home."

"Well, that's great," Don said. "You'll have to tell me where you live."

Cold fear descended on Marie at the thought of telling Don which part of town she lived in. She looked away from him and haltingly said, "We live over on North Aztec Street. It's 332 to be exact."

"Oh, sure, I know where that is," Don said lightly. "That's near where Larry Smith lives, isn't it?"

Marie answered softly, "Yes, if you know where Larry Smith lives, we're just two houses further down the road."

"I'm sure I can find it," Don said brightly. "Now we've got the place--what about the time? Will seven-thirty be all right?"

"That will be just fine, Don. I'll be looking for you."

"See you tonight," Don said cheerfully. "I'd better run now--I'll be late for class."

Marie thought the day would never end. As she walked home that afternoon, she wondered if she should call the whole thing off to save both Don and herself the embarrassment that would surely follow. A new feeling of tenderness and love filled her heart when she walked into her yard. She could see that her father had made some effort to pick up trash and straighten the front yard. When she walked in the house, she could see that Mother had scrubbed the tables and straightened the room, but it would take a lot more than straightening to cover the torn part on the couch and the worn arms of the chairs. In spite of herself, the old, helpless feeling came over her.

Marie helped her mother prepare supper and set the table. She wanted the evening meal to be over early so that she could have time to get ready for the party and allow her mother time to straighten the room again before Don came. When the evening meal was over and it was time for the dishes to be washed, her mother said, "Marie, I'll wash the dishes. You go ahead, honey, and get ready." Marie smiled her thanks and went to her room.

Marie's bedroom door had scarcely closed when her young brother, Douglas, came tearfully to his father and said, "My sheep is sick. She won't even get up." Father rose quickly and left the house with Douglas. In a few minutes he and Douglas returned, the sheep held in his arms. Her father spread some old canvas and blankets on the floor, and Doug placed the sheep on them. Her father knelt and began doctoring the sick animal.

While they were in the midst of their administrations, Marie came from her room in her new dress. A horrified look came over her face as she saw the animal in the middle of the living room floor. What if Don should come now?

"Oh, Father, how could you?" she wailed.

Her father looked up and spoke briefly. "This animal is sick, and we need the light and warmth of the house. It will only take a few minutes for us to fix her, and we'll have her out of the way. You wouldn't want Douglas to lose his sheep, would you, Marie?"

Her attention was riveted on the sick animal and then, just as Marie had feared, a knock came at the the door. It was Don.

"Come in, Don," her mother said without apology. "Marie will be with you in a few minutes."

Marie's father looked up from the sick animal and smiled a greeting to Don. "You must be Don. We've heard a lot about you. We're happy to have you in our home, Don. If you'll excuse us for a minute, Douglas and I need to take care of this animal so we can remove it from the house."

Marie came from her room quickly, not looking at her parents, but walking straight to the door that would take her from the house.

"Let's go, Don," she spoke tersely. She wanted him out of the house as quickly as possible.

Father rose from his position on the floor and said, "Just a minute, young folks. Don, we're happy you're taking our daughter out tonight. We're trusting her to your care. We want you to have her back to us by twelve o'clock tonight."

Don smiled and replied, "Of course, Brother Enos. The party and dance should be over by then."

Marie left the house quickly, with Don hurrying to keep up with her. When she saw the bright, beautiful car he was driving, she almost forgot her disappointment and embarrassment. She climbed in almost before Don could open the door for her.

"Boy, you're in a hurry, aren't you, Marie?" Don laughed and seated himself next to her in the car. The motor started smoothly, and they made an exit from the Enos household.

"Tell me about the trip you took back east this summer," Marie said. "Didn't you spend two weeks in New York City?"

"Oh, sure," Don said, passing off the question lightly. Then he began laughing. "I can't get over opening that door and finding a sheep in the house!"

"Tell me about New York City," Marie said stubbornly, trying to bring him back to her question and to divert his mind from what had happened.

"Oh, it's just a big city with lots and lots of people. What was the sheep doing in the house, anyway?" he laughed.

"That sheep belongs to my brother, Douglas," Marie said angrily, "and it was sick, and my father was doctoring it. I've looked forward to going out with you for a long time, Don, but you can turn around right now and take me home."

"Wait a minute--what for?" Don asked in astonishment.

"Never mind. Just take me home right now."

A feeling of hurt and bewilderment came over Don, but, obedient to her wishes, he turned the car around and headed back for the Enos's residence. As they pulled into the yard, Marie began to open the door. Don reached over and held on to her arm. "I'm sorry, Marie. I'm sorry you feel this way, but I think you owe me an explanation. Why do you want to go home? What have I done?"

"It's just that I don't want anyone making fun of my family," she said angrily. "Maybe we don't live in a fancy house and drive a fancy car, and maybe we _do_ have sheep in our living room and drive a pickup truck, but that doesn't mean my parents aren't as good as anyone else."

"Oh, so _that's_ it," Don laughed, but his laugh made her angrier still.

"Just let me go," she said, trying to pull her arm free from his grasp.

"Just sit still a minute, young lady. I've listened to your explanation. Now I think you need to listen to mine. I wasn't laughing at your father and your brother and your home, at least not in the way you thought I was. I was laughing because I was thinking how much fun it must be to live at your place. I could never imagine a sheep being brought into the living room at our house! A father must really love his son to take that kind of care of his son's sick animal. Marie, I'm sure you know that our family joined the Church only about two years ago. When I told my father that I had asked you to go to the party with me tonight, he was really happy. He said, 'Don, tell me why you asked Marie to go with you. What attracted you to this girl?'

"I suppose I hadn't really thought about it very much until my father asked. But it was an easy question for me to answer. I said, 'Father, I guess it would be wrong to say that I'm not attracted by Marie's pretty face or beautiful hair. But it's more than that. I'm attracted to Marie because she is different. She is kind of special. I've noticed that Marie doesn't follow the extremes in makeup or fashion. I noticed that when Marie is with the kids that her language is always clean. She is always smiling and acts like she would be a pleasant person to be around. A couple of times I've been to school parties where the cigarettes were passed or where the drinking was taking place, but Marie would have none of that. I knew that she came from a large family, and her girlfriends told me that she often was the one to stay home and care for her brothers and sisters.'

"My father smiled and said, 'Let me tell you why I'm happy you're going with Marie, Don. It is because I have such great respect for her parents. You know it was the example of her father that attracted me to the Church of Jesus Christ. He's one of the men that works for our company. I had noticed there was something different about him. He was always to work on time, and was honest and hard-working. His language was clean, and everyone knew that the most important thing in the world to him was his family and his church. When Brother Enos and another man knocked at our door two years ago, I was happy to let them in because of the kind of people they were. It was Brother Enos who first introduced me to the Book of Mormon and to the gospel of Jesus Christ. Brother Enos has done more to change my life than any man I know. The Enos family doesn't live in a very fancy house and they don't have a great deal of money, but they have something money can't buy. They have love in their family. They have the gospel of Jesus Christ to guide them. I am proud, son, that you can see these values as I do and that you've asked Marie to go to the party.'"

Don had released his grasp on Marie's arm. She looked up at him slowly, tears forming in her eyes. "I'd still like to go with you tonight, Don, if that's all right."

"Of course," he replied softly.

"Just a minute, Don. I'd like to go into the house first, and then I'll be all ready to go."

Marie ran to the house and threw open the door. Her parents were seated on the couch engaged in a serious conversation. Douglas was in a nearby chair. As Marie entered, they spoke almost with one voice, "We're sorry, Marie."

"Sorry for what?" she asked, smiling through her tears. She threw her arms around her mother, kissed her father, ruffled Doug's hair, and said, "We'll be back before twelve. I'll see you later."

FATHER

A SON'S LETTER

Dear Dad,

I am writing this to you, although you have been dead thirty years. From your seat in the place beyond, I hope you can see these lines. I feel I must say some things I didn't know when I was a boy in your home--things I was too stupid to say.

It's only now, after passing through the long, hard school of years-- only now, when my own hair is gray--that I understand how you felt.

I must have been a bitter trial to you. I was such a fool! I believed my own petty wisdom, and I know how ridiculous it was compared to that calm, ripe, wholesome wisdom of yours.

Most of all, I want to confess my worst sin to you: I was convinced that you didn't understand.

When I look back over it now, I know that you _did_ understand. You understood me better than I did myself. Your wisdom flowed around mine like an ocean surrounding an island. And how patient you were with me! How full of long-suffering and kindness! And how pathetic, I now realize, were your efforts to get close to me--to win my confidence, to be my pal.

I wouldn't let you. I couldn't. What was it that held me aloof? I don't know. But it was tragic--that wall that rises between a boy and his father, and their frantic attempts to see through it and climb over it.

I wish you were here across the table from me just for an hour, so I could tell you there's no wall any more. I understand you now, Dad, and God knows how I love you. How I wish I could go back to be your little boy again!

I know what I could do to make you happy every day. I know how you felt.

Well, it won't be long, Dad, until I am over--and I believe that you'll be the first to take me by the hand and help me over the further slope. And I'll put in the first thousand years or so making you realize that not one moment of your yearning over me was wasted. It took a good many years for this prodigal son (and all sons are, in a sense, prodigal) to come to himself. But I've come. I see it all now.

I know that the richest, most precious thing on earth--and the thing least understood--is the mighty love and tenderness and craving to help that a father feels toward his boy. For I have a boy of my own. And it is he that makes me want to go back to you and get down on my knees to you.

Up there somewhere in the stillness, hear me, Dad--and believe me.

--Your Son

THE FACTS OF LIFE AFTER FIVE. . .

When I call two-year-old Joshua "Joshy-baby" he corrects me with great indignation, "I'm not a 'bobby'" (because he can't say long a's).

"What are you, then?"

"A 'leedle' boy" (because he can't say short i's or t's).

I can't resist pursuing the conversation. "What is Jayson?" (five-year-old brother).

"A 'beeg' boy."

"What is Daddy?"

With great emphasis he answers, "A <u>beeeeger</u> boy."

"What is Mommy?"

"Not a boy."

Surprised, I correct him. "Mommy is a girl."

"What's that?" he asks, with the curiosity he would ask, "What's a worm?"

I had just come to the realization that little boys growing up in a house full of little boys do not know the first thing about girls. When I told five-year-old Jayson that his best friend and cousin Jennifer is a girl, he was crushed.

"That doesn't change anything," I reassured him.

"Yes, it does," he insisted. "Girls are <u>not</u> as tough as boys."

"Isn't Jennifer tough enough for you?" I asked, already knowing the answer.

"Yea," he admitted, then added, "maybe she's still a boy."

Exasperated, I continued, "Don't you know the difference between Mommy and Daddy?"

Wisely, he replied, "Mommy is weaker and Daddy is stronger."

"I'm serious," I warned.

"Okay, then. A mommy is shorter and a daddy is longer."

"That's the only difference?" I pleaded.

"A mommy has things that feed babies, and a daddy uses plastic bottles."

Fascinated that the obvious differences weren't so obvious, I ventured out into the neighborhood to learn more about the adult male and female gender.

One little toughy proclaimed, "Dads kill spiders, and moms scream."

"Daddies tell you not to cry when you get hurt, and mommies cry for you," said one sweet young thing.

"Daddies drive and mommies can't," a little blue-eyed boy said.

"That's not true," I said, defending my gender.

"My dad says they can't," he insisted.

"Where do you learn such things?" I asked, aghast.

The whole neighborhood chimed in, "At school."

I marched right over to Rock Canyon Elementary School and spoke to Mrs. Polson, Mrs. Davis, and Miss Mousely--all kindergarten through second-grade teachers--and told them what I had heard in the streets. They consented to quiz their kids to determine whether they were "putting me on" or if "that's the way it really is."

That's the way it really is.

The difference between mommies and daddies has a lot to do with attitude, our research revealed.

David explains: "Dads think smart and moms think worried." Kate is a little more blatant: "Moms get mad, and dads don't." And Amy puts it poetically: "Moms get mad, and dads get glad."

Those differentiating attitudes are defined even more clearly in conversations about child care.

"Moms get up in the middle of the night, while dads have sweet dreams," Anne says. Jordan reports that dads let you have candy, and moms have a fit about it. According to John, moms let you go to the store, and dads make you stay home. David puts it like this: "I would like to tell you a little joke. While Momma has a baby, Daddy has to take care of too many children and wants to go somewhere and doesn't want to take care of the children." Susan states, "Moms do the talking, and dads do the spanking. Moms do the worrying, and dads go out looking for you."

Character also enters into the evaluation. "Dads tell jokes, and moms get mad," says Anne. "Dads are the preachers, and moms are the sleepers," observes Shannon. Anne adds, "Dads hog all the covers, while moms try to get warm."

The most obvious difference between moms and dads is revealed in their working habits. Kent simply states, "Dads work and moms don't." Wendy says, "Dads work outside, and moms work inside." Jared clarifies that "dads work with tools, and moms work with dinner."

Money, too, makes a difference. Erica explains, "Dads make the money and moms balance it." But Kenny says, "Dads work for the money, and moms blow it." And Mark emphasizes, "Dads earn the money, and moms go shopping--and that's the truth!" Lori simply states, "Dads are rich, and moms are poor."

Lori indicates that confidence separates the dads from the moms: "Dads are sure, and moms aren't."

One's lifestyle reveals a vast difference between moms and dads. "Moms go on diets," Christy divulges, "and dads read the newspaper. Moms find the specials, and dads only watch them." Lisa announces that the biggest difference between her mom and dad is that "Dad sleeps by the telephone, and mom sleeps by the clock." Denice discloses, "Moms pick out every dress at the dress shop, and dads take care of the bills."

In my research, appearance was not in the foreground of differences, but it did come up. The same Denice philosophizes, "Let's take hair for instance: moms go to the beauty parlor, and dads go to the barber shop. Some dads are bald, and moms wear wigs." Elaine goes into even greater detail: "Dads grow mustaches, and moms curl their hair." Jordan decides, "They just look different." That's because, Michele explains, "They're born different." As a result, she adds, "Moms have soft voices, and dads have hard voices." Even after all that, Heidi Jo insists that there's only one variable: "Their shoes are different."

It's just as I thought: Mommies are not girls, and daddies are not boys. They're a whole lot more in the eyes of the little one who qualifies them for that honor.

And what about the clincher? "Dads get presents on Father's Day, and moms get nothing."

--Peggy Fugal

FREE AGENCY

We cannot break the commandments. We can only break ourselves against them--or else, by keeping them, rise through them to the fulness of freedom under God. God means us to be free. With divine daring, he gave us the power of choice.

--Cecil B. DeMille

*****

FREE AGENCY. . .THE GIFT DIVINE

Next to the bestowal of life itself, the right to direct that life is God's greatest gift to man. One of the most urgent needs today is the preservation of individual liberty. Freedom of choice is more to be treasured than any possession earth can give. It is inherent in the spirit of man. It is a divine gift to every normal being. Whether born in abject poverty or shackled at birth by inherited riches, everyone has this most precious of all life's endowments--the gift of free agency, man's inherited and inalienable right.

Free agency is the impelling source of the soul's progress. It is the purpose of the Lord that man become like him. In order for man to achieve this, it was necessary for the Creator first to make him free. . . .

With free agency there comes responsibility. If man is to be rewarded for righteousness and punished for evil, then common justice demands that he be given the power of independent action. A knowledge of good and evil is essential to man's progress on earth. If he were coerced to do right at all times, or were helplessly enticed to commit sin, he would merit neither a blessing for the first nor a punishment for the second. Man's responsibility is correspondingly operative with his free agency. Actions in harmony with divine law and the laws of nature will bring happiness, and those in opposition to divine truth, misery. Man is responsible not only for every deed, but also for every idle word and thought. . . .

God is standing in the shadow of eternity, it seems to me, deploring the inevitable results of the follies, the transgressions, and the sins of his wayward children, but we cannot blame him for these any more than we can blame a father who might say to his son:

"There are two roads, my son, one leading to the right, one leading to the left. If you take the one to the right, it will lead you to success and to happiness. If you take the one to the left, it will bring upon you misery and unhappiness and perhaps death, but you choose which you will. You must choose; I will not force either upon you."

God has shown the world, through his prophets in ages gone by, that many of his people, individuals as well as nations, would choose the path that leads to misery and death, and he foretold it, but the responsibility is upon those who would not heed God's message--not upon God.

The power of choice is within you--the roads are clearly marked. In making the choice, may God give you clear-seeing, strong will, courageous hearts!

--David O. McKay

*****

FREEDOM OF TRUTH

Some people think freedom is the ability to do anything they want. We do have freedom to choose, but we do not have freedom from the consequences of our choices.

We are free to lie.

We are free to cheat.

We are free to steal.

We are free to kill.

We are also free to sluff school, skip home assignments, sneak a peak at pornographic pictures, or think dirty thoughts. We're free to smoke. We're free to eat foolishly and mistreat our bodies.

Some people forget that we lose freedom by choosing freely to do the wrong things; or by not knowing what is right, what is truth; or by refusing to listen and believe; or by ignoring laws and breaking commandments.

The consequences of wrong choices can limit our freedom in making other choices along the steps of life. For instance, we can no longer "choose" to go on a mission or enter the temple if we have already "chosen" to be unclean, unworthy. We can't go ahead with college plans if we have chosen to be a high school dropout. We're no longer free to date and enjoy the carefree times of youth if we choose to marry too young.

You want to be worthy of every blessing the Lord has in store for his choice children. Start now to build your strength to live the gospel. Exercise your spiritual muscles by:

Bearing testimony

Accepting Church assignments

Listening more and talking less

Praying, praying, praying

Living clean

Doing good

Keeping the commandments of God.

--Elaine Cannon

*****

PATHWAYS IN LIFE

The other day I followed the path that led from our house to the south pasture. The path took me out past the barn and around the place where the pond used to be. The pathway wound its way across gullies and around trees and boulders. Some of the trees and boulders had been moved long ago, but the path still made a neat circle around the places where they used to be.

I had to laugh at myself. Here I was, following a path that caused me to walk more than twice the distance that should have been required, and today I wanted to hurry, too. I asked myself why I was taking this path instead of going directly to the pasture. I answered myself by thinking, "I'm taking this path because everyone else takes it, and everyone else takes it because everyone else takes it."

I could imagine that old sheep wandering by here years ago. She must have had plenty of time and just wandered toward the barn, and the rest of the flock followed behind her. And so a path was started, and it grew deeper and deeper as days went by. Soon no one thought any more--they just got on the path, as I was doing today, and followed it.

I remembered how I used to have fun as a boy herding sheep. I would hold a stick for a sheep to jump over, and then each sheep that followed would jump in the same place, even though I had moved the stick. Finally, a sheep would come along that was brave enough to be different, a sheep that was smart enough to think for himself and not jump just because the others were jumping. He would walk quietly by the place without jumping, and then the others would follow him.

How often we are like sheep! Some character a long time ago must have been pretty hard up for something to do. He found that by rolling up a tobacco leaf and setting fire to it, he could suck smoke through the other end. He could blow smoke out of his nose and cough and spit. I guess this was so stupid that it took a while to catch on, but soon others began doing it because everyone else was doing it. Now, many years later, people follow this same crooked path because they see others doing it. Millions of dollars are spent, health is ruined, bright white teeth are stained, and breath is tainted because everyone else is doing it.

Sometimes there will be one who comes along and thinks for himself. He dares to make his own path. He dares to be different. I guess they call this moral courage, daring to be different. I think I would call it common sense. But it is not always easy to be different, and so we do many foolish things.

When I came back from the pasture today, I made my own path. It was a lot shorter, and it took me past a pleasant stream of water and near a beautiful patch of flowers I had never noticed before. Perhaps others will follow this same path. If they do, I hope they do it by choice, and not because someone else did it.

FRIENDSHIP

President Abraham Lincoln was once criticized for his attitude toward his enemies.

"Why do you try to make friends of them?" asked an associate. "You should try to destroy them."

"Am I not destroying my enemies," Lincoln gently replied, "when I make them my friends?"

*****

If a man does not make new acquaintances as he passes through life, he will soon find himself left alone. A man should keep his friendships in constant repair.

--Johnson

*****

We take care of our health; we lay up money; we make our roof tight and our clothing sufficient; but who provides wisely that he shall not be wanting in the best property of all--friends?

--Ralph Waldo Emerson

*****

The antidote for fifty enemies is one friend.

--Aristotle

*****

Someone who is very wise in the ways of men has said that there are two ways to make friends: one is to do something for people, and the other is the let people do something for you.

*****

We want to live on, not because of ourselves, but because of the people who care. It's giving and doing for somebody else--on that, all life's splendor depends; and the joy of the world, when you sum it all up, is formed in the making of friends.

--Anonymous

*****

If thou hast a thousand friends, thou hast none to spare; if thou hast a single enemy, thou wilt meet him everywhere.

*****

Friendship

By friendship you mean the greatest love, the greatest usefulness, the most open communication, the noblest sufferings, the heartiest counsel, and the greatest union of minds of which brave men and women are capable.

--Jeremy Taylor

*****

Friends bring joy that is eternal in nature.

*****

Friends are fragile things, and require as much care in handling as any other fragile and precious thing.

*****

If nobody smiled and nobody cheered and nobody helped along,
If every man looked after himself and good things all went to the strong,
If nobody cared just a little for you, and nobody thought about me
And we all stood alone in the battle of life, what a dreary old world
    this would be!

*****

It is my course in life to find,
At every turning of the road,
The strong arm of a comrade
To help me with my load.
And since I have no gold to give
And love alone must make amends,
My only prayer is while I live
God make me worthy of my friends.

*****

FRIENDSHIP

To laugh a bit and joke a bit
    And grasp a friendly hand;
To love a bit and scold a bit
    And know they'll understand;
To tell one's secrets, hopes, and fears
    And share a friendly smile;
To have a friend and be a friend
    Is what makes life worthwhile.

*****

SOMEBODY CARES!

What a world of woe
    Lifts from our hearts
When we surely know
    That somebody really

120

And truly cares
    That we're in somebody's
Thoughts and prayers.
    I want you to know
And I feel you do
    That somebody is always
Caring for you.

*****

AS THYSELF

Strange--but the more I know of you,
the better I like myself.
You always seem to take the book
of me down off the shelf,
and turn the pages of my mind
until you make me see
the finer, bigger, happier sort of
person I might be.
I grow an inch or two in height
each time you look my way.
You exhilarate my ego--
I feel happiest this way.
And quite the nicest part of all--
and this is very true--
the more I like myself, the more
I love the world and you.

--Helen Lourie Marshall

*****

I'd like to be the sort of friend that you have been to me;
I'd like to be the help that you are always glad to be.
I'd like to mean as much to you each minute of the day
As you have meant, good friend of mine, to me along the way.
I'm wishing at this special time that I could but repay
A portion of the gladness that you've strewn along my way.
If I could have but just one wish, this only would it be:
I'd like to be the kind of friend that you have been to me.

*****

TO MY FRIENDS

I look at the past with a soft sadness,
At the future with apprehensive wishfulness.
For my life has not been all I have wanted,
And the future holds not to promises, but to hopes.

But today my thoughts are filled with peace,
With a sunlight contentedness and a drowsy enthusiasm.
For I know the laughter of children,

Friendship

The warmth of kittens, and the blueness of the sky.
I know the dances of trees, the poetry of the earth.
And I hear the songs of wind.
But most of all, I know the comfort of friendship,
The comfort of a friend like you.

These things depend not upon yesterday or tomorrow.
They are what make my life worthwhile--
They are what make today.

--Pam Hunter

*****

DISCOVERING A FRIEND

If sorrow never happened and trouble never came,
The only thing you'd know about your neighbor is his name.
If all your days were bright and fair and certain was your place,
Acquaintances upon this earth are all you'd ever own
If care had always passed you by and grief you'd never known.

Time was I used to nod to one who lived across the way.
I knew his name and he knew mine; we passed the time of day.
But nothing did he mean to me, and nothing I to him,
Until one morning sorrow came and all my world was grim.
I saw his face, I felt his hand, and knew he came to lend
The strength I needed, and right then I found I had a friend.

'Tis not in sunshine friends are made, but when our skies are gray;
The splendid souls that men possess are never on display.
We cannot tell what lies behind the hasty nod or smile,
Or what of worth will come from it in just a little while.
We only know that we face the cares that life must send,
We realize the passerby has changed into a friend.

*****

I KNOW SOMETHING GOOD ABOUT YOU

Wouldn't this old world be better
If the folks we meet would say,
"I know something good about you!"
And then treat us just that way?
Wouldn't it be fine and dandy
If each handclasp warm and true
Carried with it this assurance,
"I know something good about you!"

Wouldn't life be lots more happy
If the good that's in us all
Were the only thing about us
That folks bothered to recall?
Wouldn't life be lots more happy

If we praised the good we see?
For there's such a lot of goodness
In the worst of you and me.

Wouldn't it be nice to practice
That fine way of thinking, too?
You know something good about me!
I know something good about you!

*****

ETERNAL FLIGHT

Soaring on
white-tipped
wings
goes the
swallow,
with each
tiny flick
of his feathers
lifting him
to greater
heights.

But I,
I am woman,
and how
do I fly
and soar
in the heavens
of the sky?
On the
white-tipped
wings of friendship
go I,
on golden wings
of love
I fly!

--Jan Flynn

*****

FRIEND

You came,
and with you
came new friendship.
I happily anticipated
your walks
and chatty talks
across my porch.

Friendship

Through quips
and tears,
we shared a little
of what we are,
and though the time
was short
(and in eternal view,
a second passed),
I felt your love,

knew it would last
the brief encounter
we call life.

I knew, too,
that though we part
for now,
someday, even if
our paths don't cross again,
in the realms of
unhurried forever,
I will there
declare you
"friend."

                    --Barbara Werrett Nielsen

                         *****

                    LEAF-PICKING

Sometimes
when I'm
strolling
I'll pluck
a tender leaf
from a
low-swinging
branch
of a friendly
tree
and closely
examine
the delicate
network
of veins
which
trace
its backside,
and somehow,
when I'm
through
with my examinings

and marvelings,
I know
that tree better,
and
I love it.

Sometimes
when
I'm talking
with a
friendly
soul,
I'll pull
from him
a small
part of
his
heart,
and
as I
turn
this
nature's wonder
over and
over
in the
palm
of my
hand,
I learn
to
understand
him better,
and
I love him.

--Jan Flynn

*****

I LIKE YOU

I like you,
and I know why.
I like you because
you are a good person
to like.

I like you because
when I tell you something special
you know it's special,

Friendship

and you remember it
a long, long time. You say,
"Remember when you told me
something special?"
And both of us remember.

When I think something is important,
you think it's important, too.
We have good ideas.

When I say something funny,
you laugh;
I think I'm funny, and you think
I'm funny, too.

I like you because
you know where I'm ticklish,
and you don't tickle me there
(except just a little, sometimes);
but if you do,
then I know where to tickle you, too.

You know how to be silly;
that's why I like you.
Boy, are you ever silly.
I never met anybody sillier than me
'til I met you.

I like you because
you know when it's time to stop being silly--
maybe day after tomorrow,
maybe never.

We fool around the same way all the time.
If I pretend I'm drowning,
you pretend you are saving me.
If I am getting ready to pop a paper bag,
then you are getting ready to jump.
That's because you really like me.
You really like me, don't you?
And I really like you back.
And that's the way we keep going
everyday.

If you go away,
then I go away, too.
Of if I stay home,
you send me a postcard.
You just don't say,
"We'll see you around sometime;
bye."
I like you a lot because of that;
if I go away,
I send you a postcard, too.

And if we go away together,
and if we are in
Grand Central Station
and if I get lost,
then you are the one who
is yelling for me.

I like you because
when I am feeling sad,
you don't always cheer me up
right away.
Sometimes it's better
to be sad.

You can't stand the others
being so googly and gaggly
every single minute.
You want to think about things.
It takes time.

If you find two four-leaf clovers
you give me one; if I find four,
I give you two; if we find three,
we keep on looking.
Sometimes we have good luck,
and sometimes we don't.

I like you because
I don't know why, but
everything that happens is nicer with you.
I can't remember when I didn't like you;
it must have been lonesome then.

I like you because, because, because.
I forget why I like you, but I do.
I would go on choosing you,
and you would go on choosing me
over and over again.
Why do I like you?
I guess I just like you because I like you!

--Sandel Stoddard Warburg

*****

Friendship is a bridge that leads to a garden full of flowers, where one may spend enjoyable and very pleasant hours--a bridge that leads to happiness, companionship, and pleasure; to affection, understanding, and to gladness without measure. I know, for we have walked this bridge, and found these many things. How delightful to experience the joy that friendship brings!

*****

WHAT IS A FRIEND?

A friend is someone who likes you. Someone with whom you can really be yourself. One who appreciates the good in you, overlooks the bad in you, and brings out the best in you. With a friend, you can share a laugh, a secret, a viewpoint, a success, or a disappointment--as well as a complete assortment of problems, large and small. A friend is someone who understands silence as well as words. . .stands by you. . .forgives you. One who lifts you up and never lets you down, and who makes you feel it's a pretty nice old world, after all. How would I know so well? Because you have been such a friend to me.

A blessed thing it is for any man or woman to have a friend, one human soul whom we can trust utterly; who knows the best and the worst of us, and who loves us in spite of all our faults; who will speak the honest truth to us, while the world flatters us to our faces and laughs at us behind our backs; who will give us counsel and reproof in the day of prosperity and self-conceit, but who, again, will comfort and encourage us in the day of difficulty and sorrow, when the world leaves us alone to fight our own battles as we can.

--Kingsley

*****

A FRIEND IS A TREASURE

A true friend is a priceless gem--treasured, loved, and valued as one of life's greatest blessings; for friendship is something you cannot buy. It only comes about when two people are honest, kind, and sincere with one another. A true friend can belong to all who seek the best things in life, and everyone can become a friend.

The outside appearance reveals very little about a person's real worth, for beauty and goodness are found within the heart--and every loving heart radiates a beauty no eye can miss.

A true friend is someone we can turn to in time of need, and through his love and understanding we gain the strength to overcome many of the trials and tribulations in life. A friend is someone special who listens with enthusiasm to our hopes and our dreams; someone who overlooks our faults and failings, but never forgets to give praise when it is deserved. With just a touch of the hand or the warmth of a smile, a friend can bring a ray of sunshine into the darkest day. True friends do not fade into yesterday, for time has a way of taking and sealing them into cherished possessions within our heart. A true friend is here to linger throughout the years and treasure forever.

--Fern Hughes Hunt

*****

128

ENCOURAGE! IT'S COURAGE

I couldn't believe what I was hearing as I sat in that testimony meeting. A sister I shall call Katie--in my opinion the most attractive and talented young woman in our ward--was tearfully admitting that she didn't feel accepted. She felt that nothing she did was good enough because no one ever complimented or appreciated her.

But everything Katie did was special. I liked her immensely, and was awed by her abilities. Each time she gave a talk or a lesson that touched me, I wanted to compliment her--but I always procrastinated, thinking, "Surely she hears so many compliments, mine would be meaningless." Apparently everyone else thought the same thing. When I'd been in her home, too, I had always wanted to tell her of my admiration, but it's hard to say those special words that draw people close. Consequently, we remained "casual friends." A wave of self-incrimination swept over me. I had thought so many good things about her. Why hadn't I said them?

All the kind thoughts in the world give a person no help if he never knows about them. So if you feel uplifted by Brother Wilson's solo in sacrament meeting, tell him! If you feel a real sense of kinship with a neighbor, tell her! If you like the way your husband or roommate smiles at you, let that person know!

The art of encouraging others is a basic part of the gospel of Jesus Christ, because it is a means of helping others progress.

--Darla Larsen Hanks

****

FRIENDS

Friends are never earned--they're a gift from the love in God, and they're precious beyond human evaluation. But you dare not take them for granted, or they'll drift away like smoke. The warmth of their caring will vanish like the chill of the endless nights.

Most of my friends are unknown, and they probably won't rate an obituary unless they live and die in small towns where nothing much ever happens. But a few of my friends are big people; they've made the world ring with laughter down through a gaseous, burning core. They're famous, sensitive, and talented, and their names are household words. Yet they are no more precious in God's eyes or in mine than those wonderful nobodys who live and die in small towns.

Who is your friend? He's someone who warms you with a nod or the unspoken word in hard times when you're hurting beyond words. Who is your friend? She's someone who holds you to her breast and sighs softly into your hair when no other medicine can stop the pain. A friend is someone who clinks his glass against yours or answers the phone at three in the morning when you're lost--and, with a few words of encouragement or concern, makes you realize you're not really lost at all.

Friends come in both sexes and in all shapes and sizes. The most important thing to have in common is the ability to share with you your most skysplitting joy or your deepest, most awesome sorrow. For they are your friends.

--Glen Campbell

*****

THE SIGNIFICANCE OF FRIENDSHIP

Six months ago, by appointment from the First Presidency, we attended a mission-wide conference in South Africa. After four glorious days with the wonderful people of that nation, and as we were leaving, many members said, "When you return, please give our best regards and love to our friends all over the world." Little did they realize--and little did I realize at that time--that I would have this kind of an opportunity to extend their love to their friends worldwide.

Since this responsibility has come to me, I have thought a great deal about friends in the gospel of Jesus Christ. I am reminded in the 84th Section of the Doctrine and Covenants, that great revelation on priesthood, of how the Savior reported through the Prophet Joseph Smith, ". . .you are mine apostles, and even God's high priests; ye are they whom my Father hath given me; ye are my friends." (D&C 84:63.) This verse shows the important blessing of being recognized as the Savior's friend.

I would like to leave this thought with you as we think about friends and the part they should play in our lives as Latter-day Saints. Perhaps this simple illustration will help us realize the need of being friends in the home, in the neighborhood, and in the community.

Several months ago my wife and I were in our front yard when the newspaper boy came down the street on his bicycle, which was loaded with papers. About twenty or thirty yards behind him was another boy, following on a bicycle. I was not sure at that time what their relationship was, but I did notice they were coming down the street at a pretty good clip.

When the newspaper boy reached our sidewalk, he was traveling too fast to make the approach to our home; as a result, he went one way, the bicycle went another, and the newspapers went everywhere. Noticing the boy had fallen on the lawn and was not hurt, but realizing he would undoubtedly be embarrassed from falling in front of his friend, we moved toward him.

At the sight of this perfect three-point landing, if we may refer to it as that, his companion shouted his pleasure and laughed heartily with complete and full enjoyment at his associate's misfortune.

Trying to relieve the embarrassment of the paper boy, knowing he didn't want help but <u>did</u> want to have his pride repaired a little, I took a few more steps toward him and said, "It's kind of a low blow to have your friend laugh when you've had a bad spill, isn't it?"

He went on picking up the papers without even looking up. Finally, he had the papers back in place, and he got on his bicycle. As he started to pedal away from us, he mumbled, "He isn't my friend--he's my brother."

His words have been ringing through my ears ever since. I sincerely feel that one of the great purposes of family home evening and home teaching is to have family members realize that a brother <u>can</u> be a friend; that a sister <u>can</u> be a friend; and that a father and a mother can be more than parents--they can be <u>friends.</u>

I hope and pray that we might catch the wisdom and inspiration of building a home so that our members in that sacred unit can look upon a father and say, "He is my best friend," or, "My mother is more than my mother; she is my friend." When we realize that parents and family members can be more than blood relations and are in very deed friends, then we will have a glimpse of how our Heavenly Father wants us to live-- not only as brothers and sisters, but as very close friends.

--Marvin J. Ashton

*****

THE HAND-ME-DOWN BOX

When ten-year-old Leigh Baugh got home from school, she found her mother rummaging through a big cardboard box of clothes.

"What are those?" Leigh asked, reaching for a warm molasses cookie cooling on the kitchen counter.

"Those are for dessert, little one," warned her mother, "and this is another box full of hand-me-downs from the Ellers."

Her mother held up a green corduroy jumper and asked, "How do you like this one?"

Leigh reached for a red velveteen party dress with a ruffle of lace at the collar and said, "I like this one better."

"That's lovely, Leigh!" her mother exclaimed. "It hardly shows any wear at all."

"Why do the Ellers give us their hand-me-downs?" Leigh asked, examining a white silk blouse.

Her mother looked up and reached out to stroke Leigh's copper hair, then turned away and sighed, "Because we need them, Leigh."

The Ellers were a rich family who had a large, lovely home in town. They had two daughters just a year older than Leigh and her sister, Tina. The Ellers girls went to a private school that required uniforms, so more often than not they outgrew their other clothes long before they were worn out.

The Baughs were a poor family who lived in a little old farmhouse outside town. Their two daughters had been wearing hand-me-downs for as long as they could remember. Despite their differences, the Baughs and the Ellers were good friends. So, it was with great pleasure that the Ellers gave the Baughs their hand-me-downs, and it was with much gratitude that the Baughs accepted them.

Leigh didn't mind wearing hand-me-downs, particularly the Ellers's hand-me-downs. The Ellers shopped only at the finest stores in the city, and all their clothes were fashionable and well made. Since the Ellers went to a different school, no one in Leigh's school recognized her "new clothes." If anything, her friends marveled that she dressed so well. Leigh never told anyone about the hand-me-down box.

One day in school Mrs. Kratz, Leigh's fourth-grade teacher, announced, "It's time to decide what you want to be when you grow up." All the children moaned, except Leigh. Leigh had wanted to be a writer ever since she had first learned how to read.

"I want you to tell us what you've decided in a little speech next Wednesday." The children groaned even louder.

"A speech!" Leigh gasped, quietly. She had never spoken in front of a class before. "What will I say?" she wondered. "What will I wear?" she worried.

When Leigh got home from school that day, she tore through the house, frantically calling her mother.

"What's the matter, Leigh?" her mother cried. "Are you hurt?"

Leigh explained breathlessly, "I have to give a speech, and I don't have anything to wear!"

"A speech?" questioned her mother. "Whatever for?"

"I have to talk about what I want to be when I grow up, and I have to do it in front of the whole class! I'll be so nervous! I want to look my best so no one will laugh at me. . . ."

Trying not to laugh at what her daughter considered to be a serious problem, Mrs. Baugh stepped down from the ladder where she'd been standing to hang some hand-sewn curtains made of worn-out sheets. "Let's look in that new box of hand-me-downs."

"<u>Not</u> hand-me-downs," Leigh protested. "Not this time. For once, can't I have a new dress?" she pleaded, eyeing the homemade curtains.

"I don't have the fabric to make you one," offered her mother.

Leigh looked more closely at the sheet curtains and almost stomped her foot before she remembered the punishment for such behavior. Once when her mother had reminded her to do the dishes, Leigh had stomped away in a fit of anger. "If you like stomping so much," her mother had suggested quietly, but firmly, "then you may stomp the entire time you are washing the dishes." Leigh had washed and stomped until she thought her arms and legs would fall off. But she had learned her lesson and decided not to stomp, despite her frustration.

Looking at her still feet, she barely whispered, "Not a hand-me-down dress. Not a homemade dress. A store-bought dress. Like the Ellers wear. Just this once. Please."

Mrs. Baugh knelt before her daughter, placed her hands on Leigh's shoulders, and looked straight into her troubled eyes. "We'll go look on Saturday."

Leigh was triumphant as she hugged her mother. Later that night, Leigh lay awake in bed thinking about her first store-bought dress. "She said 'look'," Leigh reminded herself, "<u>not</u> buy. But I have twelve dollars I have saved in babysitting money, and surely that will buy a dress as nice as the Ellers wear." Then she drifted off to sleep, dreaming about her first trip to one of the fine shops in the city.

But when Saturday came, they didn't go to the city. They went to the next town. They didn't go into a fine shop, either. They went to a factory outlet store that didn't look much different than the local grocery store. Leigh tried hard to conceal her disappointment as her mother lead her to the rack in the corner full of dresses her size. One by one, they pulled dress after dress off the rack and held each up to Leigh, looking for the perfect one for her first speech. The dresses were pretty, but they were all made of cotton. There were no corduroys, velveteens, or silks--just plain old cotton dresses like Leigh used to wear before the Ellers started sending their hand-me-downs. Leigh hesitated to ask, but ventured, "Where are the velveteen dresses, Mother?"

"Oh, Leigh," her mother laughed good-naturedly. "There are no velveteen dresses in here, and if there were, we couldn't afford them."

Leigh wandered to the front of the store and peered out the big plate-glass window to the quaint shop across the street. A little girl in a blue fur coat, hat, and muff was just leaving with her mother, who was laden with ribbon-tied boxes. Leigh turned to the check-out counter in her store and watched the cashier stuff purchases into brown paper bags. Leigh returned to her mother in the back corner. "Let's go back to the hand-me-down box, Mother," Leigh offered, trying to smile. "I'll save my money until I have enough to buy something better. Maybe in the shop across the street."

Mrs. Baugh looked out at the shop Leigh had seen and consoled, "Maybe someday, Leigh."

It was decided that Leigh would wear the red velveteen dress with the ruffle of white lace at the collar she had first admired in the latest box of hand-me-downs. She tried it on, and was as pleased with how it felt as how it looked. The velveteen seemed to caress her and the red brought out the natural rosiness in her cheeks. Her mother pinned a new hem while Leigh twirled about planning her speech. Leigh had decided to open her speech on her career in writing by talking about how she loved to read.

Leigh practiced her speech aloud one last time while her mother carefully pressed the velveteen dress. Today was the day, and Leigh had never felt more confident in her life.

When she got to school, Leigh carefully removed her coat and patted her dress into place. It was then that she noticed Linnie Lubette staring at her. For years, Leigh had tried to get close to Linnie. Linnie had the best of both worlds. She lived in the country like the Baughs, but was rich like the Ellers. And Leigh very much wanted to be her friend.

"Is that a new dress, Leigh?" Linnie asked, almost mockingly.

"Yes," Leigh answered with confidence. "I got it for my speech today. Are you all ready?"

"Of course," Linnie answered, with even more confidence. "Are you sure that's new?" But before Leigh could respond, Linnie was gone.

Leigh began to panic. The dress was new to her, but it was a hand-me-down from the Ellers. But then, how would Linnie Lubette know that? She finally put it out of her mind to concentrate on her speech.

When Leigh passed Linnie's desk, Linnie grabbed her hand and sneered, "Didn't I see that dress at the church Christmas party?" Leigh pulled away and sat down. Then she remembered. The Ellers and Lubettes belonged to the same church. This velveteen dress might have been Cindy Ellers's Christmas party dress. She might have worn it to the church

Christmas party. If Linnie had admired it, she might remember it. Leigh suddenly grew very nervous and began fussing with the dress, wishing she could change it into another one right then and there. Suddenly, she heard her name called.

"Why don't you go first, Leigh?" her teacher asked. "We're anxious to hear about your career choice."

Leigh slipped out of her seat and walked slowly to the front of the room. Before she even had a chance to gather her thoughts, her teacher spoke again. "My, don't you look lovely today, Leigh. Is that a new dress?"

Before Leigh could respond, Linnie Lubette chirped, "It's not new. It's a hand-me-down from Cindy Eller."

Leigh was mortified. She'd been found out. Now everyone would know. She wore hand-me-downs. Tears welled up in her eyes and she hung her head to hide them. The room fell silent.

Suddenly, Leigh felt her teacher's arm around her shoulders, pulling her close. "You are so fortunate, Leigh. See this dress I'm wearing? It's a hand-me-down, too."

Leigh looked up for the first time and stared through tear-filled eyes at her teacher's pretty blue floral silk dress. "You see," her teacher turned to explain to the class, "teachers don't make very much money, so I can't afford nice dresses like this. But I have a sister who is a doctor, and she has many beautiful clothes. She shares them with me because she loves me."

Leigh slowly turned her gaze from her teacher to Linnie Lubette, who was shrinking into her seat.

"You are so fortunate, Leigh," her teacher continued, "to have a friend who is kind enough to share her good fortune with you."

Leigh perked up, wiped the tears from her eyes, brushed the skirt of her hand-me-down velveteen dress smooth, and cleared her throat.

"Now, what is it you want to be when you grow up, Leigh?" her teacher asked.

"I want to be like your sister," Leigh answered, smiling.

"A doctor?"

"No," Leigh replied, turning to face the whole class, "someone kind enough to share with others."

Then, instead of talking about her being a writer, Leigh told an enraptured class all about the hand-me-down box.

--Peggy Fugal

GOALS

WORKING WITH SINGLENESS OF PURPOSE

Those who are considered experts in the behavioral sciences emphasize the need for early identification of goals. The basis for this emphasis when applied to leadership is simple: <u>if you don't know where you are going, how do you expect to take anyone else with you?</u> No Church leader should ever forget the destination to which he is leading others, for the Savior has specifically directed, "this is my life and my glory, to bring to pass the immortality and eternal life of man."

Working with singleness of purpose to achieve this goal does not imply narrowness; on the contrary, it asks each leader to expand his abilities to the utmost so that he might motivate others to "seek God and his righteousness." To those involved in leadership roles, singleness of purpose implies complete application of the gospel--forgiving seventy times seven, turning the other cheek, going the second mile. It implies understanding, motivating, keeping an eye single to the glory of God, and never losing sight of the objective to which the Savior has called us.

To lead without singleness of purpose may be illustrated by the following:

It was a stormy night in the English Channel. Now and then one could discern a swimmer reenacting the great epoch drama of the many who aspire to conquer the Channel. Florence Chadwick had been successful in even more difficult endurance tests, but on this murky night she tossed in her victor's cap when only a few hundred feet remained.

The next day she was asked, "In view of your past accomplishments, what single factor contributed to your failure to swim the Channel?" Her response was quick and terse. Said Miss Chadwick, "It was foggy and dark. I lost sight of my objective."

Life's byways are crowded with the wanderers who lost sight of their objective. Perhaps they will never know how close they came to success. The real champion gives all he has, and then gives just that little extra bit more that makes the difference. A strength beyond one's self does not come, however, until one's whole soul is immersed in purpose, in desire, in faith.

Thus is the real leader identified as one who accepts the Savior's objectives as his own--who desires the kingdom of God, who has faith in the application of the gospel, and who serves with a singleness of purpose.

GOSSIP

IT'S A PRETTY GOOD PLAN--TO FORGET IT

If you see a tall fellow
ahead of the crowd,
a leader of men
marching fearless and proud,
and you know of a tale
whose mere telling aloud
would cause this proud head
in anguish to be bowed--
it's a pretty good plan
to forget it.

If you know of a skeleton
hidden away
in a closet, and guarded
and kept from the day,
in the dark, whose showing,
whose sudden display
would cause grief and sorrow
and lifelong dismay--
it's a pretty good plan
to forget it.

If you know of a spot
in the life of a friend
(we all have such spots
concealed, world without end),
whose touching his heartstrings
would play on and rend
'til the shame of its showing
no grieving could mend--
it's a pretty good plan
to forget it.

If you know anything
that will darken the joy
of a man or a woman,
a girl or a boy,
that will wipe out a smile
or the least way annoy
a fellow, or cause
any gladness to cloy--
it's a pretty good plan
to forget it.

--Author Unknown

137

GRATITUDE

We can be thankful to a friend for a few acres or a little money; and yet for the freedom and command of the whole earth, and for the great benefits of our being--our life, health, and reason--we look upon ourselves as under no obligation.

--Seneca

*****

THANKFUL TONGUES

On Thanksgiving morning I stepped to the fence and said to my neighbor, "I'm so glad you live next door to me."

She looked up with a surprised smile on her face and said, "Thank you so very much. Nobody ever said that to me before."

Surely all her neighbors had often thought this about my next-door neighbor, for her kindnesses on routine days of the year were varied.

She would pick up the newspaper and put it on the porch when someone was going to be late coming home so that the paper wouldn't be carried off by stray dogs.

She could be counted on to turn off the water if a mischievous child began to play with the garden hose in the owner's absence.

Yes, she was a fine neighbor, and many had reason to be glad for the blessing of her personality. Yet when I took time to tell her in simple words that I was thankful she lived next door, she seemed so surprised and happy--as if I had handed her an unexpected amount of money.

This year as Thanksgiving approaches, I am wondering if there are others who need to hear a statement of the obvious. Should I speak a word to my doctor, lawyer, merchant? Perhaps thanks is due some of those we as children listed in the familiar nursery rhyme, chanting sing-song fashion as we counted buttons on our sweaters.

The emotion of gratitude that we regrettably keep hidden during much of the rest of the year has opportunity to come plainly into view when Thanksgiving Day approaches. In the true spirit of the season, we come to know the happiness spoken of in the Bible: "A man hath joy by the answer of his mouth: and a word spoken in due season, how good is it!" (Proverbs 15:23.)

Thankful tongues can encourage a neighbor and show gratitude to God for his blessings.

--Ruth C. Ikerman

*****

138

AN OPEN LETTER TO OUR HEAVENLY FATHER

Most Mighty God:

In these times of trouble and strife, I wish to seek a moment of solitude with thee and thank thee openly for thy marvelous blessings.

First, dear God, I thank thee for the privilege of being born in the promised land of plenty--this great America. I thank thee, O God, for inspiring men of great moral stature to lead our ship of state on a peaceful course on a sea of life made treacherous by storms of greed and passion.

I thank thee, O God, for goodly parents--parents that have led me through darkness of despair to the brighter glory of thy great work and its manifold blessings. Parents that have fed me, clothed me, and passed on to me the wondrous privilege of being able to say that I am a Mormon.

I thank thee, O God, for a sound physical body, an alert, healthy mind, and a humble spirit that may someday return to thee in thy celestial kingdom.

I thank thee, God, for the paragons of faith and obedience that guide thy Church through thy divine revelation and inspiration.

I thank thee for the privilege of being able to take the girl of my choice to thy holy temple, to be united as one, for time and all eternity. For the opportunity of having my children sealed to me, and being able to rear them in thy true Church.

I am grateful, dear God, for everything thou hast placed at my command, for my use and convenience. Life is as a great kaleidoscope when lived in conjunction with thy word--each turn a new day, permeated with peerless, ever-changing patterns of glory and beauty.

Ofttimes, O God, it is difficult to realize thy presence amid the hustle and the rush that constitutes today's metropolitan society. At these moments, it is only necessary to repair to the quiet of the home, or the splendor of thy natural creations.

When ere I walk amid lofty pines, or gaze silently at the moon reflected by a black midnight sea, or listen to a coyote in mournful prayer across the desert's plains, then I know of thy presence, dear God, and offer this prayer to thee:

In gratitude, Lord, my head is bowed
In a solemn and gracious prayer.
My spirit soars like a downy cloud
With the knowledge that thou art near.

Stay by me, Lord, when I do seem
From thy straight and narrow to stray,
For I know thou lovest and will redeem
If I but remember to pray.

--Ronald Acheson

*****

GRATITUDE WITH GRANDEUR

One of our neighbors, the wife of a young attorney, told us a few days ago about the funeral services held recently for her mother. The services did not go as planned.

The neighbor's mother was a tall, slender woman of sophisticated beauty, with light blue eyes and blonde hair. A mountain-grown girl who had majored in speech at college, she had spent her last thirty-five years in New York City. There her husband had been national director of the Cub Scouts prior to his death in 1949. She had met him when she was a member of the Young Women's Mutual Improvement Association general board.

The family arranged the services, with four spekers: a prominent businessman who had been a neighbor in Great Neck, Long Island; a farmer who knew her; an attorney friend; and a woman speech instructor from the university.

The day of the funeral was a cold February day. That morning our neighbor's phone rang; the voice was a man's, and it was kindly and warm. Our neighbor could not recall ever having met the caller before.

He got to his point quickly: "Would you and your family mind," he asked, "if I played the organ at your mother's service today?"

"We should be honored," our neighbor responded.

The phone conversation ended.

The caller appeared at the service shortly before starting time. He made a further request of the family: "If there is one minute available, I would appreciate saying a few words."

His second request was also granted.

He played with deep feeling at the organ, "I Know That My Redeemer Lives." People seemed to be moved.

After he played the organ, he was called upon to speak. He explained that when he was a missionary in California some forty-five years earlier, he was presiding at a meeting. A tense situation had developed after a woman in the audience had risen to her feet and spoken.

140

"Silence followed," he explained, "and as presiding officer I was puzzled as to what to do. It was then that this good woman whom we honor today rose up. She spoke with calmness and power and conviction. It took courage on her part. The tense atmosphere was dispelled, and I was greatly relieved. I shall always be grateful."

The speaker of that brief, touching message was Alexander Schreiner, former Salt Lake Tabernacle organist.

Alexander Schreiner, a loyal friend for many years, has taught me many lessons with his quiet genuineness. What perhaps moved me most when our neighbor told us of that incident at the funeral was his courage in expressing gratitude. Too often I have given thanks if it was convenient, and let it slip if it called for extra effort or boldness.

Alexander Schreiner could have sent a spray of flowers to that funeral. Perhaps he did. That alone would have been most commendable, to remember after forty-five years.

But he chose to seek out the family of the departed woman. They were strangers to him. Then he made two unusual requests of them. That took courage. From that courage his gratitude assumed a grandeur that could lift generations--for our neighbor said, "We so much appreciate Dr. Schreiner's thoughtfulness. More than that, through his brief lines at the service, we caught a choice glimpse of mother's life we might otherwise never have known."

--Wendell J. Ashton

*****

A SPECIAL TYPE OF SOLDIER

At the request of the First Presidency, I had gone to England as coordinator for the LDS servicemen; one Saturday afternoon in 1944, I sent a telegram from London to the base chaplain near Liverpool letting him know that I would be in camp the next morning to conduct Mormon Church services at ten o'clock.

When I arrived at that camp, there were seventy-five Mormon boys, all in uniform--and quite a number in battle dress. The chaplain to whom I had sent the wire proved to be a Baptist minister from the southern United States. He, too, was waiting for my arrival. As these young men ran out to greet me--not because it was I, but because of what I represented--and as they literally threw their arms around me, knowing I was representing their parents as well as the Church, this minister said, "Please tell me how you do it."

"Do what?"

"Why," he said, "I did not get your wire until late this morning. I made a hurried search. I found there were seventy-six Mormon boys in this camp. I got word to them. Seventy-five of them are here. The other is in the hospital. I have more than six hundred Baptist men in this camp, and if I gave them six months' notice, I could not get a response like that." And then he repeated, "How do you do it?"

I said, "Sir, if you will come inside, perhaps you will see." We went in to the little chapel. The boys sat down. I asked, "How many here have been on missions?"

I think fully 50 percent raised their hands. I said, "Will you and you and you"--and I pointed to six of them--"please come and administer the sacrament? And will you and you and you"--and I pointed to six others--"please come and sit here and be prepared to speak."

Then I said, "Who can lead music?" A number of hands were raised. "Will you come and lead the music? And who can play this portable organ?" There were several more hands, and one was selected. Then I said, "What would you like to sing, fellows?" With one voice, they replied, "Come, Come Ye Saints!"

We had no hymn books. The boy sounded the chord; they all arose. I have heard "Come, Come Ye Saints" sung in many lands and by many choirs and congregations, and--without in any way reflecting adversely on what we usually hear--I think I have only heard "Come, Come Ye Saints" sung that once when every heart seemed to be bursting. They sang every verse without books. When they came to the last verse, they didn't mute it; they didn't sing it like a dirge--but, throwing back their shoulders, they sang out until I was fearful the walls would burst. "And should we die before our journey's through, happy day, all is well"; I looked at my minister friend, and found him weeping.

Then one of the boys who had been asked to administer the sacrament knelt at the table, bowed his head, and said, "Oh, God, the eternal father." He paused for what seemed to be a full minute, and then he proceeded with the rest of the blessing on the bread. At the close of that meeting I sought that boy out. I put my arm around his shoulders, and said, "Son, what's the matter? Why was it so difficult for you to ask the blessing on the bread?"

He paused for a moment and said, rather apologetically, "Well, Brother Brown, it hasn't been two hours since I was over the continent on a bombing mission. As we started to return, I discovered that my tail assembly was partly shot away, that one of my engines was out, that three of my crew were wounded, and that it appeared absolutely impossible that we could reach the shores of England. Brother Brown, up there I remembered Primary and Sunday School and MIA and home and church, and up there, when it seemed all hope was lost, I said, 'Oh, God, the eternal father, please support this plane until we reach a landing field.' He did just that, and when we landed, I learned of this meeting and I had to run all the way to get here. I didn't have time to change my battle dress, and when I knelt there and again addressed the Lord, I was reminded that I hadn't stopped to say thanks. Brother Brown, I had to pause a little while to tell God how grateful I was."

Well, we went on with our meeting. We sang. Prayers were offered, and these young men, with only a moment's notice, each stood and spoke, preached the gospel of Jesus Christ to their comrades, bore their testimonies, and again I say--with due respect to the various ones with whom I have associated and labored--they were among the finest sermons I ever heard. Then the time was up, and I said, "Fellows, it's time for chow. We must dismiss now, or you will miss your dinner."

With almost one voice, they cried, "We can eat grub any time--let's have a testimony meeting!" So we stayed another hour and a half while every man bore witness to the truthfulness of the restored gospel of Jesus Christ. Each one in turn, and in his own way, said, "I know that God lives. I know that the gospel is restored. I know that Joseph Smith was a prophet of God." Again I looked at my friend, and he was weeping unashamedly.

At the close of that meeting, this minister said to me, "I have been a minister for more than twenty-one years, and this has been the greatest spiritual experience of my life."

--Hugh B. Brown

HAPPINESS

He who enjoys doing, and enjoys what he has done, is happy.

--Goethe

*****

Dedication to some labor of love is the secret of happiness, no matter how humble or obscure.

*****

You ask, "What is the price of happiness?" You will be surprised with the simplicity of the answer. The treasure house of happiness may be unlocked and remain open to those who use the following keys: the first, you must live the gospel of Jesus Christ in its purity and simplicity--not a half-hearted compliance, but hewing to the line. And this means an all-out devoted consecration to the great program of salvation and exaltation in an orthodox manner. The second, you must forget yourself and love your companion more than yourself. If you do these things, happiness will be yours in great and never-failing abundance.

--Spencer W. Kimball

*****

Where was it ever promised us that life on this earth can ever be easy, free from conflict and uncertainty, devoid of anguish and wonder and pain? Those who seek the folly of endless happiness--who fear moods, who shun solitude, who do not know the dignity of occasional depression--can find bliss easy enough in tranquilizing pills or in senility.

The purpose of life is not to be happy. The purpose of life is to matter, to be productive, to have it make some difference that you lived at all. Happiness, in the ancient, noble sense, means self-fulfillment--and it is given to those who use the fullest of whatever talents God or fate bestowed upon them. Happiness lies in stretching the resources of the mind and heart to the farthest boundaries of which we are capable.

--Leo Rasten

*****

MY PRESCRIPTION

Take a little happiness
Well blended with a smile,
Add a bit of solo
Every little while.

Read a page of jokes
After every meal.
It's really quite surprising
How it will make you feel.

Laugh when others laugh,
And smile when'er they smile.
All these little medicines
Are every one worthwhile.

So when you're feeling bad,
As many patients tell,
Just try this doctor's remedy
And see how soon you're well!

                    --Vernelle J. Pulsipher

                         *****

Life is a mixture
     of sunshine and rain,
Good things and bad things,
     pleasure and pain.
We can't have all sunshine,
     But it's certainly true,
There is never a cloud
     the sun didn't shine through.
So always remember
     that whatever befalls you
The power of God
     is always beside you,
And if friends disappoint you,
     and plans go astray,
And nothing works out
     in just the right way,
And you feel you have failed
     in achieving your goal,
And that life wrongly placed you
     in an unfitting role,
Take heart and "stand tall"
     and remember who you are
For God is your father
     and no one can bar
Or keep you from reaching
     your desired success,
Or withhold the joy
     that is yours to possess.
For with God on your side
     it matters not who
Is working to keep
     life's good things from you,
For you need nothing more
     than God's guidance and love
To insure you the things
     that you're worthy of.
So trust in his wisdom
     and follow his ways,

Happiness

And be not concerned with
    the world's empty praise,
But seek first his kindgdom
    and you will possess
The world's greatest riches,
    which is true happiness.

HUMAN RELATIONS

The only way to compel men to speak good of you is to do good.

--Voltaire

*****

Speech is to thought what gold is to the diamond. It is needed as a setting, but only a little is required.

--Voltaire

*****

When you point the finger of scorn, look at your hand--you will find three fingers pointing back at you.

--Persian Proverb

*****

He who wishes to exert a useful influence must be careful to insult nothing. Let him not be troubled by what seems absurd, but consecrate his energies to the creation of what is good. He must not demolish, but build.

--Goethe

*****

Understanding people and getting along with them ought to be the aim of anyone serving in an executive capacity.

--Charles E. Wilson

*****

When building the staff for his newly conceived computer company, H. Ross Perot hired the best people he could find. His motto: Eagles don't flock. You have to find them one at a time.

*****

APOLOGY TO A FRIEND

The storm subsides,
    and in my heart resides
A deep regret where only
    love for you should be.
Give back my ugly searing
    words of spite

That in the night glow hot
    to torture me.
I'll hide them deep in
    cushioned dark
To keep them ever still
    and dead,
Those biting, vicious
    words of mine
I wish unsaid.

--Marian Boyle Monahan

*****

MAN'S MEASUREMENT

A man's no bigger than the way he treats his fellow man;
This standard has his measure been since time itself began.
He's measured not by tithes or creeds, nor by the gold
    that's put aside,
    Nor by his sanctity.
He's measured not by social rank when character's the test,
    Nor by his earthly pomp or show,
    Nor by displayed wealth possessed.
He's measured by his justice, right, his squareness in all
    dealings made, his honest, quiet way.
These are his measurements ever near to serve him when they can,
For man's no bigger than the way he serves his fellow man.

*****

CRITIQUE

I wonder
Sometimes
What we'll all
Look like
When we cross
That invisible
Threshold
And shed
This phony drape
Of made-up,
Costumed
Flesh and bones.

I think
That only then
We'll clearly see
The beauty
Of those
We thought
So ordinary.

And we'll see
We often judged
So wrong,
When we all
Critiqued
With our bodies on.

--Barbara Werrett Nielsen

*****

Personal and corporate honesty often pays off in dramatic ways. Donald Douglas, for example, built such a reputation for his aircraft company, and he worked to preserve it.

There was the time Douglas was competing with Boeing to sell Eastern Airlines its first big jets. Eddie Rickenbacker, who headed Eastern, is said to have told Douglas that his specifications and claims for the DC-8 were close to his competition on everything but noise suppression. He then gave Douglas one last chance to out-promise Boeing on this feature.

After consulting his engineers, Douglas reported back that he did not feel he could make that promise. Rickenbacker replied, "I know you can't. I wanted to see if you were still honest. You just got yourself an order for $135 million. Now go home and silence those jets!"

*****

Every man is said to have his peculiar ambition. Whether it be true or not, I, for one, can say that I have no other so great as that of being esteemed of my fellow men, by rendering myself worthy of their esteem. How far I shall succeed in gratifying this ambition is yet to be developed. I am young, and unknown to many of you. I was born, and have ever remained, in the most humble walks of life. I have no wealthy or popular relatives or friends to recommend me. My case is thrown exclusively upon the independent voters of the country; and, if elected, they will have conferred upon me a favor for which I shall be unremitting in my labors to compensate. But, if the good people in their wisdom shall see fit to keep me in the background, I have been too familiar with disappointments to be very much chagrined.

--Abraham Lincoln

*****

DO YOU LIKE YOURSELF?

Once a friend of mine named Ed said to me, "For a very long time I didn't like myself." It was not said in self-pity, but simply as an unfortunate fact. "It was a very difficult time," he said, "and very painful. I did not like myself for a number of reasons, some of them valid and some of them pure fancy. I would hate to have to go back to that."

"Then, gradually," he said, "I discovered with surprise and pleasure that a number of people liked me. And, I thought, if they can like me, why can't I like myself? Just thinking it did not do it, but slowly I learned to like myself--and then it was all right."

This was not said in self-love, in its bad connotation, but in self-knowledge. Ed meant literally that he had learned to accept and like the person "Ed" as he liked other people. It gave him a great advantage. Most people do not like themselves at all. They distrust themselves, put on masks and pomposities. They quarrel and boast and pretend and are jealous because they do not like themselves. But mostly they do not ever know themselves well enough to form a true liking--and, since we automatically fear and dislike strangers, we fear and dislike our stranger-selves.

Once Ed was able to like himself, he was released from the secret prison of self-contempt.

I wish we could all be so. If we could learn to like ourselves even a little, maybe our cruelties and angers might melt away. Maybe we would not have to hurt one another just to keep our ego-chins above water.

--John Steinbeck

*****

HERE'S WHAT HAPPENS WHEN YOU ARE IN TUNE

In telling about his life and how it changed when he was out of tune, renowned artist and teacher Robert Henri recollected the little attic room in which he had lived as a student in Paris.

"My place was a romance," he declared. "It was a wonderful place. . .I studied, and thought, and made compositions, and wrote home letters full of hope. It was wonderful. . . .

"But days came when hopes looked black and my art student's paradise was turned into a dirty little room with broken tiles; ashes fell from the stove, and it was all hopelessly poor."

Everything depended, he decided, on whether or not he was in tune. When he was, he liked the world and everything in it--and the world and everyone in it liked him. But when he fell out of tune, he disliked everyone--and everyone disliked him.

One of the biggest--and maybe the hardest--lessons anyone whose success depends on influencing others favorably has to learn is to stay in tune. It is easier to be out of tune--to find fault, criticize, and complain. Anyone who lives in tune with his world finds more interesting people and situations in it than he can imagine--and people find him interesting and pleasant to be around.

One of America's most successful men admitted that until he was forty he was a carping critic, able to find fault with everything and everybody, from Abraham Lincoln to Richard Nixon. Then, overnight, he changed, and he began looking for the good in people and things. Whenever he found good, which was often, he told people what he had found.

It remade his people entirely, and inside of six months he was living in a different world--a world in which he was completely in tune. And the world rewarded him bountifully, as it always will those who are in tune with it.

*****

In the year 1884 a young man from America died while visiting Europe. His middle-aged, grieving parents returned with the body.

They were heartbroken; they had loved their son very much. After the funeral they began to discuss some kind of memorial to him--not a tombstone or an ornate grave, but a living memorial, something that would help other young men like their son.

After considering many alternatives, they decided that something in the field of education would be most appropriate. It would be the kind of memorial that would go on year after year helping educate young people. That would be the best kind of tribute to their son's memory. They arranged an appointment with Charles Eliot, then president of Harvard University, and he received the quite ordinary, unpretentious couple in his offices, asking what he could do for them.

They told him about the death of their son, and apologized for taking up his valuable time. They explained that they wanted to establish a memorial to him--something that would help other young men like their son get an education.

Eliot looked at the unprepossessing couple with some impatience and a certain suggestion of aristocratic disdain. "Perhaps you have in mind a scholarship," he said crisply.

"No," said the woman, her mild manner belying the quickness and sharpness of her mind. "We were thinking of something more substantial than that--perhaps a new building or so. . . ."

"I must explain to you," said Eliot with what seemed a patronizing air, "that what you suggest costs a great deal of money. Buildings are very expensive." Obviously, Eliot did not think that from their appearance they were capable of that kind of donation.

There was a pause, then the lady rose slowly and said, "Mr. Eliot, what has this entire university cost?"

Eliot shrugged and muttered, stating a figure that amounted to several million dollars.

"Oh, we can do better than that," said the lady, who now had seemed to make up her mind about the entire thing. "Come, dear," she motioned to her husband, "I have an idea." And they left.

The following year President Eliot of Harvard learned that the plain, unpretentious couple had contributed $26 million for a memorial to their son. The memorial was to be named Leland Stanford, Jr. University.

*****

THE FACE

I saw him on the street only this morning. Already late for work, I cut through Skid Row to my 8:23 commuter. It was a miserable morning, the sky a musky gray made of factory smoke and soot and dirty rain. Even my new coat with its fashionable collar turned up against my face could not hide the dingy alleys covered with broken glass. Scrawny cats pawed through the garbage cans that lined the narrow passageways between the bars. I saw the names above the doors--The Blue-Tailed Fly, The Painted Lady, Janie's.

I berated myself for having tried to save time by the shortcut. Lowering my head deeper into my collar, I hurried around the corner, running full-tilt into a weaving, lurching man. He fell heavily to the sidewalk in front of me. I stared with horrified fascination at him. His clothes were filthy, and he reeked of garlic and liquor. His unshaven face was clean only where the rain ran down it in tiny streams. His uncombed hair was as black as the eyes that stared fully at me, devoid of any expression. For a second that stretched into an aeon, I stood there, frozen. Then, as he softly called my name, I turned and ran and ran and ran until I saw the familiar station, the people I knew, and the signs and sounds of sanity. But the soft call of my name still sounded in my ears.

Sinking exhausted into my train chair, I closed my eyes to shut out what I had seen. The derelict on Skid Row was not unknown. It was the face of Jim, a boy I had known years earlier in grammar school in the small town where I had been reared. It was a gossipy little town, closely knit by a common religion and the stand-offish attitude shown those who violated any of its codes. Jim's mother was an alcoholic, and the neighbors could hear his father and mother cursing and swearing long into the night. As this news reached the ears of the townspeople, more and more of Jim's playmates were forbidden to play with him. My folks were more lenient, and as the years went by, he came often to our home.

When his father committed suicide while Jim was still in junior high school, the last of his friends drifted away, and he became more lonely, more resentful of society. To fight back at the rules that had excluded him from other groups, he began to cut school, and the boys he associated with were no strangers to police records. Finally, just like all the rest, I turned my back on him.

By leaving him in the alley, I was turning my back on him again. Our town gave him a start toward Skid Row, but I was pushing him the last mile by taking away his last hope of acceptance.

I turned and went back to him. I tried to give him my understanding, my help, and my confidence. Many years later, I received the following letter from him:

Dear Susan:

I don't know whether you remember me or not, but I remember you and I always will. You see, you are the one person I will never forget. It has been many years since you used to play badminton with me and hike up the mountains and listen to my troubles. It was you who, when I went with you for the first time and tried to get fresh with you, taught me that life is more than sex. You taught me to understand the beauty of a rose. You stimulated me to think about the meaning of life. You were the one person who had faith in me. Three years ago, I got married, and my wife and I now have a beautiful little daughter. With my wife's full approval, we are going to name her after you.

Always,
Jim

*****

SHANNA'S GIFT

Robin and Shanna were almost the same age. They lived on the same street, and as little girls had often played together. But, as they grew, their interests became quite varied, and by the time they reached high school, they had little in common.

Shanna had been born with a birth defect that caused her to walk with difficulty and have poor control over some muscular reflexes. Robin had enjoyed being with Shanna when they were younger, but now she had a new group of friends who would have little to do with Shanna--and, besides, they were interested in things Shanna would never be able to participate in, such as sports and gymnastics.

Robin knew that she was intentionally leaving Shanna out of her life, and felt somewhat guilty over it--because she knew that Shanna still very much wanted to be her friend. She would offer small favors and often ask Robin to walk to school with her, but Robin would decline, offering some excuse or another, and she'd tell herself that she didn't want to get up early enough, since Shanna's disabilities caused her to walk so slowly. But deep down, she knew that the real reason was that she was embarrassed to be seen with her. You see, Shanna was clumsy, and when the girls at school saw her struggle with some obstacle, they giggled and made fun. They didn't mean any harm, and Shanna never noticed--at least, Robin didn't think Shanna noticed. Although Robin never made fun of her and

153

she really did like her, she told herself that she was more like the other girls and had more in common with them--so she went on leaving Shanna out of her life.

Then one night Robin had a dream.

She saw herself in a beautiful place and in a time she imagined to be before this life. She was a little girl again, surrounded by what seemed to be happiness and love. But she was not alone. She had a playmate with shiny golden hair and deep blue eyes that sparkled when she smiled. They were inseparable, and did everything together. They ran and danced and played little girl games, and Robin marveled at how beautiful and graceful her friend was.

Days joyfully passed, and a time grew near when Robin was going to have to say goodbye--to take her step into this life. Her friend walked with her as far as she dare, and with big tears in her eyes, stood nearby to watch the event unfold.

Robin approached with anticipation and hesitation, and was told at the threshold of her new life on earth that a tiny little body had been injured in some way, and that it was necessary for her to meet a special life-long challenge. Tears flooded her eyes, and the words around her seemed to fade in the distance as she stood, trembling and fearful of what was to come. Her trance-like state was gently interrupted by a familiar and loving touch, and she turned to see her little friend leaving. But she was not going back--she was going on ahead, in Robin's place.

Robin had to be restrained as she called to her, and she wept as she saw her friend wave a final, loving goodbye from what seemed to be a long way away. But she could still see the unmistakable evidence of a walk that suddenly became painfully familiar to her. Robin fell sobbing to the ground.

Robin awoke with a start, looked at her clock, and, with tears streaming down her face, she dressed and left the house without stopping to eat. She knew Shanna would have a head start, but she knew she had to find her. She hurried on with a firm resolve in her aching heart. As she turned the corner, she saw Shanna up ahead. As Robin approached, Shanna dropped an armful of papers on the sidewalk. She was awkwardly bending down to retrieve them when Robin reached her. She knelt to help, and met with a startled but pleased expression on Shanna's face.

Robin asked if she could walk with her; Shanna, still a little surprised, said, "Sure!" As they walked on together, Robin thought she detected a familiar sparkle in Shanna's deep blue eyes.

--Susan Empey

KINDNESS

DON'T POSTPONE THOSE KIND WORDS

When I leave this mortal shore
And mosey around the earth no more,
Don't weep, don't sigh, don't sob--
I might have struck a better job.

Don't go and buy a large bouquet
For which you'll find it hard to pay,
Don't mope around and seem all blue--
I may be better off than you.

Don't tell the folks I was a saint
Or any other thing I ain't.
If you have jam like that to spread
Just hand it out before I'm dead.

If you have roses, bless your soul,
Just pin one in my buttonhole
While I'm alive and well today,
Don't wait until I've gone away.

*****

CANCER CAN'T DEFEAT HIS OLD FRIENDS

Jim Wilhelmy, weak with cancer, could only watch as his two hundred acres of soybeans and corn grew ripe and heavy. He knew the time had come for harvesting, and he feared all would be lost.

Wilhelmy, fifty-two, was receiving chemotherapy for the lung cancer that was soon to take his life. He could no longer work the fertile fields he and his wife, Eileen, had nurtured for twenty years. As harvest time approached, word of Wilhelmy's plight spread through the Will County countryside southwest of Chicago. A few weeks ago, an army of neighbors arrived at the Wilhelmy spread in a caravan of tractors, combines, huskers, and wagons--fifty farmers and twenty-five of their sons.

The women brought fresh pies, covered hot dishes, jugs of steaming drink. Their men already were at work in the fields taking in the corn crop.

Old Charlie Jackson said, "I elevated six thousand bushels of corn myself for Oscar Wallin the time he caught his hand in a picker and tore it off. Dunno why you do these things. Hard to explain. You just do it. You're neighbors."

Gordon Walsh, fifty-two, stood by the corn crib. "This is just the natural thing farm people do for each other," he said.

Mrs. Wilhelmy's eyes filled with tears, touched by the display of humanity as old and dependable as the land itself. Her husband, once a vigorous man--farmer, township clerk--stopped by and shook hands, grateful he had such friends.

For two Saturdays the army in bib overalls rolled across the farm land, bringing in the soybeans. Wilhelmy wept at their kindness. On the final Saturday, they tackled the corn crop worth $25,000. But Wilhelmy couldn't stop by. He stayed home.

Mrs. Wilhelmy said, "How do you thank people? There's no way. Jim and I are very grateful."

The harvesting was all done by nightfall Saturday.

At midnight, Jim Wilhelmy died.

*****

TRUE BENEVOLENCE

A young lad, a student in a university, took a walk one day with his professor, who was commonly called the students' friend because of his kindness to those he instructed. While they were walking together, they saw a pair of old shoes lying in the path; the shoes were supposed to belong to a poor man employed in a field nearby, a man who had nearly finished his day's work. The student turned to the professor, saying, "Let's play a trick on that man. We'll hide his shoes and conceal ourselves behind those bushes, and watch to see his perplexity when he can't find them!"

"No," said the professor, "we must never amuse ourselves at the expense of the poor. But you are rich, and may give yourself a greater pleasure than amusement by means of this poor man. Put a dollar in each shoe, and then we will hide."

The student did so, and then hid with the professor in the bushes nearby, from a point where they could easily watch the laborer. The man soon finished his work, and came across the field to the path where he had left his coat and shoes. While he put on his coat, he slipped one foot into a shoe--but, feeling something there, he stooped down and found the dollar. Astonishment and wonder swept across his face. He gazed at the dollar, turned it over in his hand, and looked at it again and again. He looked around him, but could see no one. Finally, he put the money in his pocket, and proceeded to put on his other shoe. How great was his surprise when he found the other dollar!

His feelings overcame him; he fell upon his knees, and there uttered aloud a fervent thanksgiving, in which he spoke of his wife--sick and helpless--and his children--without bread--whom this timely bounty from an unknown hand would save from suffering. The young student stood there, deeply affected, and tears filled his eyes. "Now," said the professor, "aren't you much more pleased than if you had played your intended trick?"

"You have taught me a lesson I shall never forget," answered the youth, "for I feel now how true it is that it is more blessed to give than to receive."

*****

I WAS JUST THINKING

The letter you didn't write dims the light for a lonely friend.

The phone call you didn't make is a soundless void for someone who loves you.

The flowers you didn't send are immortal, but death came to the woman who never received them.

For the crime of thoughtlessness, remorse seems a mild penalty.

I didn't write the letter. I didn't make the phone call. I didn't send the flowers. The friend is lonely still. The loved one is far away. My flowers mark a grave.

Perhaps all this would not be so poignant except for a letter that came today. I had managed to send a brief note to a girl in a hospital. It was a mere acknowledgement of her misfortune, written in the time it would take me to change my nail polish. But this is what she wrote to me:

"Your letter came on my very lowest day. It's surprising what a kind word from another person can do for one's morale. You go along from day to day thinking that sometimes life isn't very rewarding, and then someone lets you know that you are appreciated. I think we all need that once in a while."

I think I needed her letter more than she needed mine. I needed to be reminded that I am well and that my life is filled with happiness and contentment and love and, often, joy. I needed to be reminded that in these riches of my heart, there is ample room for the lonely and the ill and the tired. Only by remembering that are my riches truly mine. The letter from the girl in the hospital had one last paragraph. I hope I never forget it:

"God put us on earth to love and care for one another. How wonderful it would be if only everyone could realize that life is so terribly short, and that we could gain so much by helping each other."

--Patty Johnson

*****

BLESSINGS IN DISGUISE

Two months before our baby boy was born, the doctors found it necessary for me to have major cancer surgery. During the time of my convalescence and as we awaited the arrival of the baby, we prayed frequently. The stake, under the leadership of President Ezra Taft

157

Benson, united in fasting and prayer. Later, a prayer circle of high priests was held in our home. I was administered to often; and many, many times the voices of our three children (the baby could not talk) were raised in the petition, "Help Mother to get well soon." The doctors shook their heads. I had one chance in one thousand--it was only a question of time.

What I want others to know is the experience that came because of my situation.

The spirit of humility was poured upon us, and the knowledge that God is all-powerful was made known to us. Through frequent prayers, we were led to trust in his plan and to know that all would be well.

The spirit of repentance permeated our home. We felt that we must live better and do better if we would expect the Lord to bless us and give us what we wanted so very much.

We felt the spirit of love toward each other, toward the children, and the children toward each other. We showed each other every day the affection and appreciation we had; days might be numbered, but love would guide us through.

The spirit of appreciation for our blessings came to us, and we felt as if our cup would run over. Our little boy was born and was perfect. The children remained well. Harold was blessed with health to carry on his work and Church activities. Life took on new meanings. God had been good to us.

And then there came to us a display of friendliness. A neighbor across the alley, whose antagonism against anyone who would have so many children in the city had made little unpleasantries on various occasions, sent with the children large bouquets of flowers she had grown and picked from her own garden. For the first time in the year we had lived there, she smiled and waved at me.

There came to us gifts of all kinds--flowers, food, and clothing. Money came through the mail with the simple greeting, "Merry Christmas." Interested friends who knew we had not been able to can produce during the summer brought us more than a hundred quarts of fruits and vegetables. A young lady who had never met me knitted a wool sweater for the baby.

Blessings came to us because Harold continued his calling as a bishop. When asking about financial arrangements, the doctors said, "You're a bishop in your church. We will give you service at a minimum charge." When I returned to the hospital for a second surgery, there was no one to care for my family; a young lady, who was visiting her sister, volunteered to come to our home. She had never met us, but for two weeks she had complete charge of five children and the house. When she was ready to return to her family, we gave her a little gift and hid some money in the package, too--money we knew she would not accept from us outright. The next day she came back with it, and with tears in her eyes, she said, "It has been an honor for me to be in the home of the bishop. My husband is in the South Pacific, and I do not want to be deprived of any blessing by taking pay. I know that my reward will come in other ways." She would not accept any remuneration.

People say to me, "Oh, how terrible! What an awful experience your sickness has been. You must try to forget it, and start a new life."

It must not be that way! I never want to forget. I know the memory of it will make me a happier and better person.

--Virginia Driggs Clark

LIFE

Life is the childhood of our immortality.

--Goethe

*****

Knowledge comes, but wisdom lingers.

--Tennyson

*****

Fifty years ago people finished a day's work and needed rest. Today, they need exercise.

*****

Never get so busy making a living that you forget to make a life.

*****

He who thinks wisdom is greater than virtue will lose his wisdom.

--Hebrew Proverb

*****

Don't believe the world owes you a living. The world owes you nothing--it was here first.

--Robert Jones Burdette

*****

The surest way to get somewhere is to know where you're going.

*****

A small-town paper reported that a newcomer, who had moved there to escape the traffic and congestion of the city, was run over by the Welcome Wagon.

*****

When we look into the long avenue of the future, and see the good there is for each one of us to do, we realize, after all, what a beautiful thing it is to work and to live, and to be happy.

--Robert Louis Stevenson

*****

Don't worry about your station in life. Someone will always tell you where to get off.

*****

If you're feeling low, don't despair. The sun has a sinking spell every night, but it comes back up every morning.

*****

In the inscrutable wisdom of God, knowledge is not without its price-- everything that has been learned comes by effort, by someone's agonizing study.

*****

There is no point in quaking with the impact of every hour. We have to have faith, the faith to quiet our hearts in the midst of confusion and uncertainties. We can't run away from everything; we can't keep on running from anything--for, sooner or later, we would run out of the strength to run. We have to live life, face it, honor it, enjoy it, adjust to it.

--Richard L. Evans

*****

Finish every day and be done with it. You have done what you could. Some blunders and absurdities have crept in; forget them as soon as you can. Tomorrow is a new day; you will begin it well and serenely, and with too high a spirit to be cumbered by your old nonsense.

--Emerson

*****

Once in a while we should stop and ask ourselves in whose army we are fighting. Whose battle lines are we defending--the Savior's, or Satan's? The battle lines are being drawn. And, like it or not, our actions signal our true allegiance.

*****

Learn to make the most of life,
Lose no happy day.
Time will never bring them back,
Chances swept away.
Leave no tender word unsaid,
Love while love shall last;
The mill cannot grind
With water that is past.

--Sarah Dounedney

*****

161

THE MONUMENT

God,
Before he sent his children to earth,
Gave each of them
A very carefully selected package
Of problems.
These,
He promised, smiling,
Are yours alone. No one
Else may have the blessings
These problems will bring you.
And only you
Have the special talents and abilities
That will be needed
To make these problems
Your servants.

Now go down to your birth
And to your forgetfulness. Know that
I love you beyond measure.
These problems I give you
Are a symbol of that love.
The monument you make of your life
With the help of your problems
Will be a symbol of your
Love for me,
Your father.

--Author Unknown

*****

MY NEIGHBOR'S ROSES

The roses red upon my neighbor's vine
Are owned by him, but they are also mine.
His was the cost, and his the labor, too,
But mine as well as his the joy, their loveliness to view.

They bloom for me and are for me as fair
As for the man who gave them all his care.
Thus I am rich, because a good man grew
A rose-clad vine for all his neighbors' view.

I know from this that others plant for me,
And what they own, my joy may also be.
So why be selfish, when so much that's fine
Is grown for you upon your neighbor's vine?

--Abraham L. Gruber

*****

KITH AND KIN

If you could see all your ancestors
    all standing in a row,
would you be proud of them, or not,
    or don't you really know?
Some strange discoveries are made
    in climbing family trees,
and some of them, you know, do not
    particularly please.
If you could see your ancestors
    all standing in a row,
there might be some of them, perhaps,
    you wouldn't care to know.
But here's another question, which
    requires a different view:
if you should meet your ancestors,
    would they be proud of you?

*****

No matter what else you are doing
From cradle days through to the end,
You're writing your life's greatest story,
Each day sees another page penned.
Each month, the end of a chapter,
Each year, the end of a part.
And never a word is mistaken,
Or even a thought of the heart.
Each morn when you wake the book opens,
Revealing a page pure and white;
What thoughts, what actions, what doings
Will cover its surface by night?
God leaves that to you, you're the writer,
And never one word will grow dim,
Until someday you write the word
         finished
And give your life's book back to Him.

--Anonymous

*****

CHILD-STEPS

I stood once with my Father
Not long before my birth.
He gave me words of wisdom
To guide my steps on earth.

I'm sure his words were simple,
He knows no complex ways;
He must have shown me child-steps
To shape and form my days.

163

Now I'm an earthbound child;
I seek his words, and fail.
Were all those words of wisdom
Left somehow at the veil?

But then I think I hear him
Say, "Seek and ye shall find,
But first, you must remember
My words aren't in your mind.

"The veil can rob a child-mind,
But you've got another part
That holds my words where none can rob:
I placed them in your heart.

"Just listen as you live each day;
When you do right, you'll know.
For every time you do what's right,
Your heart will start to glow."

I need no man to teach me;
God's words are with me still.
I simply notice day by day
How each act makes me feel.

I love those glowing child-steps,
It seems so simple now
To make my way through life's hard times;
The child-steps show me how.

                        --Dean Black

                    *****

                  A NEW DAY

I walked along the deserted beach
    with its air of calm and quiet.
The sea, usually green and clear,
    was dark in the fading light.
The whitecaps seemed to reflect my mood
    of sadness and remorse,
For instead of dancing on the wave,
    they retreated from its force.
The waves seemed to say to me,
    "Now you are at summer's end,
Another day has passed from life,
    a new day will soon begin.
What will you do with that day
    that has been granted to you?
Will you live it to its fullest,
    so when that day is through
You can rest contented, knowing
    that on that day,

                  164

You lived its every second
   and threw not a minute away?"
I thought about the advice
   the waves had given me,
And slowly the sad mood lifted
   as I began to see
That life is not only existing,
   but living and loving, too.
So as the waves told me,
   I will also tell you,
"Let not one moment slip by
   and catch you unaware,
But live life to its fullest
   and the wonder of moments share
With me and with all others
   who on this earth shall stay;
For moments make a minute,
   and minutes make a day.

--Betty Helveston

*****

MY OPPORTUNITY

I want that somehow I may live,
Some bit of inspiration give,
Some word or deed of mine be spent
To lend someone encouragement,
That he may nobler live each day. . .
For just once will I pass this way.

I want to live and have clean fun,
Enjoy each day from sun to sun;
To have within my heart real joy,
To keep the spirit of a boy.
I want to laugh and sing and play. . .
For just once will I pass this way.

I want, ere all my race is run,
To see some work of mine begun
To mark, for trav'lers following me,
The danger spots, so all may see;
To put some beauty here to stay. . .
Though just once will I pass this way.

Then I would add some brotherhood,
Allay what hate and fear I could.
And whether we be great or small,
See truth and justice govern all;
Help righteousness to have full sway. . .
For just once will I pass this way.

To use my talents by some plan
That seeks to serve my fellow man;
To try to soften grief and pain
And help restore the smiles again.
All this to do while yet I may. . .
For just once will I pass this way.

I pass this way but once, 'tis true.
And yet, 'tis given me and you
To add some happiness and cheer
For other pilgrims trav'ling here.
So when we're gone, some may say
They're glad that we have passed this way.

--Thomas Simpkin

*****

WHAT DOES A FATHER SAY TO HIS SON BEFORE HIS FIRST GAME?

This is your first game, son.
I hope you win.
I hope you win for your sake,
not mine.
Because winning's nice.
It's a good feeling,
like the whole world is yours.
But it passes, this feeling.
And what lasts is what
you've learned.

And what you learn about
is life.
That's what sports are all about.
Life.
The whole thing is played out
in an afternoon.
The happiness of life.
The miseries.
The joys.
The heartbreaks.

There's no telling
what'll turn up.
There's no telling
whether they'll toss you
out in the first five minutes,
or whether you'll stay for
the long haul.

There's no telling how
you'll do.

You might be a hero,
or you might be
absolutely nothing.
There's just no telling.
Too much depends on chance--
on how the ball bounces.

I'm not talking about the
game, son.
I'm talking about life.
But it's life that the game
is all about,
just as I said.

Because every game is life.
And life is a game.
A serious one.
Dead serious.

But that's what you do
with serious things.
You do your best.
You take what comes.
You take what comes,
and you run with it.

Winning is fun.
Sure--
but winning is not
the point.

Wanting to win is the point.
Not giving up is the point.
Never being satisfied
with what you've done
is the point.
Never letting up is the point.
Never letting anyone down
is the point.

Play to win.
Sure.
But lose like
a champion.
Because it's not
winning
that counts.
What counts is
trying.

*****

I LEARNED TO LOVE LIFE

Dear Abby:

Not long ago I was shy, ugly, poorly groomed, unhappy, and without a boyfriend. I never smiled. I wrote to you, and you gave me the best advice I've ever received. Here it is:

"The key to being popular with both sexes is to be kind. Be honest. Be tactful. If you can't be beautiful (or handsome), be well-groomed, tastefully attired, trim of figure, and keep a smile on your face!

"Be clean in body and mind. If you're not a 'brain,' try harder. If you're not a great athlete, you can be a good sport. Try to be a standout in something. If you can't dance or sing, learn to play an instrument.

"Think for yourself, but respect the rules. Be generous with kinds words and affectionate gestures, but save heavy artillary for later. You'll be glad you did. If you need help, ask God. If you don't need anything, thank God."

I have followed your advice step by step, and kept it handy when I felt down. I am now president of the sophomore class, and I play the guitar.

Smiling comes naturally to me, and I love life. I have a boyfriend who plays football, and he is kind and respectful. My grades are better, and I have more friends than I ever dreamed I'd have.

Abby, you're not the only one who helped me. God helped me. He answered my prayers.

--Happy in St. Louis

*****

JUST FOR TODAY

1. Just for today, I will try to live through this day only, and not set far-reaching goals in an effort to overcome all my problems at once. I know I can do something for twelve hours that would appall me if I had to keep it up for a lifetime.

2. Just for today, I will try to be happy. Abraham Lincoln said, "Most folks are about as happy as they make up their minds to be." He was right. I will not dwell on thoughts that depress me. I will chase them out of my mind and replace them with happy thoughts.

3. Just for today, I will adjust myself to what is. I will face reality. I will try to change those things I can, and accept those things I cannot change.

4. Just for today, I will try to improve my mind. I will not be a mental loafer. I will force myself to read something that requires effort, thought, and concentration.

5. Just for today, I will exercise my soul in three ways. I will do a good deed for somebody without letting them know it. (If they find out I did it, it won't count.) I will do at least two things that I know I should do but have been putting off. I will not show anyone that my feelings are hurt; they may be hurt, but today I will not show it.

6. Just for today, I will be agreeable. I will look as good as I can, dress becomingly, talk softly, act courteously, and speak ill of no one. Just for today, I'll not try to improve anybody except myself.

7. Just for today, I will have a program. I may not follow it exactly, but I will have it, thereby saving myself from two pests--hurry and indecision.

8. Just for today, I will have a quiet half hour to relax alone. During this time, I will reflect on my behavior and will try to get better perspective on my life.

9. Just for today, I will be unafraid. I will gather the courage to do what is right and will take the responsibility for my own actions. I will expect nothing from the world, but I will realize that as I give to the world, the world will give to me.

LISTENING

When your work speaks for itself, don't interrupt.

--Shelby

*****

Where the river is deepest, it makes the least noise.

*****

THE ART OF VISITING

One day I was asked to sit with a friend who was recuperating from a long, serious illness. I arrived carrying my work basket jammed with mending, a folder of material on a PTA project, and some patterns to cut out for Relief Society.

I was greeted at the door by the Relief Society president of my friend, Elizabeth, who explained that Elizabeth needed no special bedside care; my responsibility was to visit with her. As I started toward the bedroom, basket in hand, the Relief Society president gently took my arm and said, smiling, "You do know how to visit, don't you?"

My puzzled expression must have answered her question, for she asked, "May I give you some ideas on visiting?" I nodded.

She then said, "First, when you are visiting for a short time, try to leave your busy work at home--unless, of course, it is really urgent. Bringing work with you might tell Elizabeth that you are so busy you really should have stayed home. If, on the other hand, you walk in empty-handed, you are telling her that visiting with her is the most important thing you could possibly do during your stay. It says that you are here to enjoy her company, and you're doing it by choice.

"Second, your visit is more important than any well-prepared food you might carry. A casserole without companionship does not taste very good; the hunger for friendship is as important as the need for good food. Of course, it's best to try to satisfy both appetites.

"Third, be careful not to upstage the stories of your friend while you are together. I fear that many of us unconsciously do just that. If Elizabeth tells you she is planning an exciting weekend thirty miles from home, don't tell her about going surfing in Hawaii. If her complicated surgery took a team of twelve specialists, don't tell her about your exotic acupuncture. If she exclaims about her daughter who just had twins, don't tell her that your cat had a litter of nine. Let her recount, relive, and relish her memories without any competition.

"Fourth, respond to her conversation. Respond, but do not judge or assess her thoughts or ideas. Verbally show her that you care about the conversation. It's certainly supportive to say to a companion, 'Oh, yes! Really? Hmmmmmmm. For goodness sakes, is that right? Uh, huh. Well!'

Even when you simply respond with 'oh,' you are constantly reminding her by the tone of your voice that you are listening to her stories.

"That's all it takes," she concluded. "Visiting, simply, is really listening. Have a nice visit. There is therapy there for both of you!"

--Evalyn D. Bennett

LOVE

Love may not make the world go around, but it sure makes the trip worthwhile!

*****

If I love someone, I will do things for them that will help them gain eternal life.

*****

We need the influence and love of others, "for none of us liveth to himself." (Romans 14:7.) The very essence of life is lost when there is no one else who really matters to us.

*****

LOVE: A TOUCH OF GODHOOD

The word **love** is the most used, misused, understood, misunderstood, simple, yet profound word in language.

It is the most poignant, powerful, beautiful, and fulfilling concept placed in the heart of man--a thought given man of God so that man might be God.

--<u>The New Era,</u> June 1971

*****

If you love something,
   set it free;
If it comes back to you,
   it is yours.
If not, it never was.

--Irene

*****

INVENTORY

In marriage, his young hand held mine in sacred vow;
In childbirth, his kind hand caressed and soothed my brow.
In love, his hands cared for each tiny one who came;
In priesthood, his hands humbly blessed and gave each name.
In parenthood, his busy hands signed school report cards;
In guidance, his hands lifted chins and gave awards.
In sorrow, his strong hands console the ones in need,
With thoughtfulness, his calloused hands perform each deed.

In wisdom, his hands reassure our destiny,
In faith, his hand will hold mine through eternity.

--Dana Benson

*****

MY GIFT

Our only purpose, as we live,
Is something of ourselves to give
To others, as they pass hereby--
But what give I?

The painter paints for all to see.
The singer gives a melody.
The rich upon cash gifts rely--
But what give I?

I have no talents, large or small,
Nor have I wealth; it seems that all
I have is love that cannot die--
And this give I.

A picture's cold when paints are dry,
And songs and poems are heard, then die.
There is no peace that wealth can buy--
Still, what give I?

The art and riches fade away.
All tangible belongings stray;
I learn that but one gift will live--
The love I give.

*****

LOVE

There is no difficulty that enough love will not conquer; no disease that enough love will not heal; no door that enough love will not open; no gulf that enough love will not bridge; no wall that enough love will not throw down; no sin that enough love will not redeem. . . .

It makes no difference how deeply seated the trouble may be, how hopeless the outlook, how muddled the tangle, how great the mistake. A sufficient realization of love will dissolve it all. If you could only love enough, you would be the happiest and most powerful being in the world.

*****

LOVE IS A SPECIAL WAY OF FEELING

Love is a special way of feeling.

It's the safe way we feel when we sit on our mother's lap, her arms around us tight and close.

It's the good way we feel when we talk to someone, and they want to listen--and don't tell us to go away and be quiet.

It's the happy way we feel when we save a bird that has been hurt. . .or feed a cat or calm a frightened colt.

Love is found in unexpected places. It is there in the quiet moment when we first discover a beautiful thing. . .when we watch a bird soar high against a pale blue sky. . .when we see a lovely flower that no one else has noticed. . .when we find a place that shelters us and is our very own.

Love starts in little ways. It may begin the day we first share our thoughts with someone else. . .or help someone who needs us. . .or, sometimes, it begins because, even without words, we understand how someone feels.

Love comes quietly--but you know when it is there, because, suddenly, you are not alone anymore, and there is no sadness inside you.

Love is a happy feeling that stays inside your heart for the rest of your life.

--Joan Walsh Angland

*****

THE MYSTERY AND MAGIC OF LOVE

Moses Mendelssohn--the saintly German-Jewish philosopher who was hunchbacked as a result of boyhood curvature of the spine--fell in love with Guggenheim's charming daughter, Fruntje, nearly two hundred years ago in the city of Hamburg.

"Well, you are a philosopher and a wise man," Guggenheim said, "so you will not take it amiss. The girl said she became frightened when she saw you because of your appearance."

"I thought as much," Mendelssohn nodded, and asked permission to say farewell to the girl. He went upstairs, and found her busy with her needlework.

She avoided looking at him during their conversation, which he skillfully led around to the subject that was on his mind. Finally, she asked him timidly whether he, too, believed that marriages were made in Heaven.

"Certainly," he replied, "and something quite unusual happened
As you know, they call out in Heaven at the birth of a boy, 'T
will get that girl for a wife.' When I was born, my future wife
thus announced, but it was added, 'She will, alas, have a terrible ——.

"I shouted, 'Oh, Lord, a girl who is humpbacked will very easily
become bitter and hard. A girl should be beautiful. Good Lord, give the
hump to me, and let her be handsome and well formed!'"

The girl, deeply moved, stretched out her hand for Mendelssohn's. She
became his faithful and loving wife, devoted to him for the rest of his
life.

--Theodor Reik

*****

BROTHERHOOD

Abram and Zimri were brothers, and tilled their lands in a happy vale
together. The same plow turned the sod of both their farms in the
spring, and when autumn came with its fruitful harvest, they shared
equally the bounteous product of their common labor, and each stored his
portion in his barn.

Abram had a wife and seven sons, but Zimri lived alone. One evening
as Zimri lay upon his lonely bed, he thought of Abram and his family.
Within himself, he said, "There is my brother, Abram. He has a wife and
seven sons, for whom he must provide, while I have neither wife nor
child, and yet we share our crops alike. Surely this is an injustice to
my brother. I will arise, and go down to the fields, and add to my
brother's store."

The moon looked out from between the murky clouds, and threw a
shimmering light upon the stubbled field, newly reaped. He took a
generous third of his sheaves from his own abundant store, and carried
them to his brother's pile. He returned to his home with a light heart,
and slept soundly.

As Abram lay upon his bed that night, he thought of his brother.
Within himself, he said, "There is my brother, Zimri. He is alone. He
has no sons to help him. He does his work without assistance, while I
have seven lusty sons who bind my sheaves. Yet we divide our gains
equally. Surely this is not pleasing in the sight of God. I will arise
and go down to the field, and will add to my brother's store."

The trees stood straight in the light of the cold, round moon, and
their yellow leaves were shown, then hidden, as the playful moon sported
with the clouds. Abram arose and, guided by the doubtful light, stole
softly to the fertile field. From his ample store he took a generous
third, and carried it to add to his brother Zimri's pile. He returned to
his home with a good heart and slept, for his soul was untormented.

175

When morning came, and each surveyed his store of sheaves, he wondered how it was that his own store had not decreased, although the night before he had given away a third--but neither of the brothers spoke in explanation. At length, their day's toil was ended, the sun reclined upon its bed covered by the western hills, and the brothers returned to their homes.

Before the generous Zimri slept that night, he arose--and, led by the beneficient thought that Abram's share should be greater than his own, again visited the scene of his exploit the night before. The tall cedars stood up black against the sky, and the moon silvered their high tops with a mellow, slanting light. Again he carried from his sheaves a third, and stored them with his brother Abram's lot. He then retired behind his pile to keep watch.

It was not long before Abram came stealing softly down the silent field. He turned now right, now left, as if he wished not to be seen. He took from his sheaves again the third, and placed it in Zimri's store.

The brothers met. Zimri saw it all, but could not speak, for his heart was full. He leaned upon his brother's breast, and wept.

MARRIAGE

THE CHOICE

". . .Until death
You do part. . . ."

And another
Marriage begins,
With words
That speak
Of its ending.

You try hard
Against all
The forces
That undermine
Your love.

And then
At death,
It ends
Anyway.

". . .For time and
All eternity. . . ."

And another
Marriage begins,
With words
That speak
Of forever.

You try hard
With the help
Of eternal bonds
That enhance
Your love.

And then
At death,
It lives
Always.

--Sue Dean

*****

A MOTHER'S PRAYER

If you could know the joy that filled my heart that day
When you were placed within my arms,
Your tiny hands touched mine, and somehow I knew
I needed help to guide your feet from harm.

177

My cup was overflowing, and with tears of thankfulness
I bowed my head to pray.

The years have passed; you cannot know the pride that
    filled my heart today
When your eyes met mine--and I saw mirrored there
A maiden, lovely, innocent, and fine.
My thoughts raced back;
And I knew God had guided me each time
I knelt to pray.

Do you remember the white rose you picked from our garden
    one day?
Your childish voice cried out, "Mommy, come see!"
I told you then your life, like the white rose,
Pure and spotless should be.
Again I felt the need of him, and fervently I prayed,
    "Dear God, show her the way."

If you could know the joy that fills my heart this day,
You'd never take the wider path that beckons to us all.
You'd never carelessly forget, or let one petal fall,
That you may kneel
And marry for time and all eternity
My darling, for this I pray.

*****

TEMPLE WEDDING

With stars in her eyes and a smile on her face
A lovely young girl stood in a wonderful place,
Her dream of a lifetime about to come true;
Her months of waiting were finally through.

She entered the temple, the House of the Lord,
With her fiance to be sealed with an unbreakable cord.
Being married for time and all eternity--
The thought filled her soul with peaceful serenity.

She stood for a moment in a semblance of prayer
To thank her Heavenly Father for the reason she was there,
For the gospel revealed to her, true and dear,
And the knowledge she had that the Lord is near.

Her heart was filled with joy untold
As the events of the day began to unfold;
As she put on her robes, so white and so pure,
She was where she belonged--of this she was sure.

Together through the temple, one heart and mind,
They knew in these sweet moments great treasures they'd find.
They made many covenants with their Lord that day
And were promised many blessings if the commandments they'd obey.

As she knelt before the altar with her husband-to-be,
She was glad it meant togetherness for all eternity;
For she loved this man with all her heart
And knew he loved her, and they would never part.

As they left the temple, now man and wife,
To enter a world filled with toil and strife,
They vowed that often they would return to the place
The beauties and spirit of the gospel to embrace.

And now by her side her proud husband stood,
They knew the things that had happened had been for their good.
They were so happy they could scarcely talk,
As down the path of life they started to walk. . . .

****

WHAT IS A BRIDE?

A bride is a girl with a mother trailing behind her. She is an angel with rollers in her hair. She is the picture of calmness, yet she doesn't know which end is up. She is filled with happiness, yet she is holding back tears a great deal of the time. She holds forth bravely, yet a small glimpse of fear shows in her face. She dresses with speed, unlike any girl; but, of course, this is done with the help of at least three other people.

She's a small girl's idol, a teenager's dream, a young woman's future, a mother's past, and an old maid's hope. No other person can smile quite so patiently at her father, scream quite so loudly at her brother, hold her sister's hand quite so tightly, and say more than a million words with one swift glance to her mother. Yes, she's scared and brave; worried and calm; impatient and patient; tearful and happy; and very much in love.

She is a woman with a halo over her head. And at last, when she looks at her beloved and says those two magic words, "I do," she's a wife.

*****

A BLUEPRINT FOR A HAPPY HOME

Marcia was packing her trunk, and I, sitting near the window, was doing a bit of hand sewing.

"Mother, do you think I'll ever again be as happy as I am right now?"

I did not look up from my sewing. "Of course you won't be--not every hour, but you can be even happier."

"Not happier! I couldn't possibly be that. You know how I love Steve, and I don't for a minute doubt his love for me. The temple ceremony was much more impressive than I had ever expected it to be. And the reception was simply perfect. I just couldn't be any happier!"

179

"I say happier, Marcia, because today your love is young--untested. It will deepen as it matures. I say happier, because the greatest benefits of love are as yet unrealized. I see no reason why you shouldn't have one of the happiest homes in the world, if--"

"If what?"

"If you build wisely on the sound and firm foundation that you and Stephen have now."

"But we haven't done anything special. We just knew what kind of person we wanted to marry, and then we found each other and fell in love."

"That's what I mean. You knew the kind of person you wanted for a husband. You didn't just become emotionally involved without thinking about the future."

"It wasn't really so difficult. I wanted someone stable, purposeful, and good--like Dad, I guess. I wanted a husband who would be a good father, and Stephen seems to be that kind of person. We like to do the same things, and we both want a home and children and--"

"That's what I mean by the foundation, Marcia. It is built in the years before marriage. I like to think that your father and I have contributed the first factors for your future happiness. You have been reared in a home where you have developed a desire for the things that make for happiness in the home--a home where all members are active in the Church."

Marcia laughed. "We've had to be Church-active to keep up with you and Dad."

"Well, perhaps, but at any rate, you have approached marriage with the correct view of its purpose and importance. The fact that you both wanted a temple marriage indicates that you believe the marriage covenant is sacred and that the family unit continues into eternity."

It was difficult to think of Marcia as a bride (though four college years were behind her), ready for the great adventure of wifehood, but it was evident that she wanted to make it a success.

"Well, since you want a happy home, I have something for you." I went into the study and, returning with a page I had clipped years earlier from the Church News, I said, "Here it is, a blueprint for a happy home. You'll want to keep it, Marcia. In his address, President David O. McKay enumerated ten contributing factors for a happy home. Read it often; as the months and years go by, you'll see how basic and wise and true it is."

"Perhaps I'd better paste it on the inside of a kitchen cabinet." She was teasing, but I didn't mind. "Mother, how could I forget all the little clippings you've pasted on the inside of our kitchen cabinet doors--about everything from vitamins to 'Things Wise Wives Should Do'?

Of course, they were meant just for you, but we girls read them, too, whenever we did the cooking."

"Well, Marcia, it isn't a bad idea. You may want to do the same thing. And if you do, check number seven on President McKay's list for special emphasis." I read from the list, "Learn the value of self-control. There will be differences of opinion, and irritations are inevitable, but self-discipline can keep most of them from becoming mountains."

This was the first opportunity we had had for a serious conversation since the wedding flurry had begun, and I meant to make the most of it. "Life is a serious business, Marcia, and a great challenge; but there is plenty of wonder, of everyday enjoyment in it, too, and lots of room for romance."

I scanned the page. "I don't worry in the least about the atmosphere of your home, knowing so well your interest in music and other cultural things. Continued Church activity and family prayer will keep the atmosphere reverent. That's mentioned here on the page, too. Number eight is, 'Foster home ties by continued companionship.' That's important, too, and it involves parents, children, grandparents, and grandchildren, enjoying whenever possible the association of each other."

Marcia sighed audibly. "Too many people, Mother. At present I'm interested in only one person--Steve. How about the romance you mentioned?"

"Of course," I said, retracing my thought, "you and Stephen. Well, never let other people or other interests come between you. Nourish the love you have for each other, by word and in little concrete ways."

"For instance?"

"For instance, there will be separations--brief ones, at least--when you can't go along. Slip a surprise note into his suitcase telling him how much his love means to you, how lucky you feel having married so fine a man. A wonderful bond for a man away from home! He will find ways to reciprocate."

I waited for her response.

"Sounds wonderful--pretty idealistic," Marcia said. She added, "Do you remember Jane Lewis, Mother? She insists that I am much too idealistic. She says that couples aren't ever as happy as they pretend to be, and that I should be more practical."

"Jane is right," I said, "that there are millions of unhappy homes. But she's wrong about the idealism. It's the most practical aspect of life. Keep it, Marcia, my dear, and make good use of it."

She did not answer, but I watched with gratitude as she folded the printed page, almost reverently. Then she slipped it within the pages of a gift cookbook, as if she intended it for daily use.

--Alberta H. Christensen

President McKay's Ten Contributing Factors
to a Happy Home

1. Lay the foundation of a happy home in your premarital life.

2. Choose your mate by judgment and inspiration as well as by emotion.

3. Approach marriage with the lofty view it merits.

4. The noblest purpose of marriage is procreation.

5. Let the spirit of reverence pervade the home so that if the Savior happened to call unexpectedly, he could be invited to stay and not feel out of his element.

6. Let husband and wife never speak in loud tones to each other "unless the house is on fire."

7. Learn the value of self-control.

8. Foster home ties by continued companionship.

9. Make accessible to children proper literature, music, and appropriate movies.

10. By example and precept, encourage participation in Church activity.

--From an address delivered May 6, 1962,
in Chicago, printed in the Church News
May 19, 1962

MISSIONARY WORK

TO A MISSIONARY AT CHRISTMAS TIME

I know it can get lonely
Away from home at Christmas time,
And that your thoughts must wander,
Longing for that homey clime.
You think of all the folks back home,
You wonder what fun's brewing;
You gaze at your girl's photograph
And wonder what she's doing.
A gentle tugging at your heart
Tells you you're far away
From the familiar hearth
That has kept you safe from the fray.
But you, my dearest elder,
Are the most blessed of us all,
For you've a special Christmas; yes,
You've a certain call.
For you and only you can give
The greatest Christmas gift--
A gift that's sent straight from God
To saddened hearts uplift.
Yes, it is the choicest gift,
This Christmas gift you're giving,
The gift of truth, of faith in God,
That makes our life worth living.

*****

HAVE YOU BEEN A MISSIONARY?

Have you ever preached a sermon with an awful stomach ache?
And your head so full of throbbing that you thought it soon would
     break?
Have you ever read your Bible under shelter of some tree
While the rain fell all around you til it formed a little sea?

Have you ever sailed six miles to bless a member's baby?
Have you eaten a Christmas dinner made of common spuds and gravy?
Have you ever tried to twist your tongue around another country's
     lingo,
And said, "I'll learn this language yet, if it's the last thing I
     do, by jingo!"?

Have you ever tried to bring comfort to a family rent with pain?
Have you told a crying mother that her son would live again?
Have you ever watched jeering eyes as you preached upon the   street?
Have you ever thrilled with unbound joy when with some interest
     you chanced to meet?

Did you ever feel the least bit slighted because someone forgot
    to write?
Did you ever think, "She'll never wait, but, then again,
    she might"?
Did you ever come home discouraged after preaching had gone   wrong?
Did you ever change your feeling just by singing a happy song?

If you've hiked along the highway, if you have stood in the rain,
If you have preached on an empty stomach without a thought
    of gain,
If you have been discouraged, if you have seen the work go
    contrary,
If you have done these things and laughed, my friend, then you
    have been a missionary!

*****

THE BEST TWO YEARS

Taking a bath in cold water with a spoon
And trudging up five flights of stairs,
Trying to digest my companion's home cooking,
And thinking nobody cares.

Are these the best two years of my life?
Surely, it's got to get better.
If these are the best two years of my life,
Then, at least, can't I get just one letter?

Keeping appointments where no one shows up
And sitting around on the floor,
Mosquitoes eating my face and my feet
And being too tall for the door.

Are you sure these are the best two years of my life?
I miss all my family and friends;
If these are the best two years of my life,
Why can't I wait til it ends?

Eating my fill of strange foreign food
And taking my shots for malaria,
Having another door slammed in my face
While I'm trying to calm Mom's hysteria.

Are these really the best two years of my life?
Are you sure I'm going to live through it?
If these are the best two years of my life,
I'd better get busy and get to it.

Then watching a person's life change for the better
And teaching of God's great love and care;
Then hearing his halting, humble attempt
To offer his first simple prayer--
Oh, these _are_ the best two years of my life!

They couldn't possibly get any better!
I'm happy, I'm fine, I'm doing just great,
So please disregard my last letter!

--Susan Hiatt Biggs

*****

HUNGRY SPIRIT

She gently turned the pages
Warmed by words of truth;
With hungry spirit,
Knelt to ask (as Joseph knelt),
Seeking light, expecting affirmation.

She cast her searchings
On this new-found God,
Looked heavenward, and listened.

Then, as Joseph Smith beheld,
As Moroni did reveal
The light of truth descended,
A sacred knowledge
Within her grasp.

She traveled as with Nephi,
Beheld the promised land,
Felt the spirit of prophecy
As Abinidi stood before the king
And called him to repent.

She heard the things that Alma taught
And saw the wars and wickedness.
She saw the Lord extend his hand,
Protect those who were faithful,
And bless them in his mercy.

Oh, sweet revelation,
A history saved at Moroni's hand.
Translated by the gift of God,
That all might have that certain faith,
A testimony in wisdom's light.

She walked into waters of baptism,
Compelled by sacred history
To stand uprightly before the Lord.

A convert to concepts redeeming,
Her thirsting soul refreshed,
Her hungry spirit fed.

--Suzanne Dean

*****

A lonely young Persian student was in Munich, struggling to find meaning to life but deeply disturbed by the materialism and selfishness that seemed to fill postwar Europe. He heard a knock at the door one day, and two humble Mormon missionaries stood before him. He was not the least interested in religion; in fact, cynicism and doubt had filled his soul until he was nearly persuaded that there was no God or any real meaning to life. The only thing that interested him about these two young men was their English accent--he had mastered four languages, but English was not one of them.

He invited them in, but as they began their discussion, he cautioned, "I don't want to hear about your God, nor do I want to hear how your religion got started. I only want to know one thing: what do you people do for one another?"

He waited, and a look of doubt crossed his dark features as the elders exchanged glances. Finally, the spokesman for the two said, softly, "We love one another."

Nothing he could have said would have been more electrifying than this simple utterance, for the Holy Ghost immediately bore witness to his soul that these missionaries were true servants of the Lord. Shortly thereafter, he was baptized, moved to America, and began studying for his doctorate--all because a young missionary declared a simple truth.

--Russ Price

*****

DAVID O. MCKAY, A YOUNG MISSIONARY

In 1957 our family was traveling by automobile from Glasgow to Edinburgh; we stopped in Sterling, Scotland, and father escorted us through this ancient city, his first field of missionary labor. After showing us the magnificent castle and the house in which he lived as a young missionary, he said, "Now I want to find a certain house. It is near the foot of the castle." We drove around and soon located it. It was an old house, with a plaque on the wall. Father told us this story:

When father received his call to go on a mission, it came at a most inopportune time. He had just graduated from college, and had been offered a fine teaching position at Weber Academy. He discussed it with his father, and told him, "I'd like to go on a mission someday, but this just isn't the time."

His wise father said, "It is your decision to make, David, but this is a call from the Lord." Father reluctantly accepted.

Then, he said, "I began tracting streets here in Sterling. The people tore up the tracts and threw them in our faces, slammed the doors on us. They cried, 'You cannae steal our lassies to take them to the walled city in Salt Lake.' They wanted no part of us, and no part of the gospel. I was disgusted, homesick, and discouraged. Then I came to this house and read these lines on this plaque: **What ere thou art. . .act well thy part.**

"I decided that I was here as a missionary--so I would act the part, and be a good missionary!"

--Edward R. McKay

*****

THE FIRST MISSIONARY JOURNEY OF SAMUEL SMITH

Samuel Smith, the first missionary of the Church, had the following interesting experience, told by his mother:

On June 30, 1830, Samuel started on the mission to which he had been set apart by Joseph. In traveling twenty-five miles, which was his first day's journey, he stopped at a number of places in order to sell the Book of Mormon, but he was turned out as soon as he declared his principles. When evening approached, he was faint and almost discouraged; coming to an inn that was surrounded by every appearance of plenty, he asked if the landlord would buy one of his books--a history of the origin of the Indians.

"I don't know," replied the host; "how did you get hold of it?"

"It was translated," rejoined Samuel, "by my brother, from some gold plates he found buried in the earth."

"You liar!" cried the landlord. "Get out of my house--you shan't stay one minute with your books!" So saying, he thrust the young elder from a door of plenty.

Samuel was sick at heart, for this was the fifth time he had been turned out of doors that day. He left the house, and traveled a short distance, then washed his feet in a small brook as a testimony against the man. He then walked five miles further on his journey, and, seeing an apple tree a short distance from the road, he decided to spend the night beneath it. There he lay all night, upon the cold, damp ground.

Two weeks later, when Samuel returned that way, he saw a sign on the tavern door; it read, "Smallpox." He was informed that the innkeeper and two of his children had recently died, and that several other members of his family were ill with the malady. No other people in the village, however, had contracted the disease.

Following an arduous missionary trip that appeared to be a complete failure, Samuel returned home, carrying all his books but two. One he had given to a poor widow who had fed him, and the other he had presented to a new friend, John P. Green, a Methodist minister. After listening to Samuel's earnest testimony, he read the book prayerfully and received a conviction of its truthfulness.

Eagerly, Green carried the new volume to his brother-in-law, Phineas T. Young, who also read and believed. Phineas, in turn, presented it to his brother, Brigham Young, who read it and received a testimony of its truthfulness. The acceptance of that sacred volume of "American scripture" started Brigham Young along the road to a famous destiny--one that was to influence greatly the history of the Church as well as the history of western America.

This same copy of the Book of Mormon also helped convert Heber C. Kimball--and, in fewer than two years, the Greens, the Kimballs, and the Youngs, together with their households, were baptized. Thus did Samuel, a young, unselfish servant of God, cast bread upon the waters, to find it returned a hundredfold.

--Carter E. Grant

MOTHER

The mother bounced her four-year-old daughter on a chair and told her to stay there, because she had been naughty. The little girl sat there a while very quietly, and then exclaimed, "I'll bet if Daddy had known you were going to act this way, he wouldn't have married you!"

*****

Motherhood is the greatest potential influence in human society. Her caress first awakens in the child a sense of security; her kiss the first realization of affection; her sympathy and tenderness, the first assurance that there is love in the world. Thus in infancy and childhood she implants ever-directing and restraining influences that remain through life.

--David O. McKay

*****

The noblest calling in the world is that of mother. True motherhood is the most beautiful of all arts, the greatest of all professions. She who can paint a masterpiece or who can write a book that will influence millions deserves the plaudits and admiration of mankind; but she who rears successfully a family of healthy, beautiful sons and daughters whose immortal souls will be exerting an influence throughout the ages long after painting shall have faded, and books and statues shall have been destroyed, deserves the highest honor that man can give.

--David O. McKay

*****

MY MOTHER

God molded you from finest clay
And sent you from above,
And that is how I came to have
The gift of life and love.

You showed me how my erring feet
Should tread the path of life,
That was so new, so strange to me,
So filled with unknown strife.

And when I stumbled on my way
'Twas you who helped me up,
And bade me on, and gave me strength
To drink the most bitter cup.

You taught me how to worship God,
And pointed out the way,
But greatest gift of all, my dear,
You taught me how to pray.

189

And now upon my knees I bend
As you have taught me to,
And bow before the heavenly throne
To thank my God for you.

                    --Thyrza Roskelley

                 *****

            LAMENT OF A COLLEGE GRADUATE

I received a college degree
With honors, no less.

But I spend my day doing laundry
And my house is always a mess.

I sit on the floor with a babe on each knee
Whom I'm trying to dress.

I sing about piggies and birds in a tree,
And I must confess

That college prepared me inadequately.
But I'll make it, I guess;

And if someone should ask if I'd do it again,
I'd quickly say, "Yes!"

                    --Susan Hiatt Biggs

                 *****

                TO WALK ALONE

All I wanted was this for you:
That you could tie or buckle your shoe.
    At night when the stars blinked loftily down
    At us and the lights in our little town,
        You read to me, I read to you
        Of the Little Red Hen and Little Boy Blue,
    And all I wanted was that you should need
    To feel this urgency to read.

And all I wanted when the noon sun shone
Was that you could walk to school alone.
    Sometimes the wind tossed leaves in our path;
    You would leave my side and chase them and laugh;
    I watched how the breeze tossed your red-gold curls
    As you dropped my apron to run with the girls;
    All that I wanted was that you should decide
    The turn of your sails with the outgoing tide.

All that I wanted too soon is here;
You need me no longer, but, oh, my dear--
Childhood, schooldays--now that you're grown,
How can I learn to walk alone?

--Mabel Jones Gabbott

*****

A MOTHER'S PRAYER

As I look in his tiny, sweet baby face,
Snuggled so peaceful in blanket and lace,
My joy seems complete, my cup runneth o'er,
But, Father, I'll need thy blessings still more.

He's pure and good and he knows no sin,
So I'll need thy help in raising him.
I'll need more wisdom than I've ever had,
That I might discern the good from the bad.

More knowlege and patience, grant me from above,
That I might teach him through kindness and love.
And guide his footsteps, where'er they trod,
That he will shun evil, and follow God.

I know in this world temptations are great,
That Satan is striving to alter our fate,
So stay by my side, both day and night,
And help me always to teach what is right.

And bless him, too, as to manhood he grows,
That he'll walk in the paths that the gospel shows.
A light to the world may he always be,
In doing good, and in serving thee.

Thanks for the loan of this precious boy,
Who brings me peace, and comfort and joy.
I'll do my best to raise him just right,
That his return "home" will be a delight.

May celestial glory be his constant aim,
And eternal life his final gain.
Am I wanting too much for this tiny lad--
To have only the good, and know no bad?

I'll strive day and night to fulfill my part,
And teach all these things from a mother's heart.

Oh! how I hope he will understand,
That we must prepare here for the promised land.

When his mission's complete, and his earth life is o'er,
May he walk with thee, on that golden shore.

191

Then, I'll know without doubt that my joy is complete,
As he takes up his work in that heavenly retreat.

--Ellen J. Eagar

*****

A COMMERCIAL MOM

My great goal in life is to be
The kind of mother I see on t.v.
The commercials are full of the perfect mom;
The kind I want to be.

My rice would be fluffy, my clothes clean and white,
My hands would look like those of my daughter.
She'd come to me often for help and advice,
And appreciate all that I taught her.

My garbage bags would never break through
And a man would float in my toilet.
I'd have my hair done while wearing my mink
And never fear that I'd spoil it.

I'd have infinite patience with mud-splattered kids,
And the mess that they track on the floor.
I'd whisk off their clothes and wash them in Tide,
And mop them right out of the door.

I'd make pitchers of Koolaid for neighborhood kids
Who play on my front lawn in bunches.
I'd send off my children each morning to school,
Remembering to put love in their lunches.

I'd bring home the bacon, fry it up in a pan,
And my skin would be soft to the touch.
I'd keep my floors shiny and my house super-clean
Without having to work very much.

I'd stay fashionably slim and I'd wear stylish clothes
And play tennis in all my spare time.
I know that I'm dreaming, but you must admit
That this kind of life sounds sublime!

--Susan Hiatt Biggs

*****

A MOTHER IS LOVE

A mother can be almost any size or any age,
but she won't admit to anything over thirty.
A mother has soft hands and smells good.

A mother likes new dresses, music, a clean house,
her children's kisses, an automatic washer, and Daddy.
A mother doesn't like having her children sick,
muddy feet, temper tantrums, loud noise, or bad report cards.
A mother can read a thermometer (much to the amazement
of Daddy) and, like magic, can kiss a hurt away.
A mother can bake good cakes and pies,
but likes to see her children eat vegetables.
A mother can stuff a fat baby into a snowsuit in seconds,
and can kiss sad little faces and make them smile.
A mother is underpaid, has long hours, and gets very
little rest. She worries too much about her children,
but she says she doesn't mind it at all.
And no matter how old her children are,
she still likes to think of them as her little babies.
She is the guardian angel of the family,
the queen, the tender hand of love.
A mother is the best friend anyone ever has.
A mother is love.

                    --Mary Dawson Hughes

                         *****

                    NEWBORN BABE

It was in heaven when, all of a sudden,
I was surrounded by a beautiful glow.
A voice whispered softly,
"It is now your time to go."

Because I was special
I left my Heavenly Father's side,
And came into another world,
So different, so spacious, so wide.

I had great fears;
I wept, and wondered where I was.
I was wrapped in soft flannel
And clean white gauze.

When, all of a sudden,
Arms of warmth cuddled me oh, so near,
Kissed me on my tiny head,
And whispered, "You are so dear."

"And your eyes are blue. . .
And just look at your toes!

You have the fairest skin,
And the sweetest little nose."

Mother

The arms that I was cuddled in
Made me feel secure.
The voice of love and adoration said,
"You are so innocent and pure."

I knew that someone loved me,
And I wasn't all alone;
But I thought at times the arms that held me
Would crush my tiny bones.

It was my mother
Who cuddled me, in her loving arms.
I knew she stayed close by my side
To keep me from all harm.

Days rolled onward;
I had such tender care.
She sang to me sweet lullabys;
She was a jewel so rare.

When I tried to crawl
I hurt my tiny knee;
She picked me up and sang again,
Her lullabys to me.

She would rock me in her arms
And kiss away my tears.
She kissed me where it hurt,
And soothed my childhood fears.

To Mom, time flew by,
But to me, life was slow.
For at last, I'm five,
And to school I can go.

My mother, with tears of tenderness, said,
"You are my little girl."
I now had eyes of brown,
And my hair in ringlet curl.

School days. . .friends. . .teachers,
Each day another step.
Mother loved and cared for me,
A vigil watch she kept.

Oh, how I thank my mother,
Who gave me life on earth;
Who suffered when I left my Lord
And gave me royal birth.

--Reeta B. Turner

*****

194

MOTHER

Somewhere between the youthful energy of a teenager and the golden years of a woman's life, there lives a marvelous and loving person known as "mother."

A mother is a curious mixture of patience, kindness, understanding, discipline, industriousness, purity, and love. A mother can be--at the same time--both "lovelorn counselor" to a heartsick daughter and head football coach to an athletic son.

A mother can sew the tiniest stitch in the material for that dainty prom dress, and she is equally experienced in threading through the heaviest traffic with a station wagon.

A mother is the only creature on earth who can cry when she's happy, laugh when she's heartbroken, and work when she's feeling ill. A mother is as gentle as a lamb and as strong as a giant. Only a mother can appear so weak and helpless, yet be the one to put the fruit jar lid on so tightly that even Dad can't get it off.

A mother is a picture of helplessness when Dad is near, and a marvel of resourcefulness when she's all alone.

A mother has the angelic voice of a member of the celestial choir as she sings a lullaby to a baby cradled in her arms, yet she can dwarf the sound of an amplifier when she calls her boys in for dinner.

A mother has the fascinating ability to be almost everywhere at once, and she alone can somehow squeeze an enormous amount of living into an average day.

A mother is "old-fashioned" to her teenager; just "Mom" to her third-grader; and simply "Mamma" to the little two-year-old sister. But there is no greater thrill in life than to point to that wonderful woman and be able to say to all the world, "That's my mother!"

--Frederick E. Kruse

*****

MOTHER WAS A HARD WOMAN

The scene is Wimbledon Stadium in London; a great crowd is gathered. An American girl has just won the women's singles tennis championship of the world. She is a tall, graceful black girl. Standing there, listening to the plaudits of the multitude, she sees walking toward her Queen Elizabeth, holding the cherished cup of victory. She curtsies before the queen and receives from Her Majesty's hand this great sports honor. In this moment of triumph, she reflects on her early life.

Born in New York to poor parents, she had to struggle with one problem after another. While she was still a child, her family lived on a little piece of land outside the city. At that time, she was ill, and was

195

sickly and weak for years. One day her mother called to her and said, "Honey, see that stone down by the barn? I want you to move that stone up here so we can use it for a stepping stone by the kitchen door."

"Mommy, I can hardly walk to the barn, let alone bring a stone up here," the girl replied.

"Well," her mother told her, "you go down to the barn as best you can, and start moving that stone. Even if you only move it half an inch in this direction, move it that much. Move it half an inch today and half an inch tomorrow, but start moving it."

The girl went down to the stone, with some effort. She pushed it half an inch. She came back to the house, exhausted. The next day, she pushed it an inch, and returned to the house. One fine day she pushed it five inches. It took her nearly two weeks to do what a child in normal health could have done in five minutes, but finally, with flushed face, she got the stone to the kitchen door.

People muttered that her mother was a hard woman. Why didn't she carry the stone herself? She may have been a hard woman, but she was a wise mother. She knew that things like moving that stone would make her daughter strong. Eventually, the girl did grow strong. The family moved back to Harlem; the girl became a street paddle tennis champion. Ultimately, she became one of the greatest tennis players in the world. Althea Gibson had many difficulties, but she had the outlook of strength gained from her experiences with a wise mother and from her faith in God.

*****

NOBODY'S PERFECT WHO'S A MOMMY

About once a year I ask myself, "Am I a good mommy?" The occasion arises annually when I do not get breakfast in bed nor a shower of gifts on Mother's Day. Determined to qualify for at least a card this year, I decided to do some honest self-appraisal.

Between parents, friends, doctors, and successful mothering books, we can all find a philosophy that fits us. But who knows better how we score than our greatest challengers?

Turning to four-year-old Jayson, I asked, "What's a good mommy?"

"A good mommy stays home and plays with her kids all day," he promptly replied.

Surprised at such misinformation, I explained, "Mommies who stay home all day do not play with their kids; they work, too." But he insisted that mommies who stay home ride bikes with their kids all day. So, what does a four-year-old know? I decided to ask someone with more insight into the facts of life--like nine- and ten-year-olds. Interviewing a third-grade class and a fourth-grade class at two separate elementary schools, I learned the requirements for "good mothering."

Good mothers help you.

Help you at what?

"Homework," says Willis Knapp.

"She helps you get dressed even if you <u>are</u> old enough to do it yourself," Jayson adds, defensively.

Nine-year-old Jan says seriously, "She helps you when you have a hard decision to make."

"So what if it's your fault it broke--a good mommy could still help you pick up the pieces."

Helping, I learned, includes "letting."

"She lets you stir the jello by yourself, even if you are a pig and splash it."

"She lets you sign your own name on the birthday card, even if no one can read it."

"A good mommy will sit on the floor and play with you. She doesn't just stand there and say, 'How nice.' She sits down and plays."

"She lets you knock down her blocks," Jayson insists.

"No matter how boring Uncle Wiggley is, she plays it again."

Julie Heimdal explains, "She <u>wants</u> to read bedtime stories. She doesn't just read; she <u>wants</u> to read."

"She crawls into your tent and pretends her hands and knees didn't get grubby."

"She teaches you how to swim no matter how she looks in a swimming suit."

"A good mommy plays fair," says Trevor Allred.

You mean a mommy would cheat?

"If she is sick and tired of this stupid game. . . ."

A good mommy understands.

John Clark says, "A good mother understands bad report cards."

Jayson says, "A good mommy understands when you don't understand, and doesn't say, 'How many times have I told you that?'"

"A good mommy understands why you forget to come home on time."

"And she never embarrasses you in front of your friends," warns Alice Oveson.

A good mommy is generous.

Jason Lewis dreams, "She lets you do and get anything you want."

Jayson says, "She gives you all her brown pennies, and some silver ones, too."

"If she has a milkshake and you don't, a good mommy will give it to you--at least half of it."

A good mother is clean.

"She washes your clothes, even if you promised not to get them dirty."

"She teaches you to wash dishes, but a good mommy does the dishes herself."

"She makes you take a bath."

You mean you <u>want</u> to take a bath?

"No, I never want to take a bath. But then she'd be a nice mommy, not a good mommy."

"She brushes your teeth in case you missed Mr. Cavity, who will monster up your mouth," Jayson says.

And a good mommy loves you.

"She has to--it's part of her job."

Gibson Arnold points out, "She kisses you <u>only</u> when you need it."

And she cares for you.

Michelle Rose says, "She does all she can to keep you alive."

"She runs when you get hurt. She doesn't just say, 'Oh, now what?' She thinks it's serious even if you're not bleeding." If you are not bleeding, "she kisses it better." If you are, "a good mommy always has bandaids."

"She tucks you into bed," says Marcia Jensen.

"And she comes when you cry in the night with a smile on her face," says Carl Brennan.

Good mommies do punish you.

"And that's good," says Barbara Miller, "because we want to do it again."

And good mommies do get mad, "especially when you wreck up the baby. If she didn't get mad, she'd faint from holding it in. If she didn't get mad, she'd be a dumb mommy, not a good mommy."

A good mommy cooks well--"real cookies, not packaged ones."

And a good mommy is pretty.

In Kevin Kelsey's words, "A good mommy does everything she's supposed to do."

Figuring I fared well, I asked my husband, "Well, what are you going to get me for Mother's Day?"

He pulled out his calculator, and a few moments later, replied, "According to my figures, I have spent as much time with the kids this last year as you have. What are you going to get *me*?"

--Peggy Ball Fugal

*****

DEAR MOTHER. . .

I'm turning thirty-two next week, and I recall the time when you were the same age. You had just given birth to Dickie, and were lovely and slender still--after five babies. I've had four, and was skinnier pregnant than I am now.

I thought you were so beautiful, with your wavy dark hair, sparkling eyes, and ringing laughter. And though people say now I look like you did then, I have never felt as pretty as I thought you were. At thirty-two, you were so full of life and energy, involved in everything.

Father had just been elected president of the Junior Chamber of Commerce, making you first lady of the Jaycee Wives. How they loved you! For the installation banquet you splurged (because we were poor then) and bought a white pleated dress of some silky, clinging fabric with a bright red, white, and blue belt. You exchanged your everyday orthopedic work shoes--a regular since your childhood bout with osteomeningitis--for a pair of red patent leather sandals, and you wore big, red baubles of costume jewelry.

You took your time bathing early that warm summer evening, powdering and perfuming yourself to perfection. I marveled that with a shake of the head, your hair was perfect. Your face was radiant without all the makeup I never fail to wear. I watched the dress float down over your body, and envied your yet-girlish figure. To me, you were a goddess. And the whole time you never said a word or minded my presence. You simply hummed a tune and reveled in your almost-privacy prior to the big event.

I don't remember what Father wore. I just remember thinking you were a handsome couple as you waved goodbye and called last-minute instructions to me, whom you'd left in charge of the baby. I was seven years old.

Earlier that day you'd taken me with you to the hall where the banquet was to be held. I can no longer remember its name or location. Several women of note were there decorating, and they all stopped to greet you when you entered, paying you for the first time the deference owed a first lady. You, the uneducated southern belle whose husband was only a tenement farmer. But I knew you were far greater than you appeared. At thirty-two, I thought you had the world by the tail, and I dreamed dreams that put me in your place.

And here I am. I haven't had a baby for five years, nor will there be another. My days revolve around a business I cannot keep up with, and my evenings around four little boys whose adoring eyes settle not on me, but on their father. And I wonder where the wonder of childhood went.

But I am here because of you. I am educated because you were not. You taught me to love books and learning because you were just then doing so yourself. I tried to imagine what it must have been like to drag a gunny sack around the field, plucking bolls of fluff all day and never going to school. It seemed like a Lois Lenski story to me, and your childhood remained a constant source of fascination.

We spoke little, because in those days children were truly meant to be seen and not heard. But when we were alone, as we seldom were, you would regale me with tales of the world from which you had sprung--so foreign to the world in which I had been reared. I treasure them to this day.

I am a businesswoman because you resented the domestic role forced upon you. You held a myriad of menial jobs just to get out of the house, and encouraged me to strive for a career of importance. From an early age you knew I had writing ability, and you made me the official keeper of family records and writer of letters. You who could not write a complete sentence read everything I brought home, including my Trixie Beldon mysteries, sometimes before I could read them myself. I received a subscription to Science Digest as grand prize winner of the school science fair, and you read every issue cover to cover-- the same way you read everything.

In an effort to make up for lost time, you never allowed me an idle moment for fear I would suffer the same fate you had. When I announced that I wanted to become a hairdresser or airline stewardess, you stated, "Your brain is too great for that." And I continued to grasp all I could right along with you in preparation for what I have today.

The adoration I had for you as a child melted away through my teen years and all but dissolved as I began my own life without you. But now, as I enter the very first years I can recall of your life, the adoration returns. Ten-fold. You were a mother to remember. You were a woman to reckon with. You were a person to know and follow. You were me in embryo. And I am only a fraction of you now. How grateful I am for even that.

--Peggy Ball Fugal

OPPORTUNITY

Use the talent you have. The woods would be very silent if no birds sang there except those who sang the best.

*****

Doing the best you can with the little opportunities that come along will get you farther than idly wishing for the big chance that may never come.

We live in the present; we dream of the future; and we learn eternal truths from the past.

--Madame Chiang Kai-shek

*****

Regard each day as a fresh start, a new beginning, a precious gift as yet unsullied, from the hand of God. Every rising sun shines on a day gleaming with infinite possibilities. Rain or shine, come what may, resolve that for at least this one day, you will find contentment in the path you must tread.

*****

OPPORTUNITY

When one door closes, another opens--but we often look so long and regretfully at the closed door that we do not see the one that has opened for us.

We cannot change the past,
It is gone forever away;
But, unforgotten, it serves
As a guide for a newer day.

The errors we made last week,
Mistakes of the month before--
Now that they're well understood,
Need never be made any more.

The past is a storage vault
From which we are able to borrow
The aid that experience lends
For a wiser, better tomorrow.

PRAYER

It is not a difficult thing to learn how to pray. It is not the words we use, particularly, that constitute prayer. True, faithful, earnest prayer consists more in the feeling that rises from the heart and from the inward desire of our spirits to supplicate the Lord in humility and in faith, that we may receive his blessings. It matters not how simple the words may be if our desires are genuine and we come before the Lord with a broken heart and contrite spirit to ask him for what we need.

--Joseph F. Smith

*****

The minute a man stops supplicating God for his spirit and direction, he becomes a stranger to him and his works. When men stop praying for God's spirit, they place confidence in their own unaided reason, and they gradually lose the spirit of God, just the same as near and dear friend, by never writing to or visiting each other, will become strangers.

--Heber J. Grant

*****

He who makes a habit of sincere prayer, and prays believing, will find his life noticeably and profoundly enriched and steadied. He will increase in tranquility and poise; he will have added courage and stamina. His physical, moral, and spiritual attitude will indicate he is aware of the presence of a powerful friend.

*****

If the devil says you cannot pray when you are angry, tell him it is none of his business, and pray until that species of insanity is dispelled and serenity is restored to your mind.

--Brigham Young

*****

It is the first principle of the gospel to know for a certainty the character of God, [that] we may converse with him as one man converses with another.

--Joseph Smith

*****

A beggar stopped a prosperous man one day to ask for a coin.
The prosperous man told him that God loved him.

"Well," said the down-and-out man, "if God loves me, why doesn't he do something for me?"

"Have you ever asked him?" came the reply.

"Er, ah, well. . .no."

"Then, do you think that I would have stopped and given you this coin if you had not asked me?"

*****

A young boy, ready for bed, interrupted a family gathering in the living room. "I'm going up to say my prayers now. Anybody want anything?"

*****

We would say to the brethren, seek to know God in your closets; call upon him in the fields. Follow the directions of the Book of Mormon and pray for your families, your cattle, your flocks, your herds, your corn, and all things that you possess; ask the blessing of God upon all your labors, and everything that you engage in. Be virtuous and pure; be men of integrity and truth; keep the commandments of God; and then you will be able more perfectly to understand the difference between right and wrong--between the things of God and the things of men; and your path will be like that of the just, which shineth brighter and brighter unto the perfect day.

--Joseph Smith

*****

You know that it is one peculiarity of our faith and religion never to ask the Lord to do a thing without being willing to help him all that we are able; then the Lord will do the rest.

I shall not ask the Lord to do what I am not willing to do.

Do not ask God to give you knowledge when you are confident that you will not keep and rightly improve that knowledge.

--Brigham Young

*****

Do you have family prayers in your family? And when you do, do you go through the operation like the grinding of a piece of machinery, or do you bow in meekness and with a sincere desire to seek the blessing of God upon you and your household? That is the way we ought to do, and cultivate a spirit of devotion and

trust in God, dedicating ourselves to him, and seeking his blessings.

--John Taylor

*****

Prayer

I have more faith in prayer before the Lord than almost any other principle on earth. If we have no faith in prayer to God, we have not much in either him or the gospel. We should pray unto the Lord, asking him for what we want. Let the prayers of this people ascend before the Lord continually in the season thereof, and the Lord will not turn them away, but they will be heard and answered, and the kingdom of Zion and God will rise and shine. She will put on her beautiful garments and be clothed with the glory of her God, and fulfill the object of her organization here upon the earth.

--Wilford Woodruff

*****

One of the greatest prayers that a man can offer, so far as I understand prayers and their consistency, is that when an elder of Israel stands before the people, he may communicate and tell some thoughts to do the people good, and build them up in the principles of truth and salvation. Prayers of this kind are as agreeable in the ears of the Lord as any prayers than an elder of Israel can possibly offer, for when an elder stands before the people, he should do so realizing that he stands before them for the purpose of communicating knowledge, that they may receive truth in their souls and be built up in righteousness by receiving further light, progressing in their education in the principles of holiness.

--Lorenzo Snow

*****

I have little or no fear for the boy or the girl, the young man and the young woman, who honestly and conscientiously supplicate God twice a day for the guidance of his spirit. I am sure that when temptation comes, they will have the strength to overcome it by the inspiration that shall be given to them. Supplicating the Lord for guidance of his spirit places around us a safeguard, and if we earnestly and honestly seek the guidance of the Spirit of the Lord, I can assure you that we will receive it.

--Heber J. Grant

*****

I hope the Latter-day Saints will not fail to say their prayers, their secret prayers and their family prayers. Children who are reared in homes where they do not have family prayers and secret prayers lose a great deal, and I fear that, in the midst of the world's confusion, of hurry and bustle, many times homes are left without prayer and without the blessings of the Lord. These homes cannot continue to be happy.

--George Albert Smith

*****

I cherish as one of the dearest experiences in life the knowledge that God hears the prayer of faith.

It is true that the answer may not come as directly and at the time or in the manner we anticipate; but it comes, and at a time and in a manner best for the interests of him who offers the supplication. On more than one occasion, I have received direct and immediate assurances that my petition was granted. At one time, particularly, that answer came as distinctly as though my Father stood by my side and spoke the words. These experiences are part of my being, and must remain so as long as memory and intelligence last. They have taught me that "Heaven is never deaf but when man's heart is dumb."

--David O. McKay

*****

PRAYER TIME

The while she darns her children's socks,
She prays for little stumbling feet;
Each folded pair within its box
Fits faith's bright sandals, sure and fleet.

While washing out with mother pains
Small dusty suits and frocks and slips,
She prays that God may cleanse the stains
From little hearts and hands and lips.

And when she breaks the fragrant bread
Or pours each portion in its cup,
For grace to keep their spirits fed
Her mother-heart is lifted up.

Oh, busy ones, whose souls grow faint,
Whose tasks seem longer than the day,
It does not take a cloistered saint
To find a little time to pray.

--Ruby Weyburn Tobias

*****

A PRAYER

Give me strength, O Lord, I pray,
A desire to live just one more day,
Give me strength my burden to bear,
Listen to my worry, pain, and care.
Strengthen me by faith in thee,
Point out the blessings bestowed on me.
Give me knowledge that I may see
Why the life of a child is trusted to me.

Prayer

Dear Lord! Let me feel your guiding arm,
Guiding and protecting me from harm.
Pour out your blessings day and night,
Open my eyes to the things that are right.
Give me strength that I may be,
All that you expect of me.

--Vernelle J. Pulsipher

*****

I TALKED TO MOTHER ABOUT PRAYER

Mother taught me God is real
And not too far away,
That he will hear and answer me
If I will kneel and pray.

She taught me to say "thank you" first
In words, and love, and deeds,
Then to very carefully
Tell him of my needs.

She taught me of his still, small voice
That tells me what is right,
How he will make me strong and wise
And fill my mind with light.

I thank him for my mother,
Who taught me how to pray.
I'll try to show my love for her
By praying right each day.

--Hortence Spencer Anderson

*****

BEYOND

I was far beyond the power of prayer, I said--
Past any fervent plea or desperate hope;
I stood within a place of solemn dread,
A black and fearsome land, no wider than one soul--my own!

Yet in that narrow way,
There crept somehow a murmured sound,
A throb of thought that whispered, "Pray!"
And somehow doubting heart, resisting soul
    refound their way to prayer.
Then courage, faith, strive on--oh, many words
    were there,
And God's own gentle peace in all was everywhere.

And this I learned from out-numbered thought,
    from need, from black despair:
There is no night too dark, no space too small,
    no void too vast;
There is no point beyond the power of prayer!

                    --Betty Ventura

                    *****

NEVER MIND, LORD

Only the top of his head could be seen bobbing up and down between the waves of the boiling, rushing, muddy waters of the river. When the waves lifted him up higher into view, his arms could be seen threshing helplessly as he attempted to pull himself toward the distant shore.

Don had been too brave in standing near this fast-moving stream so soon after the recent rains. The bank of soft dirt he had been standing on had crumbled suddenly beneath his feet, and carried him helplessly into the dirty water. Don was a strong swimmer, but his strength was no match for this powerful, swift current. When he tried to cry out and shout for help, water gushed forcefully into his open mouth, causing him to choke and struggle for air. The stream was carrying him quickly toward the waterfall and rock-strewn rapids below. It looked like no power on earth could save Don now.

Don had never believed in Jesus or in the power of prayer, but right now he had nowhere else to turn. In desperation, he sincerely whispered, "Heavenly Father, please bless me. Help me to reach the shore. I don't want to die!"

Don had hardly finished his prayer when something struck him on his back with such force that it nearly pushed him underwater. A huge log had floated downstream and was pushing against his body. In desperation, he reached for its outflung branches and, grasping them firmly, with great effort, he pulled himself onto the large floating log. Just as he did so, one end of the log struck the bank of the stream, causing it to turn toward the bank. This allowed Don to quickly and gratefully jump onto the solid earth of the riverbank. With a sigh of relief, Don said,

"Never mind, Lord, I got out by myself. I don't need your help after all."

                    *****

COVERED WITH SNOW

Judy was afraid to go home. What had started out to be a perfectly wonderful day was now ruined. She had worn her mother's best turquoise bracelet to school today, but only after Judy had asked her so many times that she had grown weary and consented. Judy had promised to be very careful with the bracelet, not only because it was worth of a lot of money, but because it had been in the family for many years. She had been careful, too, but this afternoon it had started to snow. Judy had watched the large, soft white flakes fall gently past the schoolroom windows, forming a fluffy white blanket that covered the ground to a depth of nearly six inches.

Everyone was anxious to get out into this beautiful first snow of the season. After school was dismissed, Judy had only taken a few steps from the building toward the waiting school bus when a large, soft snowball splattered against her arm. A group of boys and girls were laughing and throwing snowballs at everyone. Without even thinking, Judy was throwing back at them and having a wonderful time.

Judy's fun continued until she decided she had better get on the school bus before it left her. About then, she noticed a difference in how her arm felt. It seemed lighter, or different somehow. The realization of what had happened struck her forcefully. She lifted her coat sleeve to a bare wrist with no bracelet, and began looking frantically at the white banks of snow where she had been playing. Her heart beat rapidly as she hurried back over some of the places where she had been. Some of the students joined in the search; but when the school busses started to leave, they climbed on and left Judy to search for the bracelet alone.

Judy was desperate! She didn't dare go home without that bracelet, yet she couldn't miss the school bus--and it would be leaving soon. Judy prayed aloud, "Dear Heavenly Father, please help me find the bracelet." Just then she looked up and noticed a small depression some distance away in the center of a snow pile. There were no tracks near this place, yet she felt impressed to go over there to look. Judy could see nothing but snow until she stood exactly over the spot where the snow was depressed. There in the snow, shining up at her with its beautiful color, was the turquoise bracelet! It had probably fallen there from her wrist when she had thrown a snowball. She picked it up quickly and gratefully, and then rushed for the departing school bus.

As she slumped down into the bus seat in relief, she was very thankful. She was so glad she had found the bracelet! Judy remembered the prayer she had given, and wondered if her prayer had been answered when she had felt impressed to look in that out-of-the-way place. "No," she thought, "I probably would have looked there anyway."

*****

ABOVE THE ASHES OF NAGASAKI
(FROM A MARINE'S DIARY)

He came to our chaplain's office, a shabbily dressed Japanese man--but even dressed in rags, he radiated a dignity that commanded respect. Bowing respectfully, he spoke to us in fluent English.

"I am a Christian," he said. "I would be pleased if you would come to my home and offer a prayer in behalf of my wife. I am told the chaplain is away, but you are his assistant. I have prayed alone, but feel that an American Christian's prayer would help. Will you come?"

Help seemed far off to me in postwar Nagasaki. It had been four months since the bomb, and many people were dying of a strange illness called, simply, "bomb sickness." I told the gentleman to wait for me down where the jeeps were parked. I had heard a corpsman talking about a new medicine that seemed to help, and at the medical supply center I got a small vial of it, which I pressed into the man's hand.

We drove through the rubble and rain bordering the edge of the atomic bowl. Then we climbed for some distance over broken street stairs to what was left of a once-habitable home. Now it was a hovel, a hole in the ground with an opening in the roof and a ladder leading down to where the people lived. The single room
was cold and mostly bare, as were the children sheltered there. In an annex lay a woman, smiling, suffering, dying.

"You pray first," he said. I knelt and offered what I hoped was a comforting prayer. Then he prayed. His prayer was a masterpiece of simple Christian faith. I had expected him to ask for many things; he stood so much in need of many things. All about him was testimony of his need: the sickness, the half sack of rice, the shattered walls, the thin clothing, the winter coming on. But his was no prayer of supplication. Instead, he phrased words of gratitude and thanksgiving. He thanked the Lord for the air he breathed, for the plentiful water he drank. He expressed appreciation for his family, his heritage, and his ancestry. He was grateful for his material possessions, as if he owned the world. Mostly, he was thankful for a need for a healing. Such words were superfluous, since Jesus has said,
"Your father knoweth what things ye have need of before ye ask him."

Some time later, he came again to the chaplain's office. His smile telegraphed the glad message before he spoke. "She lives," he said. "All is well."

"Thank God for the medicine," I thought.

Then, "I would like to return this." He took from his pocket the same small bottle I had given him.

"But how did you ever get it replenished?" I asked, incredulously.

"She recovered, so I didn't need it. We prayed--remember?"

*****

LED BY THE FAITH OF A CHILD

Brother Harland was assigned to take an important genealogical assignment in England. The trip would take him back to his homeland for a period of about six weeks. Being a faithful servant of the Lord, he accepted the call without hesitation.

As preparations for the journey were being made, Brother Harland realized more each day it was going to be difficult to leave his wife and two young children for such a long period of time. He thought of the changes he could see in his children every day. Then he realized that in about six weeks' time, his one-year-old son, John, and his three-year-old daughter, Kimberly, would make great physical as well as mental growth. It became harder and harder to think of leaving them.

The children had grandparents in England whom they had never seen. His wife had not been back to England since they left to make a home in America. Wouldn't it be wonderful if he could take his family with him and let parents, children, and grandchildren get to know each other? The thought couldn't be erased from his mind. Finally, plans were completed and the way opened for him to take his family with him.

Brother Harland had served his country during World War II, and while serving in the South Pacific, he had contracted malaria. The disease had never been completely cured, and he still had recurring attacks. When these attacks came, he was very ill, and he always knew there would be a period of at least forty-eight hours that he would have to stay in bed.

One day, the family had had a long drive to Birmingham, where they were going to spend the night. The next morning, Brother Harland was to leave very early to go to London to hold another genealogical convention. He had to drive ninety miles to London, and then ninety miles back to Birmingham. But as they arrived at the place where they were going to spend the night, he became violently ill with an attack of malaria. He was so ill that he could not get to the bed without help. In fewer than twenty-four hours he had to conduct another meeting. Sister Harland did not drive. How would he get there? Sister Harland was too upset over her husband's illness to think of anything but caring for him. She decided she would have to phone one of the officials in London and tell them to postpone the meeting until her husband was well again. She knew this would mean rescheduling all of the meetings, but she could think of nothing else to do.

She was telling her husband of her decision when three-year-old Kimberly said, "But, Mommy, Daddy can get to London. All we have to do is pray to Heavenly Father, and he will help us."

For that moment when father was too ill to think and mother was too worried about him and about helping him get to his assignment, they had forgotten to pray. But a little child with a pure, beautiful faith did not forget. Because of this, she was asked if she would like to say the prayer. She did, and the prayer was a simple one: "Heavenly Father, my daddy is very sick; he has to go to a convention tomorrow. Please make him well. In the name of Jesus Christ, Amen."

The family was sharing the same room that night. About three o'clock in the morning, Brother Harland awakened, and he could not remember ever feeling sicker than he did at that moment. Little Kimberly heard him tossing in bed, and she said, "You are all better now, aren't you, Daddy?"

Not wishing to upset her nor destroy her faith, he answered, "Yes, dear, I am just fine." About three hours later, he awakened again, and he really had never felt better in his life. He was able to drive that long distance and fulfill his Church assignment successfully.

Because of this beautiful spiritual experience led by a little child, a loving family grew even closer together in their appreciation of each other and the blessings they received constantly from a loving Father in Heaven. Because of this experience, Brother Harland felt especially blessed by the beautiful spirit that was present as he conducted the convention that day in London.

--Claribel W. Aldous

*****

THE PRAYER CIRCLE

Lieutenant Roger Fenton had a lump in his throat when he said goodbye to his boys. There they were in a bunch on the station platform, the ten wayward lads into whom he had sought to instill the fear of God on Tuesday evenings in the winter, and with whom he had rambled and played cricket every Saturday afternoon during the summer. Boys of fourteen to seventeen are a tough proposition--and though Fenton would answer for their bowling and batting, he wasn't sanguine over their religion. But they had filled a big place in his lonely life in the dull little country town, and now he had to leave them and lose them. For the great call had reached him: he bore the king's commission, and in his heart was the feeling that he would never come back.

The parting words of good luck had been said, and the train was panting to be off. "Boys," he said suddenly, "I want you to do something for me--something difficult."

"Anything you like, sir," they answered, eagerly, but their faces fell when they heard their teacher's words.

"Look here," he said, "it's this. You'll meet in the old place every Tuesday evening for a few minutes and pray that I might do my duty, and, if it please God, that I may come back to you all. And I'll pray for you at the same time, even if I'm in the thick of battle."

I wish you had seen the dismay on those ten faces. It was any odds on their blurting out a shamefaced refusal, but Ted Harper, their acknowledged chief, pulled himself together just in time, and called out as the train began to move, "We'll not go back on you, sir. I don't know how we'll manage it, but we'll do it!"

As Fenton sank into his corner he was aware of the mocking looks of his brother officers. "I say," said one man, "you don't really think those chaps are going to hold a prayer meeting for you every week, do you? And if they did, you can't believe it would stop an enemy's shell, can you? It's all very well to be pious, but that's a bit too thick."

Fenton flushed, but he took it in stride. "Prayer's a big part of our religion," he said, "and I've a notion those prayers will help me. Anyhow, I'm sure my lads will do their part. Where Ted Harper leads, they follow."

And sure enough, the boys did their part. It was fine to see them starting out in the wrong direction, and twisting and doubling through the crooked lanes until they worked their way around to the Mission Hall in a rush and a scuttle so no one would see them. The doings of the "Fenton crowd," as they were known locally, were the talk of the town in those first days after Roger departed.

Would they keep it up? Would they bear the ridicule from the other boys their own age? And how in the world would they pray?

Time answered all these questions except the last. They met, and they continued to meet; they faced ridicule like heroes. But how did they pray? That mystery was as deep and unsolved as before, for whatever awful oath of secrecy bound them to silence, not a whisper of the doing of those Tuesday evenings was divulged to the outside world.

I was the only one who ever knew, and I found out by chance. Ted Harper had borrowed "Fights for the Flag" from me, and when I got it back, there was a soiled piece of paper in it with something written on it in Ted's ungainly hand. I thought he had been copying a passage, and, anxious to see what had struck him so, I opened the sheet and read these words:

"Oh, God, it's a hard business praying. But Roger made me promise. And you know how decent he's been to me and the crowd. Listen to us now, and excuse the wrong words, and bring him back safe. And, God, make him the bravest soldier that ever was, and give him the Victorian Cross. That's what we all want for him. And don't let the war be long, for Christ's sake, Amen."

I felt ashamed of myself when I came to the end of this artless prayer. I knew their secret; I could see them kneeling around the Mission farms, two or three with crumpled papers in their hands. They were unutterably shy of religious expression, and to read was their only chance. The boys on whom the fatal lot fell the previous Tuesday were bound to appear with their written devotions a week later. This war has given us back the supernatural, but no miracle seems more wonderful to me than those ten lads and their ill-written prayers. And, remember, that liturgical service lasted six months, and never a break in the Tuesday meetings. What a grand thing a boy's heart is when you capture its loyalty and affection!

It was a black day when the news came. The local territorials had advanced too far on the wing of a great offensive, and had been almost annihilated. The few survivors had dug themselves in, and held on until that bitter Tuesday faded into darkness and night. When relief came, one man was left alive. He was wounded in four places, but he was still loading and firing, and he wept bitterly when they picked him up and carried him away to first aid. That solitary hero, absolutely the only survivor of our local regiment, was Lieutenant Roger Fenton, Victorian Cross.

When his wounds healed, and the king had done the necessary bit of decoration, he returned home. We did not make the fuss they did in some places. Our disaster was too awful, and the pathos of that solitary survivor was piercing. But some of us were at the station, and there in the front row were the ten men of prayer. Poor Roger broke down when he saw them. And he could find no words to thank them. But he wrung their hands until they winced with the pain of that iron grip.

That night I got a chance to talk to him alone. He was too modest to tell me anything of his own great exploit. But there was evidently something he wanted to say, and it was as if he did not know how to begin. At last, he said, "I have a story to tell that not one in fifty would listen to. That Tuesday evening when I was left alone, and had given up all hope, I remembered it was the hour of the old meeting, and I kept my promise and prayed for the boys of my class. Then everything around me faded from my mind, and I saw the dear lads in the Mission Room at prayer. I don't mean that I went back in memory. I knew with an absolute certainty that I was watching and listening."

"How wonderful!" I said.

"That's not all. There's something stranger still," he went on. "They were kneeling on the floor, and Ted Harper was reading a prayer, and when it was done they said amen as with one voice. I got to ten right enough, but I did not stop there. I counted again, and this is the odd thing--there were eleven of them! In my dream or vision or trance, call it what you will, I was vaguely troubled by this unexpected number. I saw the ten troop out in their old, familiar way, and I turned back to find the eleventh, the comrade-in-white, and to speak to him. I felt his presence still, and was glad of it, for the trouble and perplexity were all gone. In their place was a great expectation. I seemed to know the very place where he had been kneeling, and I hurried forward. But there was nothing to be seen, nothing but the well-remembered text staring down at me from the wall: 'For where two or three are gathered in my name, there I am in the midst of them.' I remembered no more, until I found myself in the base hospital. But, of course, I knew then how I had been saved, and what my boys had done for me.

"It makes a man feel strange to have his life given back to him like that; it's as if God would expect a great deal in return. But there's a stronger feeling still in my heart. I believe the lads got their answer not for my sake, but for their own. Think what it means to them! They've got their feet now on the rock of prayer. They know the truth of God. I'm not sure, but I don't think I'll ever tell them that I saw Christ in their midst. They know it in their own way, and perhaps their own way is best."

--W. H. Leatham

PREPARATION

There is no road too long to the man who advances deliberately and without undue haste. There are no honors too distant to the man who prepares himself for them with patience.

--Jean de La Bruyere

*****

PREPARE THE MIND BEFORE PLANTING

The farmer never plants his seed until he has prepared the soil. He plows deep or shallow, according to the quality of the earth. It may be depleted in certain chemicals; these he supplies. Huge clods are broken down and the ground is turned to the sun, which adds vitality.

So with life. It is necessary to prepare the mind for planting right thoughts. Turn over the soil of thinking; break up the clods of fear, doubt, and selfishness. Throw out the stones and old dead roots of negative thinking and failure. Let the sun of faith and love and the breadth of abundant living vitalize the mind. Prepare! Then plant the seed of positive, wholesome thinking.

--Leone Kahl

*****

I CAN SLEEP WHEN THE WIND BLOWS

Many years ago the old country fair in parts of England was, besides being the place of exhibition for farm products, the place where employer and employee met. A farmer here sought his help for the coming year, and young and old went to the fair to seek employment.

Farmer Smith wanted a boy to work on his farm. He was interviewing some candidates when a thoughtful-looking lad of about sixteen attracted his attention. The gruff old agriculturist asked the boy, "What can you do?" The boy swung back at him in the same style, "I can sleep when the wind blows."

It was no wonder at all that the farmer turned about-face to others for help in receiving the answer. Even though he didn't particularly like the teenager's answer, there was something about his gray eyes that got under the farmer's skin.

He asked the lad the same question: "What did you say you could do?" Again the same answer bounced back: "I can sleep when the wind blows."

Smith was still disgusted with the answer, and he went to other parts of the fair to look into the faces of other young men who might want a job on his farm--but there was something about that answer that stuck to him like glue. First thing he knew, his feet were carrying him back to meet the steady gaze of those deliberate eyes of the boy with such strange language.

"What did you say you could do?" he thundered for the third time. For the third time, he got the same answer: "I can sleep when the wind blows."

"Get into my wagon; we'll try you out."

One night several weeks later, Farmer Smith awoke about two o'clock in the morning to what sounded like a cyclone. It seemd that gusts from the north had developed with such intensity that they threatened the roof over his head. The trees cracked, and noises outside electrified his nervous system. The speed with which he jumped into his trousers was outdone only by the lightning that split the darkness outside. With shoes half-laced, he rushed out into the farmyard to see if anything on the premises was still intact, and he knew he would need the services of the new boy he had hired. He called up the stairs of the attic where the boy slept, but the response was the healthy lung-heaving of a healthy lad. He went halfway up the stairs and thundered again, but only a snore echoed back. In excitement, he went to the boy's bed and did everything but tear the bedclothes from the youth. The lad slept on.

With a mixture of desperation and disgust, he faced the gale, and plunged out into the farmyard. He first approached the cow barn. Lo and behold, the milk producers were peacefully chewing their cuds, and inside their abode they were as snug as a mouse under a haystack. It didn't take him long to discover how the boy had chinked up the cracks of the cow abode and reestablished the locks and hinges. In the pigpen he discovered the same tranquility, even though the wind howled on.

He turned to the haystack. As he groped in the darkness, it didn't take him long to determine again the preparation of the lad with the gray, steady eyes. Every few feet on that feed stack, wires had been thrown and weighted on each side. With this construction, the alfalfa was peacefully under control, laughing at the elements.

The farmer was stunned with the revelations he had in a few short minutes on the night of that cyclone. He dropped his head. His mental maneuvers shot like lightning to the boy snoring in the attic. Again, the peculiar answer of a few weeks ago slapped him in the face: "I can sleep when the wind blows."

PROPHETS

BROKEN SILENCE

Religious scholars
Requested knowledge,
Imploring Him
To show His hand.

Some sought Him
Clothed in ritual,
Insisting to
Bear His powers.

Mighty, exemplary men,
Humble men,
Looked for his
Endorsement.

Without manifest,
The millennial silence
Echoed,

"If any of you lack wisdom,
Let him ask of God
That giveth to all men
Liberally. . . ."

A young boy knelt
To know the truth--
To bear its great
Responsibility.

Not the first to ask,
But pure in heart,
Joseph sought
His wisdom, His intent.

The silence was broken
With joyous translation
Of God's truths.

--Suzanne Dean

*****

THE RESTORATION

In a moment of quietude
And spiritual meditation
My thoughts delved deeply
Into our Heavenly Father's creation.
It was in the springtime;
I gazed up as evening grew nigh.

The beautiful heavenly bodies
Gave light and meaning on high.

My soul overflowed with assurance,
For I knew God so well--
He who created the heaven and earth
And our spirits that within us dwell.
I knew undauntedly,
Because the gospel had been restored
By our prophet, Joseph Smith,
Who had been visited by the Lord.

It was 1820 in the springtime,
When there was much doubt and dismay.
Which church was right? Which should he join?
He knelt in the woods to pray.
He was a lad
And believed just what the Bible said--
To pray and ask in faith,
To the truth he would be led.

The heavenly messengers appeared to him
And answered his anxious prayer;
God and his son, Jesus Christ,
With Joseph the truth did share.
It was 1830, April sixth,
When the gospel was finally restored.
Now in April 1987,
The membership to millions has soared.

Our prophet paid with his life,
As Christ, the Savior, did, too,
But they gave to the world a way of life
That no other faith could do.
So as I gazed again into heaven,
I wondered why I was so blessed,
For I know the world is crying out
And seeking for such a quest.

God grant that all may find their way
In this stormy world at sea;
If only their hearts will open wide
To the message he gave to me.

--Reeta B. Turner

*****

Joseph Smith was in person tall and well built, strong and active; of a light complexion, with light hair, blue eyes, very little beard, and of an expression peculiar to himself. His countenance was ever mild, affable, beaming with intelligence and benevolence, mingled with a look of interest and an unconscious smile or cheerfulness entirely free from all restraint or affectation of gravity. There was something connected with the serene and steady penetrating glace of his eye, as if he could penetrate the deepest abyss of the human heart.

He possessed a noble boldness and independence of character; his manner was easy and familiar; his rebuke terrible as the lion; his benevolence unbounded as the ocean; his intelligence universal. His language abounded in original eloquence peculiar to himself--not polished, not studied, not smoothed and softened by education and refined by art, but flowing forth in its own native simplicity, and profusely abounding in variety of subject and manner. He interested and edified while, at the same time, he amused and entertained his audience. None listened to him that were ever weary of his discourse. I have even known him to retain a congregation of willing and anxious listeners for many hours together, in the midst of cold or sunshine, rain or wind, while they were laughing at one moment and weeping at the next. Even his most bitter enemies were generally overcome if he could once get their ears.

I have known him when, chained and surrounded by armed murderers and assassins who were heaping upon him every possible insult and abuse, he rose up in the majesty of a son of God and rebuked them in the name of Jesus Christ until they quailed before him, dropped their weapons, and, on their knees, begged his pardon and ceased their abuse.

Had he been spared a martyr's fate until mature manhood, he had the powers and ability to have revolutionized the world in many respects. He would have transmitted to posterity a name associated with more brilliant and glorious acts than has yet fallen to the lot of mortal. As it is, his works will live to an endless age, and unnumbered millions yet unborn will mention his name with honor as a noble instrument in the hands of God. During his short and youthful career, he laid the foundation of that kingdom spoken of by Daniel, the prophet, which should break in pieces all other kingdoms and which should stand forever.

--Parley P. Pratt

*****

A CHURCH SERVICE IN SOVIET RUSSIA

(In 1959, President Ezra Taft Benson, who was then serving as both a member of the Council of the Twelve and as Secretary of Agriculture in the Eisenhower Administration, toured Europe and Russia with his family. The following copyrighted news article appeared in U. S. News and World Report on October 26, 1959, page 76.)

The night we left Moscow to fly to Kiev, Secretary Benson literally took us to church.

Many of the reporters laughed about it on the way, because Mr. Benson, who is a leading Mormon, had arranged earlier for us to attend a service at the Latter-day Saints Church in West Berlin, but all the newsmen found one excuse or another for not going. In Moscow, we had no choice, because the cars picked us up at the hotel and stopped at the church on the way to the airport. It was around 7:30 on the chilly, rainy evening of October 1.

As the cavalcade of cars arrived at the Central Baptist Church, on a narrow side street not far from Red Square, somebody wisecracked, "Well, boys, you're going to get to church whether you like it or not."

It turned out to be one of the most moving experiences in the lifetime of many of us. One newsman, a former Marine, ranked it with the sight of the American flag rising over the old American compound in Tientsin, China, at the end of the World War II.

The small church was packed, with people standing wherever they could find room.

Secretary Benson and his family were ushered to the rostrum. After a hymn, sung beautifully by the congregation, Mr. Benson began to talk, drawing on his experiences as one of the leaders of the Mormon Church in America. Watching the Russian congregation, you could see tears welling up in the eyes of the people as the Secretary's words were relayed to them through a translator.

"It was very kind of your minister to ask me to extend greetings to you," Mr. Benson began. "I bring you greetings from the millions and millions of Church people in America and around the world."

A soft, fervent "amen" came from the congregation. The Secretary continued, "Our Heavenly Father is not far away. He can be very close to us. I know that God lives. He is our Father. Jesus Christ, the Redeemer of the world, watches over this earth. He will direct all things. Be unafraid, keep his commandments, love one another, pray for peace, and all will be well."

By now there was scarcely a dry eye in the church. Even the few young people wept openly.

"This life is only a part of eternity," Mr. Benson went on. "We lived before we came here as spiritual children of God. We will live again after we leave this life. Christ broke the bonds of death and was resurrected. We will all be resurrected."

At the mention of the promise of life hereafter, muffled sobs could be heard in the small church. These people, after all, were sacrificing their chances of participating in the gains of the Communist society of Russia. Though worshiping God is no longer forbidden in the Soviet Union, those who do so are usually cut off from advancement.

Communism in Russia remains avowedly atheistic. In Moscow, there is one other Baptist church; there are twenty-three Greek Orthodox churches, two synagogues, and one Moslem temple. In a city of 5.4 million people, it is a comparatively tiny crack in the godless society. The dedicated Communists, when talking to visitors about religion, usually claim that those Russians who do go to the few churches in the city do so out of curiosity--much as they would visit a museum--and not because of their devotion.

"I leave you my witness as a church servant for many years that the truth will endure," Mr. Benson concluded. "Time is always on our side. God bless you and keep you all the days of your life, I pray in the name of Jesus Christ."

As the Secretary returned to his seat, the congregation broke into the familiar hymn, "God Be With You Till We Meet Again." They were still singing and waving their handkerchiefs as we followed Mr. Benson out of the church. All the way along the crowded aisle, hands were outstretched to shake our hands.

On the drive to the airport, one of the interpreters--a young Russian girl who has never known any life save that under Communism--said, "I felt like crying."

--Grant Salisbury and Warren K. Leffler

*****

THE COAT

Heber shivered in his thin coat as the cold November wind whipped around him. All he really wanted for his birthday was a warm overcoat, but he knew that asking for one would upset his mother. He remembered how she had cried the Christmas before, because she didn't have enough money to buy him even a stick of candy.

Nine days after Heber was born, his father had died, and his mother had moved from the fine house where Heber had been born to a small one, where they lived for many years. The roof leaked and sometimes they went to bed early because there was no coal for heat. Sometimes they went to bed hungry, for the fried bread hadn't been sufficient supper and there was no money for anything else.

There were days and nights when Heber's mother would sew and sew, even though she was really too tired to finish a dress for a customer. Then Heber would go under the sewing machine and push the pedal up and down so that his mother's tired legs might have a rest. As they worked together in the lamplight, she would tell him stories and they would plan together for the time they would have plenty of coal, food, and all the clothes they could wear. Neither of them dreamed that one day Heber J. Grant would be the seventh president of The Church of Jesus Christ of Latter-day Saints.

November 22 dawned clear and cold. "Happy birthday, Heber," called his mother as she handed him the most beautiful coat he had ever seen. It was made of material his mother had been sewing, and it fit him perfectly. He hugged it to himself, and could hardly wait to go out in the cold day and feel its warmth about him.

A few weeks later as Heber was hurrying on an errand, he saw a boy just his size who was crying with cold. The boy was wearing a thin sweater, and Heber shivered, even though he had on his new overcoat.

As Heber hurried by, the crying boy looked at his coat with such longing that, almost before he knew what he was doing, Heber had stopped, taken off his coat, and insisted that the boy wear it.

That very afternoon Heber's mother saw him wearing his old coat instead of the new one. "Heber," she called, "what have you done with your lovely new overcoat?" For a moment he wondered how he could tell her he had given it away. He wondered what she would say. He hoped she wouldn't cry. "Oh, Mother," he finally explained, "I saw a boy who needed it lots worse than I did, so I just gave it to him."

"Couldn't you have given him your old one?" she asked.

Heber longed to have her understand, and yet he despaired of her doing so. And then he looked up anxiously into her face. Her eyes were misty with tears, and he threw his arms around her as she answered her own question, "Of course, you couldn't, Heber, of course you couldn't."

--Lucile C. Reading

REGRET

Three things never return: the past, the neglected opportunity, and the spoken word.

*****

FADED BLOSSOMS

Just a sweet, little childish letter
And a ribbon-tied soft brown curl,
Stained with the tears of sorrow
Of a broken-hearted little girl.

I promised someday I would tell you,
Let your judgment be not too severe;
For my heart has been kept in prison
By sorrow for many a year.

You see, we had planted a flower
In a pot on the windowsill--
They're not easy to grow in these cold parts,
Nor quick to obey one's will.

My little daughter had helped me,
And I explained it would be its birth
When small, green leaves were born to life
Out of the dear mother earth.

We thrilled when first we noticed
Its first green leaves start to show,
And smiled, as with admiration,
Each day we would watch it grow.

It had grown quite tall and princely,
And my child was the first to have seen
A beautiful, bright, red blossom
Nestled in leaves of green.

It was such a priceless blossom
In this land that was bleak and bare,
And we almost seemed to caress it,
For its beauty we both could share.

My little girl had been ailing--
I had kept her in all day;
She had been so hot with fever,
And had not wanted to play.

Spring was in its early dawning;
The air was still very cool.
She was standing by the window
Watching the children come home from school.

I was busy in the kitchen,
When I heard an awful crash,
And hurried into the parlor
To see in an instant's flash--

There lay our precious blossom,
Broken right off at the base--
And my child knelt there beside it
With dirt all over her face.

I felt a terrific anger--
It was wrong, how well I know,
But remember when you judge me
How long we had watched it grow.

I seized my child by the shoulders,
And shook her time and time again;
I took her into her bedroom.
She tried in vain to explain.

"You're a careless child!" I told her,
As I seated her down on her bed.
"How could have been so naughty?
You must stay in your room," I said.

Then I closed the door behind me,
And cleaned up our broken prize;
The plant and the blossom wilted,
But I was cruel and so unwise.

I held the blossom a moment--
It seemed to droop in my hand;
The beauty of its short life ended,
It seemed hard to understand.

Then I went back into the kitchen
To bake for the evening meal--
Probably an hour or so had passed
When remorse I began to feel.

She could not have meant to do it--
She had loved the blossom so,
Her dear, little hands helped plant it,
And with joy she had watched it grow;

So I hurried into the bedroom--
It was cold in there I knew,
And she had been feeling so feverish--
What a foolish thing to do!

She lay on her bed in a stupor,
But murmured as I came near
Something about the blossom,
Though the words I could not hear.

Regret

Her dear head was hot with fever,
And the tears had made a streak
Where dirt had clung from the blossom
On each little burning cheek.

I took her tenderly in my arms
While dread fear gripped at my heart.
I said, "Dear, it doesn't matter,
Another plant will soon start."

I could not make out her answer,
Though she tried in her childish way--
"I did not mean to, Mamma,"
Was all I could hear her say.

No use of telling you further,
God knew I had failed, you see.
I was not fit as a mother,
And he called her back from me.

For ten long years I had loved her--
Ten years of glorious bliss,
How could I ever endure
To part in a way like this?

Then I saw a slip of paper
Folded, and nearby the bed,
Wet with the tears of my darling,
And this was the message I read:

"I'm so very sorry, Mamma,
We loved it so much, I know--
But I'll pray real hard, dear Mamma,
And a new, pretty plant will grow.

"I started to turn from the window,
And--" but that was all she could write.
I stood like a marble statue,
My face was so numb and white.

"Dear God, forgive me," I murmured,
As I pressed the note to my breast--
"If I could just live this day over,
I would not fail in the test."

I cut a lock from her forehead--
The soft curls I loved so well,
And placed it within the letter,
Where her hot little teardrops fell.

The two little blossoms had faded,
And two little lives were o'er--
My heart died, too, with their passing,
And my lips will not smile anymore.

Do you think that God will forgive me?
You say that he will? Then, today,
I will start to live each day better
While on earth I am destined to stay.

Oh, mothers, please gain from my story,
And learn from a heart in pain
That earthly things matter so little,
And moments we cannot regain.

Just a sweet, little childish letter,
And a ribbon-tied, soft brown curl--
Wet with the tears of sorrow
Of a broken-hearted little girl.

*****

HAVE YOU EVER BEEN CONVICTED OF A FELONY?

In sentencing two high school boys who had thoughtlessly made a practice of "borrowing" automobiles to go joy riding, a midwestern district judge made the following remarks:

You come from good homes, both of you. Yet now you have been convicted of a felony--a crime for which you might be sent to the penitentiary. In this case, I do not have to send you to the penitentiary; I am permitted to give you a parole.

But even if you never see the inside of a penitentiary or jail, you will not have escaped the penalties of your crime. The record of your conviction will be here as long as the courthouse stands. No amount of good conduct in the future can ever erase it.

Next year, or ten years from now, or when you are old men, if you are ever called to be witnesses in any court of law, some lawyer will point his finger at you and ask, "Have you ever been convicted of a felony?" You will hang your head and admit that you have--because if you deny it, the records of these proceedings will be brought from the vaults and read to the jury.

The question will be asked for the sole purpose of casting doubt on your testimony. Convicted felons are not believed as readily as other persons.

Someday you may have a chance to live and work in one of the expanding countries of South America, and you may apply for a passport. You may not get it. You might enter Canada for a fishing trip, but you would not be allowed to stay.   No country will allow you to become a resident. Your world is so much smaller now than it once was.

Someday you may seek a position in the civil service of your state or nation.   On the application blank, you will find this question: "Have you ever been convicted of a felony?"   Your truthful answer will bar you from appointment.   An untruthful answer will be detected, because appointments are made only after investigation.   The record is here to be found by anyone interested.

In a few years, you will be eighteen, and others your age will have the right to vote--but you will not.   You will be a citizen of your state and country, but you will not have any voice in public affairs.

Someday the governor may pardon you and restore your rights, but it is going to be humiliating to ask him.   He'll want to know your whole record.   It is a bad one.

I am granting you parole.   A parole is in no sense a pardon.   You will report to the men who have accepted your parole as often as they ask you to.   Your convenience is not a matter of importance.   You will also obey your parents.   If your parents send you to bed at nine o'clock, you will go without complaint.   You will perform such tasks as are assigned to you.   Your parole is a fragile thing.

Should the slightest complaint of your conduct reach this court, your parole will be revoked immediately and you will begin serving your sentence.   You will not be brought back here for questioning and/or explanations.   You will be picked up and taken to prison--without notice to you and without delay.

REPENTANCE

Forgiveness does not change the past, but it does enlarge the future.

--Paul Boese

*****

HEAVENLY FATHER
TO A BELOVED, WAYWARD DAUGHTER

She steps,
Crumpled, weary,
Into the
Glassed, tiled
Enclosure
And breathes
The warmth
Of soothing
Water.

Limb by limb,
Oh, so carefully,
She washes away
The sleep
And clutter
Of night
And previous
Day.

She creams
And softens,
Brushes
And adorns.
Fresh and lovely
From her bath
She is born.

A new beginning.
Fresh with promise,
Bright with awareness
Of herself.

"Oh, daughter!
Wouldst that thou
Would meticulously
At the beginning
Of thy day
Repent,
And wash thy sins
Away!"

--Barbara Werrett Nielsen

*****

I'm sure all of us have wondered at some time if all of our sins will truly be forgiven. In the Doctrine and Covenants, we read that they will be. We have the assurance, then, that the Lord will remember them no more. But what about our neighbors, who never seem to forget our wrongdoings? Will they forget what we have done?

Many years ago, two young brothers were caught trying to steal some sheep. As part of their punishment, the letters ST were branded on their foreheads to show that they were sheep thieves. This caused much embarrassment and shame to them and their families.

One brother was so shamed that he left the small town and wandered over the whole country trying to forget his past. People would notice the letters on his head, and he was shamed and ridiculed. He finally died penniless as a vagabond--a completely broken man.

The other brother stayed in the small town and tried to make amends for his actions. For some time the people also shunned and ridiculed him, but he would keep doing the best he could. Everything he did was now just and fair. He tried hard to change his way of life.

Many years later in the same town, a visitor was walking through the streets with a long-time resident. The brother who stayed, with the imprint still on his forehead, walked by.

"Why does that man have an ST on his forehead?" asked the visitor.

"I'm not sure--I can't quite remember," said the resident, "but I think the letters stand for 'the saint that he is.'"

SABBATH

And when you come to meeting, bring your minds with you.

--Brigham Young

*****

This very day upon which we meet to worship, the Sabbath, has become the play-day of this great nation--the day set apart by thousands to violate the commandments that God gave long, long ago. I am persuaded that much of the sorrow and distress that is afflicting and will continue to afflict mankind is traceable to the fact that they have ignored his admonition to keep the Sabbath Day holy.

--George Albert Smith

*****

"Remember the Sabbath day, to keep it holy." That seems such a little thing for us to do in return for the blessings we enjoy. But to forget that it is the Lord's day, as some of us appear to do, is ungrateful. He has set apart one day in seven--not to create a burden, but to bring joy into our lives and cause that our homes may be the gathering place of the family, that parents and children may assemble around the family hearth, increasing our love for one another. And if we do what our Heavenly Father would have us do, we will go to his holy house upon the Sabbath Day, and there partake of the sacrament, in remembrance of the sacrifice that was made for us by the Reedemer of mankind. Honor the Sabbath day and keep it holy, Latter-day Saints, and it will bring you great joy. And our Heavenly Father will bestow upon you the blessings that result from obedience to his advice and counsel.

--George Albert Smith

*****

One good but mistaken man I know claimed he could get more out of a good book on Sunday than he could get by attending church services, remarking that the sermons were hardly up to his standards. But we do not go to Sabbath meetings to be entertained or even simply to be instructed. We go to worship the Lord. It is an individual responsibility, and regardless of what is said from the pulpit, if one wishes to worship the Lord in spirit and in truth, he may do so by attending his meetings, partaking of the sacrament, and contemplating the beauties of the gospel. If the service is a failure to you, you have failed. No one can worship for you; you must do your own waiting upon the Lord.

--Spencer W. Kimball

*****

229

The story is told that President Wilford Woodruff entered into the spirit of worship so completely at sacrament meeting that he was often seen with tears running down his face. Few people actually worship when they attend sacrament meeting.

--<u>Family Home Evening Manual</u>

*****

Now remember, my brethren, those who go skating, buggy riding, or on excursions on the Sabbath day--and there is a great deal of this practiced--are weak in the faith. Gradually, little by little, the spirit of their religion leads out of their hearts and their affections, and by and by they begin to see faults in their brethren, faults in the doctrines of the Church, faults in the organization, and at last they leave the kingdom of God and go to destruction. I really wish you would remember this, and tell it to your neighbors. We are under the necessity of assembling here from Sabbath to Sabbath, and in ward meetings. In addition, we have to call our solemn assemblies, to teach, talk, pray, sing, and exhort. What for? To keep us in remembrance of our God and our holy religion. Is this custom necessary? Yes--because we are so liable to forget, so prone to wander. We need to have the gospel sounded in our ears as often as once, twice, or thrice a week, or, behold, we will turn again to our idols.

--Brigham Young

*****

HAPPY TO BE ALIVE

Every morning for several weeks I was disturbed in my early morning hours of sleep by a pesky little mockingbird perched high atop a telephone pole just outside my bedroom window. Just before dawn, I was awakened by his chirping and mimicking of every bird in the neighborhood. This would go on for five minutes or more.

One night when I retired to bed, the weather outside was miserable: the wind was blowing, and there was a drizzling rain. The following day was Sunday, so I thought the bad weather would be a good excuse to stay home from Sunday School. This was no weather to be out in.

Just at dawn the next morning I was awakened as usual by my little feathered friend. As I looked out my window at the bleak and gloomy weather, I could scarcely believe what I saw. Perched high on the pole was the bird, singing louder than I had ever heard him before. I could just make him out through the drizzling rain, and I could tell he was soaked through the feathers to the skin; he looked half drowned. I wondered how in the world he could muster up so much courage on such a dismal morning. He seemed to be trying to tell the world that he was happy just to be alive.

Needless to say, I went to Sunday School that morning, glad for the lesson learned from a little bird.

As I drove to Church, I thought of the many excuses we sometimes make for not attending our scheduled Church meetings. How simple it is to say, "The weather is bad," or, "I'm sure they won't miss me just this once," or, "I don't seem to learn anything anyway."

If we apply ourselves, you and I individually receive the inspiration and blessings that come from attending and participating in our Church meetings. We who make excuses and stay home are slipping behind, while our brothers and sisters who do attend are moving ahead. We are engaged in the Lord's work, so let us not allow anything to dampen our spirits. Even when we think we have a good excuse to stay home, let us not take advantage of it. We might ask ourselves, "Do I have the courage and vigor of the little mockingbird?"

--Harold E. Chapman

SACRAMENT

No more sacred ordinance is administered in the Church of Jesus Christ than the administration of the sacrament.

--David O. McKay

*****

The sacrament of the Lord's Supper is a very important and sacred ordinance; however simple it may appear, it is one that will add to our acceptance before God or to our condemnation.

--Joseph F. Smith

*****

The sacrament is of great importance. The Lord himself ordained that we partake of these emblems. It was regarded of such importance by our Father in Heaven that, through his beloved son and the apostles and prophets, as recorded in the scriptures, the saints were admonished to partake of it regularly. Our Father in Heaven does not give us commandments or advice that are not of importance.

--George Albert Smith

*****

Its [the sacrament's] observance is as necessary to our salvation as any other of the ordinances and commandments that have been instituted in order that the people may be sanctified, that Jesus may bless them and give unto them his spirit, and guide and direct them that they may secure unto themselves life eternal. Impress the sacredness of this important ordinance upon the minds of your children.

--Brigham Young

*****

Before partaking of this sacrament, our hearts should be pure; our hands clean; we should be divested of all enmity toward our associates; we should be at peace with our fellow men; and we should have in our hearts a desire to do the will of our Father and keep all of his commandments. If we do this, partaking of the sacrament will be a blessing to us and will renew our spiritual strength.

--Heber J. Grant

*****

How long do you suppose a man may partake of this ordinance unworthily and the Lord not withdraw his spirit from that man? How long will he thus trifle with sacred things, and the Lord not give him over to the buffetings of Satan until the day of redemption?

--Joseph Smith

*****

Then Jesus, weak from torture, his shoulders cut and sore,
Was forced to carry his own cross, as all our sins he bore.
And when he felt exhausted, the jeering crowd drew near
To laugh at him and mock him, and all his sufferings cheer.
And when they reached the summit of the round and sandstone hill,
The birds were singing sweetly and the air was clear and still.
Jesus thought how lovely and glorious it would be
To live with loving friends again, those days of Galilee.
But the soldiers took no thought of this, they had a job to do,
They hoisted him upon the cross and drove long nails through.
They put a nail through hands and feet, and then to make more sure,
They drove a cruel nail through his wrists to finish the chore.
His blood again began to flow, some drops he shed for you.
He suffered, bled, and died for all, that we might live anew.
So when we drink the water and eat the broken bread,
Think back upon the Savior and the precious blood he shed.
Let us remember, and be sure, our heart and hands are clean
    as they can be;
Let's bow our heads and whisper, "We do remember thee."

*****

THOUGHTS DURING THE SACRAMENT

Are you thinking of our Savior,
Little child, this Sabbath day,
As the emblems of his body
Are prepared a special way?

Are you thinking of the baby
Who was born in Bethlehem,
To live, and learn, and suffer,
And to die for fellow men?

Are you thinking of the twelve-year-old,
Young deacon, of that day
When Jesus taught the wise men
In the temple far away?

Are you thinking, teacher, priest,
As the emblems you prepare,
Of the blood and flesh of Jesus
And the meaning that they bear?

Sacrament

Young adult, and you who've served him
As a missionary long,
Are you thinking of that teacher
Who through life did nothing wrong?

Or, as parents, are we thinking
Of our Christ--the light, the way,
Of his love, and death, and glory
On his resurrection day?

Why should not we, our Father's children,
Sent to earth with his great plan,
Let our minds and hearts remind us
That he came to die for man?

As we take these holy emblems,
Let's remember that he trod
With one purpose in his life here:
To lead us back to God.

                    --Arline Martindale Scott

SCOUTING

A hundred years from now it will not matter what my bank account was, the sort of house I lived in, or the kind of car I drove. But the world may be different because I was important in the life of a boy.

*****

Scouting is not a science to be solemnly studied, nor is it a collection of doctrines and texts. No--it is a jolly game in the out of doors, where boy-men and boys can go adventuring together as older and younger brothers, picking up health and happiness, handcraft and helpfulness.

--Lord Baden-Powell

*****

"On my honor, I will do my best. . . ."

Ever since 1910, when an American businessman named William D. Boyce brought the Scouting movement from England to the United States, the young men of the Boy Scouts of America have been doing their very best: by being a credit to their communities, their country, and a way of life that can survive only so long as the youth of the nation are brought up to believe in and practice its principles.

Scouts also do their best by reliving the wilderness adventures and learning the skills that made our frontier forefathers strong; by discovering the important and delicate balance that must be found between self-reliance and cooperation; and by acquiring and sharing human values like faith, courage, honesty, dignity, respect, and friendliness. In all these things, a Boy Scout does his best.

*****

MISSION STATEMENT, BOY SCOUTS OF AMERICA

It is the mission of the Boy Scouts of America to serve others by helping to instill values in young people and, in other ways, to prepare them to make ethical choices during their lifetime in achieving their full potential.

The Boy Scouts of America's legacy is not only of the past, but also of the future. Today, as never before, we must live the principles of Scouting and strive to preserve the American ideals of life and government. The work toward honor, liberty, and true equality never ends. This has not changed in the past three-quarters of a century. It is as relevant today as it was in 1910.

Softly falls the light of day
As our campfires fade away.
Silently each Scout should ask,
Have I done my daily task?

Have I kept my honor bright?
Can I guiltless sleep tonight?
Have I done and have I dared
In everything to "be prepared"?

*****

JUST A CHANCE

If I were president of a bank
and owned a railroad, too,
and had Aladdin's magic lamp,
do you know what I'd do?

I'd wish to be a boy again
with patches on my pants,
a good, old-fashioned appetite,
some playmates, and a chance.

A chance to join a Boy Scout troop
with leaders such as you;
men who would give me of their best,
all upright, kind, and true.

To know what "on my honor" means,
to say "I'll do my best";
to learn to really "be prepared,"
brave, clean--and all the rest.

To give all boys that kind of chance,
this is our chosen task.
Let's give them fun the Scouting way;
isn't that all they ask?

So til all boys have had that chance,
we haven't done our best.
But when their wish is realized
we'll know we've passed our test.

For someday when I'm standing
before the great white throne
where I can hear the angels sing
and see the sinners moan--

I'll want no better advocate
to make my final plea
that just some little boy who'll say
"Gee, God, he did a lot for me."

--Author Unknown

*****

SCOUTMASTER'S DREAM

The Scoutmaster sat in a big chair and groaned.
His week's camping ended, at last he was home.
Tonight he could sleep in his own nice, soft bed,
No shouts from the Scouts would ring in his head.
A hot bath and then he was soon fast asleep,
Content, for tonight no vigil to keep.

But somehow in dreamland great men he did meet,
And they called him by name as he walked down the street.
At first he was puzzled; now, who could they be?
And then he remembered--Scout camporees!
The lads were grown men now, no longer just boys,
The lines on their faces showed sorrows and joys.

His head was made glad, they remembered his name;
Perhaps all his Scouting had not been in vain.
The nights by the campfire, the stars in the sky,
The hand held in reverence, "On My Honor" pledge I.
The boys of today, men tomorrow will be,
And the Scoutmaster's dream fulfilled we shall see.

--Mildred Goodwin

*****

SCOUT LEADERS' WIVES

Hers is the sacrificial life
Who is the Boy Scout leader's wife,
For all alone at home she stays
While he is tramping woodland ways.
While she sits waiting for her squire,
He teaches boys the art of fire;
And while the hours go dragging by,
He teaches boys how knots to tie;
And while for him she burns a lamp,
He spends a week or more in camp.

The Boy Scout leader's wife must be
As wise in many arts as he;
Must learn to stretch a meal for four
At times for eight or nine or more
When friends of his drop into town;
And never scold and never frown
At midnight when he brings them back
And asks for milk and a snack;
And never sigh, when on the phone
He tells her she must dine alone.

The Boy Scout leader's wife must be
As fond of boyhood as is he,
And see the far-off future when

Our country will have need of men--
Good men, intelligent and true,
And able men, her tasks to do,
And honest men, and clean and strong,
And men too big to stoop to wrong--
Or never she'd consent to be
The wife of such an absentee.

*****

'TWAS THE NIGHT BEFORE. . .
A Mother's View of Her Son's First Outing

'Twas the night before campout
When all through the house
Not a creature was stirring,
Not even my spouse.

The stockings were packed
In the duffle with care
Right next to the toothbrush
And clean underwear.

My Scout was all nestled
All snug in his bed,
While visions of Eagle Scouts
Danced through his head.

I slipped on my nightgown
Turned the blanket on high,
And crawled in my bed
For a little shut-eye.

When out in the driveway
I heard such a clatter
I leaped out of bed
To see what was the matter.

Tents and camp stoves--
My yard a disaster!
"Hello, good morning!"
Called our cheerful Scoutmaster.

"Tom, Kurt, Chuck, and Darrel,"
He called, checking his role.
It was obvious everything
Was under control.

"Dave, Scott, Jeff, and Ryan.
Michael, Jason, and Steve.
At last here comes Buddy,
So now we can leave!"

I couldn't believe it!
I'd just closed my eyes.
I threw on my robe
To say my goodbyes.

"Be careful while hiking.
Stay out of the snow!
Take care of the backpack.
It's borrowed, you know.

"As you roll out the sleeping bag,
Put papers underneath.
Stay clear of all bears,
And please brush your teeth."

They raced to the Blazer
With a toot of the horn,
Away they all drove.
My feelings were torn.

His very first campout,
And proud as can be.
"Happy camping to all"--
I'm glad it's not me!

--Lynda Hadley

*****

THE SCOUT LAW

A SCOUT IS
TRUSTWORTHY.
I told him I would do it--
It was a simple task;
And though I didn't get it done,
It wasn't really much to ask.
The outcome now is crucial;
An important job needs done!
But he simply doesn't trust me,
So he's picked another one.

LOYAL.
What's in it for me?
What can I gain?
A badge? Some money?
Or even some fame?
Ask not these questions
Focused on "me,"
But, "How can I help you?"
It points toward "thee."

HELPFUL.
I helped him just a little bit--
Expected nothing in return,
But was repaid a thousandfold,
Much more than I did earn.

FRIENDLY.
Faithful friends are hard to find,
We must select with care.
One is great, two divine,
And three extremely rare.
We find them in our times of need--
How 'oft they number none,
But if I wish to earn a few,
I only need be one.

COURTEOUS.
Hearts, like doors, will open with ease
With very, very, little keys,
And don't forget that two of these
Are "I thank you" and "If you please."

KIND.
Have you had a kindness shown? Pass it on!
'Twas not given for thee alone. Pass it on!
Let it travel down the years, let it wipe another's tears,
'Till in Heaven the deed appears--Pass it on!
                              --Henry Burton

OBEDIENT.
We must do the thing we must
Before we do the thing we may;
We are unfit for any trust
'Till we can and do obey.
                    --George MacDonald

CHEERFUL.
Cheer is a peculiar thing
Unlike much that one attains--
The more of it that we can spend,
The more of it remains.

THRIFTY.
If I don't save for a rainy day,
I may think I'm avoiding a drought,
But if I never put into my purse,
I can never take anything out.

BRAVE.
Some measure their bravery and show they are tough
By the number of times they win.
Indeed, it's okay to even get rough
Or to walk away with a grin.
But it's the coward who strikes when there's nothing to fear,

When nothing his progress bars;
But it takes a man to stand up and cheer
When some other fellow stars.
For the test of your bravery and the proof of your worth
Is not in the blows you can deal,
But the blows that you take on this good old earth
Show whether your stuff is real!
                    --Adapted from The Test of a Man

CLEAN.
We cup our hands to take a drink,
We fill our mind each hour;
Unless the vessel's clean inside
Whatever's poured in turns sour.

REVERENT.
Give ear, my children, to my words,
Whom God hath dearly bought,
Lay up his laws within your heart
And print them in your thought.
                    --John Rogers

*****

TEN ESSENTIALS OF SCOUTMASTERSHIP

A belief in boys that will make you want to invest yourself and your time on their behalf.

A zeal focused upon one point--the boy's happiness through his formative years--because "a happy boy is a good boy, and a good boy is a good citizen."

An immense faith in Scouting as the program that will best serve to mold our youth into fine men.

A realization that to the boys, Scouting is a game, while to you it is a game with a purpose--character building and citizenship training.

A knowledge that to your boys you are Scouting. "What you are speaks so loudly that I cannot hear what you say!"

A steadfastness of purpose to carry out a planned program with energy and perseverance, patience and good humor.

A willingness to submerge yourself and make boy leaders lead and grow through an effective application of the Patrol Method.

A desire to advance in Scoutmastership by making use of training material available on the subject.

A readiness to work hand in hand with home, church, sponsoring institution, school, local council, and national council for the good of the individual boy and for the good of the community as a whole.

A <u>love of the outdoors</u> in all its phases, and a vision of the hand that created it.

*****

The Scout, in his promise, undertakes to do his duty to his king and country only in the second place; his first duty is to God. It is with this idea before us and reckoning that God is the one father of us all, that we Scouts count ourselves a brotherhood despite the differences among us of country, creed, or class. We realize that in addition to the interests of our particular country, there is a higher mission before us--namely, the promotion of the kingdom of God; that is, the rule of peace and good will on earth. In the Scouts, each form of religion is respected and its active practice encouraged, and through the spread of brotherhood in all countries, we have the opportunity of developing the spirit of mutual good will and understanding.

There is no religious side of the movement. The whole of it is based on religion--that is, on the realization and service of God.

Let us, therefore, in training our Scouts, keep the higher aims in the forefront, not let themselves get too absorbed in the steps. Don't let the technical outweigh the moral. Field efficiency, backwoodmanship, camping, hiking, good turns, jamboree, and comradeship are, by all means, not the end. The end is <u>character</u> with a purpose.

And that purpose, that the next generation may be sane in an insane world, and develop the higher realization of service, active service of love, and duty to God and neighbor.

Our objective in the Scout movement is to give such help as we can in bringing about God's kingdom on earth by inculcating among the youth the spirit and the daily practice in their lives of unselfish good will and cooperation.

--Lord Baden-Powell

*****

Recently I was in New York on business, and as I was walking into a building I passed a fellow who was coming out of the building. Our eyes met, and I was immediately swept with memories from many years earlier. We greeted and exchanged only a few pleasantries, because neither of our schedules permitted us to spend much time at that moment, but we made an appointment to have lunch the next day to catch up on old times.

The next day I met Bill, who had been a member of a Scout troop over which I had served as Scoutmaster many years before. I learned that during that time he had grown up and married, and they had had one child, a boy. A while later his wife became pregnant with their second child, but had a very difficult pregnancy and a very difficult labor. She died in childbirth, but the young baby girl lived. Bill and his two young children lived with his parents for two months before he had the courage to move back into his own home. The first night after their return, he

242

stayed up as late as he could, trying to muster the courage to go back and have his first night in the bedroom in which he had spent so many nights with his beloved wife. The baby girl fell asleep in his arms, and his now two-year-old son and he stayed up watching television; finally, they decided they had better go to bed. His son pleadingly asked if, just this once, he could sleep with his dad. Of course, that would be fine. In fact, it relieved Bill of having to face the loneliness of that room by himself. So the two of them got back into that same bed in which he and his wife had spent so many nights; the boy snuggled up with his little fanny in the small of his father's back, and went to sleep. Bill laid there in the darkness of that familiar room and all of the loneliness and depression in the world seemed to settle in on him. He wept for the rest of the night.

As I sat across the table from Bill listening to this story, I looked him in the eye--and I had a tear in mine--and I said, "Bill, where did you get the strength to endure that trying experience in your life?" And he looked me right back in the eye, and he said, "From you, my Scoutmaster. Back in that Scout troop you taught me all the things I needed to know to face life. I can never thank you enough for being an example of greatness."

--Julian Dyke

*****

WHY SCOUTING IN THE LDS CHURCH

Not long ago, J. L. Tarr, then Chief Scout Executive, visited Provo's Missionary Training Center; during his visit, he met with missionaries in their orientation meeting, and was invited to speak. He asked the elders with Scouting background to stand. Almost all stood. He then asked those who had achieved the rank of Eagle to remain standing. Very few sat down. Mr. Tarr then turned to the MTC leaders and said, "Do you know why you have Scouting in your church?" Motioning to the audience of young men, standing tall, he said, "To prepared your young men for missions."

That came from one who is not a member of the Church, but one who knows Scouting and its value in the lives of young men being prepared!

Dwan Young, General Primary President, adds that Scouting not only helps the family be involved and strengthened as they work together, but it directs positive attention to their Scout.

It is an interesting sequence that the Cub Scout, at age eight, starts very simply, competing only with himself, as he accomplishes simple tasks, "passed off" by his parents and involving family members in monthly pack meetings. By age ten, the Scout's requirements are a little more involved and his activities are accomplished with and signed by his Webelos leader. The next year, his merit badges are not only accomplished with his troop and signed by his Scoutmaster, but he is also required to meet and work with trained merit badge counselors outside of his troop.

The highest achievement in Scouting is the rank of Eagle, requiring at least two years of service and earning awards as he is involved in the community, and which represent proficiency in a host of areas helping the young man to build character.

And, step by step, he is being prepared for his life's experiences.

In April General Conference in 1967, Elder Robert L. Simpson simply stated, "People ask, 'Why do we have Scouting in the Church? Why don't we just make up our own program?' Well, there is only one real answer. More than fifty years ago, the First Presidency designated Scouting as the activity program for boys, and they have never changed their mind. And until they do change their mind, it will be the activity for boys in the Church. The Church program included Scouting because we have a great interest in showing a boy the way to a more abundant life.

"We also have Scouting in the Church because we want to see liberty, freedom, and democracy perpetuated by means of tomorrow's leaders, who will be adequate to meet that challenge. We have Scouting in the Church because we believe in light and truth, in the dignity of the human soul. There is no darkness in Scouting. There is no untruth in Scouting. There is no degradation of the human soul in Scouting. Today's evils of pornography, immorality, disrespect for authority, and selfishness are all the products of darkness. They disintegrate in the bright light of Scouting."

--Sharon Miller

*****

TRAIN SCOUT LEADERS

"I challenge you to develop a program to prepare this generation of youth to meet the Savior when he comes."

With this statement, Elder Robert L. Backman of the First Quorum of the Seventy and general president of the Young Men, concluded his keynote address at "Hawaii Philmont." The four-day conference, aimed at training LDS leaders how to integrate Scouting into their youth programs, was held at BYU-Hawaii Campus.

Elder Backman joined Primary General President Dwan Young and John Warnick, national director of Mormon Relationships for Boy Scouts of America, on the conference faculty.

"Too many of our youth grow up as spectators," Elder Backman said. "The Scouting program is the activity arm of the priesthood to help our young men prepare for the great Second Coming."

Elder Backman said that while the Church is the largest sponsor of the Boy Scout program in the United States, with
18,783 units, "we still have a poor record of trained leaders in

Scouting." He added, "We can't teach something we don't know. That's why we're at this conference--to remedy that sad record."

"Scouting works in concert with the goal of the Church, which is to save souls," he said. "We deal with eternal lives when we work with young men. They are the future of the Church. In 1990, when our membership will be doubled, who will be our leaders? We must train our youth now."

Elder Backman advised bishops to "put your best men in Scouting, and leave them there long enough to be trained and get the job done.

"A good Scouting program makes a good Aaronic Priesthood quorum program," he said. "There is direct coorelation between the number of Eagle Scouts and the number of boys who go on missions and marry in the temple.

"Leaders, learn the Scouting program, and let it bless the lives of your youth. It's the program of the Church."

--<u>Church News,</u> August 7, 1983

SERVICE

No one is useless in the world who lightens the burdens of it to anyone else.

--Charles Dickens

*****

We begin to live only when we begin to love. And we begin to love only when self dies, and we live to bless others.

*****

You get more than you give when you give more than you get.

*****

Our lives are like shoes, to be worn out in the service of God.

--Spencer W. Kimball

*****

You must give some time to your fellow man. Even if it's a little thing, do something for those who have need of help, something for which you get no pay but the privilege of doing it.

--Albert Schweitzer

*****

I expect to pass through this world but once. Any good work, therefore, any kindness, or any service I can render to any soul of man or animal, let me do it now! Let me not neglect or defer it, for I shall not pass this way again.

--Carlyle

*****

Do all the good you can,
By all the means you can,
In all the places you can,
In all the ways you can,
At all the times you can,
To all the people you can,
As long as you can. . . .

--John W. Wesley

*****

No man has ever risen to the real stature of spiritual manhood (this applies to sisters and sisterhood, too) until he (she) has found that it is finer to serve somebody else than it is to serve one's self.

*****

SACRIFICE

When he has more than he can eat,
To feed a stranger is not a feat.

When he has more than he can spend,
It isn't hard to give or lend.

Who gives but what he'll never miss
Will never know what giving is.

He'll win few praises from the Lord
Who does but what he can afford.

The widow's mite to heaven went
Because real sacrifice it meant.

--Edgar A. Guest

*****

MY TODAY

I have no other day than this;
Oh, Father, grant I shall not miss
The service sweet of doing good,
And living truly as I should.

Oh, Father, in this day that's mine,
Let all thy sweetness through me shine;
Let all my ways acknowledge thee,
May Christ be manifest in me.

Oh! Let me by thy voice to speak
The truth to those who vainly seek;
And through me let thy love o'erflow
To all the world that needs it so.

Oh! Let today be this for me,
A day of glorifying thee.
'Tis all the day that my soul knows;
'Tis from today tomorrow grows.

So, for today, this is my prayer--
Tomorrow, Lord, is in thy care.

--Mabel F. Ricard

*****

OPPORTUNITIES TO SERVE ARE HERE

A very busy businessman was recently called to jury duty. He begrudged somewhat this interference with his life, but accepted the call as a good citizen should. His first trial involved a young man accused of "selling stolen goods." The youth was found not guilty, but the businessman was disturbed. He knew that the youth went free, not necessarily because he was innocent, but because the prosecution had failed to make its case. He called on the exonerated youth and, in the quiet of his home, counseled with him for three hours on the ethics of protecting buyers as well as sellers. Why did he do this? Because he felt a love for this young man and believed in him.

To believe in another is Christlike. It calls for faith when others doubt. It calls for work, time, care, and a helping hand when others fail. To see such an opportunity and to seize it is the kind of "living the gospel" that inspires us all to do better. Our opportunities to serve come, sometimes, in the form of a seeming annoyance.

--Lorin F. Wheelwright

*****

The longer we live, the more we realize that the people who want to help themselves can only do so by helping others. It's a basic law of success.

People who begin by asking how they can find success solely within themselves are doomed from the start. The rewards go to people who have searched diligently for ways to help others.

One of the many successful men who have used this principle was James Cash Penney. The fabulous Mr. Penney, starting with a small general merchandise store in Kemmerer, Wyoming, in 1902 built a multi-million-dollar business empire on one simple principle--the golden rule.

For years the Penney stores were called The Golden Rule Stores. And it was Mr. Penney's faith in that principle--always treating a customer as he himself would want to be treated--that made them grow and prosper.

But perhaps even more important was Mr. Penney's attitude toward his employees. In the first place, he did not like the word "employee"; he preferred to treat everyone as a partner, so he called them "associates." And he devoted himself to treating them as he would want to be treated were the situations reversed. Most of all, he knew that by helping them make money, his own success would be assured.

"No man is an island," wrote John Donne. Yet too many of us still fear the loss of self that comes through serving others. Actually, such service is the only true way to "find" yourself.

*****

FOR THE SAKE OF GIVING

John Chapman was a nurseryman in Pittsburgh. He loved all the beautiful things in the world. But he especially loved his great apple orchards when they were in bloom in the spring and when they were loaded with luscious fruit in the fall. He wished everyone could have an apple orchard. He was generous with the young trees and apple seeds. To the many families moving west to make new homes who came to buy young trees, he gave apples for their journeys and seeds, as well as saplings for the orchards they would start in distant prairie lands.

When discouraging letters came back to him, stating that the saplings and seeds did not grow, he felt that it was because the pioneers did not know how to care for their young orchards. This worried him. He thought of the blessings apple orchards would be out in the new country, to homes, to villages, and to the entire new land.

Finally, he decided he must go himself in defense of his trees. It was "as if he heard a call to go and plant orchards in the wilds, to give apple trees to the deprived pioneers." So he dedicated the rest of his life to that kind of giving.

He collected all the apple seeds he could buy or beg and made arrangements so that he could send for more. "Then he went out into the wilderness, vowing that with God's help, he would give the flowers and the fruit of a thousand orchards to the discouraged homesteaders."

He endured many hardships and dangers as he traveled about, putting small nurseries next to isolated cabins, small churches, scattered communities. As the orchards grew, "they helped to bring love and hope and joy where there had been only bitterness and despair."

As the years went by, the trees in orchard after orchard took root and bore blossoms and fruit. The people, too, took root. He had the satisfaction of knowing that he had given a priceless gift to humanity, to civilization. He said that the only reward he hoped for was that there would be orchards to plant and nurture in heaven. Truly Johnny Appleseed gave for the sake of giving, and he gave of himself.

--Eleanor Atkinson

*****

MAGNIFY YOUR CALLING

The telephone rang. The voice of the young lady on the other end of the line was familiar. "Has the copier paper we ordered arrived yet? I have a report to run off for a member of the high council, and he is anxious to get it to use in a meeting being held tomorrow."

I replied that the paper had arrived, but I added, "Virginia, I don't quite understand. When you were married a month ago, you moved out of our stake. We are most grateful to have you continue to help us, but, actually, now that you have moved, we have no further claim on your services. In fact, my responsibility is to encourage you to attend the ward in which you live and to become active there."

"Oh, don't worry about me," was her answer. "The bishop of the ward where we have moved has already given me two jobs, and I am busy working at both of them. But before I left the stake, I promised the high council member I would help him--and it's really no trouble. In fact, I believe the job where I am presently employed came about as the result of my experience working in the Church, and I would feel ungrateful if I did not show my appreciation by trying to help where I can."

I thanked her, hung up the phone, and then sat back, reflecting on the conversation that had just taken place.

I remembered when we first interviewed Virginia and asked her to help out with our typing and copying. She was only sixteen--sweet, shy, frightened, but anxious to do whatever was asked of her in the Church. She moved right in, and for nearly four years took over the complete responsibility for the typing and copying needs of our stake. No job was too big or too time-consuming. She was working for the Lord, and she wanted to do her best.

When it came to her attention that the stake patriarch was losing his secretarial help and needed assistance, it was Virginia who volunteered her services. With the passing months, I saw her grow into a beautiful, talented young woman. She had acquired a reputation not only for great competence, but for her willingness of spirit. She had the love and admiration of all her associates in the Church.

As I sat in reflection, there came to my mind a swatch of conversation I had overheard just the previous Sunday as I stood in the foyer of one of our ward meetinghouses. This time it was another woman speaking--the mother of two children, talking with a friend. She said, "I told them when I was asked to teach Primary that, if I said yes, they might as well know I had no intentions of coming to any other meetings except Primary. I have no time for prayer meeting, monthly teacher preparation meetings, or even sacrament meetings. That's the trouble with ever taking a job in the Church in the first place--someone is always putting the pressure on you to do more."

Her conversation became lost in the crowd, but I was aware, because of other circumstances, that this young woman had neither the respect of her class members nor that of her fellow teachers. She was unwilling to give any extra time or effort to her calling. In fact, her whole attitude was one of giving even less than the minimum--and, in so doing, she deprived herself of the blessing of enlarging her whole soul.

One soon becomes aware that every person falls generally into one or two major categories. The first is the one who can always be counted on to give his best and carry his load; the second is the one who fails to meet his responsibilities and who is content with going halfway. Each person establishes his reputation by his performance.

We learn another great lesson: those who accept willingly and who magnify each call they receive in the Church are the ones who, in the final analysis, receive the greatest benefits. These are they whom the Lord magnifies, to whom he adds the extra "talents," and to whom he makes his promises.

*****

AFTER MANY DAYS IT SHALL RETURN TO YOU

An LDS chapel was to be built in a northern California town. The members of the branch there had been looking forward to this time since six years earlier, when a little old woman, one of the most faithful converts, had handed the branch president five dollars and asked that it be used to start a building fund for a branch chapel. From this small beginning, the fund grew--as did the branch.

Now that the time had arrived to start construction of their Church home, the members of the branch presidency and building committee were determined that nothing should happen to delay the speedy completion of it. So they proceeded to consult the building trade unions. They explained to union officials that they were not asking for donations, although they would not refuse any donations that were offered, but that they wished to do their own work on the building as far as they could; that most of it would be donation work and much of it evening and Saturday work; and asked if there were any objection to union members working on the chapel at these times if they so desired.

No objection was made by any of the building trade unions until an LDS carpenter met with his union to discuss the matter with them. They did not like the idea of carpenter work being done on Saturday, as union carpenters are pledged not to work on Saturday--even for themselves. They told him they would prefer that the work be done on Sunday. It was finally decided that the union would make no objections to Church members doing their donation work whenever they wished.

Then Mr. C, a prominent member of the carpenter's union, asked which church it was that was beginning the new building. He was informed that it was the Church of Jesus Christ of Latter-day Saints, or the one he probably knew as the "Mormon" Church.

Mr. C's attitude changed, and he addressed the entire group. "Brothers," he said, "I would like to tell all of you my experience with the Mormon Church." Mr. C is one of the most respected members of the carpenter's local union, and is a delegate to the central labor council and to the state conventions. When he speaks, they listen.

"A few years ago," he continued, "I was in Casper, Wyoming. The Mormons were remodeling their church building. They were doing it by donation work, and I helped them for two days. They thanked me kindly and gave me a Book of Mormon.

"Sometime later I was working in Salt Lake City, and I became sick. I was staying in a hotel room and was full of misery. The weather was hot, and it seemed like I couldn't breathe. I opened my door, and a Mormon elder who was going through the hotel came in to see me. When he found out what kind of condition I was in, he said he would report it to his bishop right away. A little later that bishop, who appeared to be a businessman, came to see me. He got me a good doctor, and I was soon on my feet again. That Mormon bishop not only paid my doctor bill, but my hotel bill as well. Don't ever hesitate to help the Mormons, for you will never lose anything by it."

The building of the LDS meetinghouse went ahead speedily with the enthusiastic work of the missionaries.

The townspeople were pleasantly surprised when the LDS members did not canvass the city for donations, as other churches did when they constructed their buildings. Some of them said it was too large a building for so small a congregation, and it would put the LDS branch in debt for many years. There were several other churches in the city that had been in the process of building for five to ten years, and there was still a heavy debt burden on them. Many people were very much surprised when the LDS meetinghouse was dedicated less than a year after construction was started--and that the indebtedness was completely satisfied.

--Alvin D. Day

SUCCESS

Aim for service, not success--and success will follow.

*****

If at first you don't succeed, you'll get a lot of advice.

*****

To do for the world more than the world does for you--that is success.

--Henry Ford

*****

The most successful man is the man who holds onto the old just as long as it is good, and grabs the new just as soon as it is better.

*****

Successful people do those things a failure won't do. Sow an action, reap a habit; sow a habit, reap a character; sow a character, reap a destiny.

--William James

*****

Failure may be a real possibility, but refusal to act is to deny all chance of success or happiness.

*****

Get involved despite the threat of failure; he who rises quickly and continues his journey is as though he had never fallen.

*****

If one advances confidently in the direction of his dreams and endeavors to live the life which he has imagined, he will meet success unexpected in common hours.

--Henry David Thoreau

*****

One day back in the Gay Nineties, a fourteen-year-old Brooklyn boy sat down on a curb in the New York shipping district. There he put his brain to work on the problem of how an eighth-grade graduate whose father had just died could earn a living for himself and his family. Emmet J. McCormack had been trying to hook on as an office boy, but four successive firms had told him that they didn't have enough work to keep a boy busy.

After considerable thought, young McCormack rose from the curb and went back to the firms, offering each of them one-fourth of an office boy for $1 per week. They hired him.

McCormack later became co-founder of Moore-McCormack Lines, the second-largest American flag shipping company. But this was his first coup--and, until his death in 1965, he was proud of having been the world's first "syndicated office boy."

*****

RECIPE FOR SUCCESS

To laugh often and much; to win the respect of intelligent people and the affection of children; to earn the appreciation of honest critics and endure the betrayal of false friends; to appreciate beauty; to find the best in others; to leave the world a bit better, whether by a healthy child, a garden patch, or a redeemed social condition; to know even one life has breathed easier because you lived--this is to have succeeded.

--Ralph Waldo Emerson

TEACHING

I hear, and I forget. I see, and I remember. I do, and I understand.

--Chinese Proverb

*****

The great end of education is to discipline rather than to furnish the mind; to train it to the use of its own powers, rather than to fill it with the accumulations of others.

--Tryon Edwards

*****

The aim of education should be to teach rather how to think than what to think--rather to improve our minds so as to enable us to think for ourselves than to load the memory with the thoughts of other men.

--Beattie

*****

THE LESSON

I was given an assignment to be here today,
And, of course, when they ask you, you want to obey.
So I went out and purchased some paper and paint
And proceeded to make this board look like what it ain't.

I worked through the night and into the next day
To make up my posters and figure out what they'd say.
I painted my nails and curled my hair
So that when you looked up here you wouldn't be scared.

I really spent time on my typing and such,
For two days I didn't do mothering much.
I remembered the staples and papers and pins,
And I searched for cute things for beginnings and ends.

I made up some handouts so you wouldn't be guessin'.
And now I just wish I had studied the lesson!

--Barbara Werrett Nielsen

*****

COACHES NEVER LOSE

A team can lose.
Any team can lose.
But in a sense,
A coach never loses.

For the job of a coach
Is over and finished
Once the starting whistle
Blows.
He knows
He's won or lost
Before play starts.

For a coach has two tasks.
The minor one is to
Teach skills:
To teach a boy how to run faster,
Hit harder,
Block better,
Kick farther,
Jump higher.

The second task,
The major task,
Is to make men
Out of boys.

It's to teach an attitude
Of mind.
It's to implant character
And not simply to impart
Skills.
It's to teach boys to
Play fair.
This goes without saying.

It's to teach them
To be humble in victory
And proud in defeat.
This goes without saying.

But, more importantly,
It's to teach them
To live up to their potential
No matter what the
Potential is.

It's to teach them
To do their best
And never be satisfied
With what they are,
But to strive to be
As good as they could be
If they tried harder.

A coach can never make a
Great player
Out of a boy who isn't

Potentially great.
But he can make a
Competitor out of any
Child,
And, miraculously,
He can make a man
Out of a boy.

For a coach,
The final score doesn't mean
So many points for my team,
So many points for theirs.
Instead, it reads:
So many men
Out of so many boys.

And this is a score that
Is never published.
And this is the score
That he reads to himself,
And in which he finds
His real joy
When the last game is over.

*****

THE TYPICAL TEACHER
(We Hope Not!)

There once was a teacher; this tale will be sad,
For he had some habits, and all of them bad.
His intentions were good, as his wish to succeed.
Some ambition was all that this teacher would need.

He felt that he needed a rest for just five
Between each class, to keep him alive.
So into his office he'd rush for his break,
Sit down and relax til the bell would him wake.

Then into the classroom he'd dash for devotion,
But find that his students were caught in commotion.
He'd shout and he'd rave and he'd call them a name,
On all but himself he placed all the blame.

The devotion is over, but as you suppose,
When the teacher stepped forward, a disturbance arose.
"Please, students. . ." he calmly asked them to hush.
But they weren't impressed with that silly old mush.

Twelve minutes gone, he would now call the roll,
Calling each name in his raspy, dull droll.
At the end of the roll there arose such a roar
That our teacher was ready to flee for the door.

Teaching

"Will you please be quiet!" he exploded from the lung;
And the students all chuckle, "He's a funny one."
And finally the silence lies thick as black smoke,
So our teacher decides to tell a good joke.

With the class now in stitches, the spirit all gone,
Our teacher says, "Let's let the lesson get on."
So he pulls out some papers and calls out each name;
This daily procedure is always the same.

With students now reading their papers with care--
Oh, no! It can't be our teacher there,
Giving his lesson, carefully choosing each word,
And the students not listening to this silly old bird.

But this is not all--our man has only begun.
Not realizing that now his time is half gone.
So he has the students copy from the board
The questions; the students moan with single accord.

It's time for discussion, a question he poses,
Not a move, not a sound, the class now transposes.
Blank looks, stupid stares is all he receives.
So he answers the question, the pressure relieves.

Then he sees a twinkle, and a light in an eye,
And a hand shoots up with a soul-rending sigh.
"At last some interest I've finally inspired;
This class isn't listless, or bored, or tired."

So he calls on our student with a satisfied grin,
For the lesson is on faith and works and sin.
"Teacher, what will we eat when we are a spirit?"
The question was good, but the subject not near it.

The student soon leads him off on a byway,
But he's right at home on this oft-traveled highway.
And soon the students are laughing and singing,
They've been saved by the bell with its musical ringing.

Tomorrow he'll play a record or tape,
For he's unprepared and in a bad scrape.
The next day's for study, the students sleep on.
No good will be gained, but another day's gone.

The third day a speaker will be at our school,
For a teacher's vacation, 'tis a wonderful tool.

And question-and-answer periods are always so fine.
Can you think of a better way to waste lots of time?

The year hurries on, and if you're like me,
Moses will still be in the Red Sea.
For I talk about things of no great import,
Just things that come up of any old sort.

So on goes our story--oh, isn't it fun?
Except when you realize you're the son-of-a-gun.
Yes, the teacher above, you'll recognize, too,
For the teacher above is none other than you!

So don't you start planning your lessons ahead,
Or the teacher above soon will be dead.
And born in his place, a servant of God,
Following the trail where the Master trod.

                    --M. Palmer and A. Stringham

                    *****

                    THE LITTLE BOY

Once a little boy went to school;
He was quite a little boy,
And it was quite a big school.
But when the little boy
Found that he could go to his room
By walking right in from the door outside,
He was happy.
And the school did not seem
Quite so big any more.

One morning,
When the little boy had been in school awhile,
The teacher said,
"Today we are going to make a picture."
"Good!" thought the little boy.
He liked to make pictures.
He could make all kinds--
Lions and tigers,
Chickens and cows,
Trains and boats.
And he took out his box of crayons
And began to draw.

But the teacher said, "Wait!
It is not time to begin!"
And she waited until everyone looked ready.

"Now," said the teacher,
"We are going to make flowers."
"Good!" thought the little boy.
He liked to make flowers,
And he began to make beautiful ones
With his pink and orange and blue crayons.

But the teacher said, "Wait!
I will show you how."
Her flower was red, with a green stem.

Teaching

"There," said the teacher,
"Now you may begin."

The little boy looked at the teacher's flower.
Then he looked at his own flower.
He liked his flower better than the teacher's,
But he didn't say anything.
He just turned his paper over
And made a flower like the teacher's.
It was red, with a green stem.

On another day,
When the little boy had opened
The door from the outside all by himself,
The teacher said,
"Today we are going to make something with clay."
"Good!" thought the little boy.
He liked clay.

He could make all kinds of things with clay--
Snakes and snowmen,
Elephants and mice,
Cars and trucks.
And he began to pull and pinch
His ball of clay.

But the teacher said, "Wait!
It is not time to begin!"
And she waited until everyone looked ready.

"Now," said the teacher,
"We are going to make a dish."
"Good!" thought the little boy.
He liked to make dishes.
And he began to make some
That were all shapes and sizes.

Then the teacher said, "Wait!
And I will show you how!"
And she showed everyone how to make
One deep dish.
"There," said the teacher,
"Now you may begin."

The little boy looked at his teacher's dish.
Then he looked at his own.
He liked his dishes better than the teacher's,
But he didn't say anything.
He just rolled his clay into a big ball again
And made a dish like the teacher's.
It was a deep dish.

And pretty soon,
The little boy learned to wait,

And to watch,
And to make things just like the teacher.
And pretty soon,
He didn't make things of his own anymore.
Then it happened
That the little boy and his family
Moved to another house
In another city,
And the little boy
Had to go to another school.

This school was even bigger
Than the other one,
And there was no door from the outside
Into his room.
He had to go up some big steps,
And walk down a long hall
To get to his room.

And the very first day
He was there,
The teacher said,
"Today we are going to make a picture."
"Good!" thought the little boy,
And he waited for the teacher
To tell him what to do.
But the teacher didn't say anything.
She just walked around the room.

When she came to the little boy,
She said, "Don't you want to make a picture?"
"Yes," said the little boy,
"What are we going to make?"
"I don't know until you make it," said the teacher.
"How shall I make it?" asked the little boy.
"Why, any way you like," said the teacher.
"And any color?" asked the little boy.
"Any color," said the teacher.
"If everyone made the same picture,
And used the same colors,
How would I know who made what,
And which was which?"
"I don't know," said the little boy,
And he began to make a red flower with a green stem.

--Helen E. Buckley

*****

A TEACHER'S PRAYER

Lord, give me the wisdom to discover in each child his spark of divinity, the gift that you have given him, and through love and guidance to nurture this spark into a glowing flame.

261

Let me not favor any one child at the expense of others. Let all be equally worthy of my devotion without regard to their intelligence, their religion, their race, or their wealth.

Let me teach a love of America, by keeping ever alive her commitment to the greatest good for the greatest number in the belief that these children are your greatest good and your greatest number.

Lord, help! They're coming into the room right now, all thirty-two of them. Any small miracle will be greatly appreciated. Amen.

--Sam Levenson

*****

A little more than fifty years ago a Johns Hopkins professor gave a group of graduate students this assignment: Go to the slums. Take two hundred boys, between the ages of twelve and sixteen, and investigate their background and environment. Then predict their chances for the future.

The students, after consulting social statistics, talked to the boys, and, compiling much data, concluded that 90 percent of the boys would eventually spend some time in jail.

Twenty-five years later another group of graduate students was given the job of testing the prediction. They went back to the slum. Some of the boys--now men--were still there; a few had died; some had moved away. But they got in touch with one hundred and eighty of the original two hundred. They found that only four of the group had ever been sent to jail.

Why was it that these men, who had lived in a breeding place of crime, had such a surprisingly good record? The researchers were continually told, "Well, there was a teacher. . . ."

They pressed further, and found that in 75 percent of the cases it was the same woman. The researchers went to this teacher, now living in a home for retired teachers. How had she exerted this remarkable influence over a group of slum children? Could she give any reason why these boys should remember her?

"No," she said, "no, I really couldn't." And then, thinking back over the years, she said musingly, more to herself than to her questioners, "I loved those boys. . . ."

*****

A BOY BECOMES A MAN

It was his second day of school when the little brown-eyed, tousle-haired boy in blue overalls came home early. Shuffling his five-year-old feet heavily in the dust, he trudged up the long road to the ranch house near Jackson, Wyoming. Mother, alerted by his untimely return, went to the porch and dropped to her knees beside him.

His lips were tightly shut, but trembling. His cheeks were smeared where there had been tears. The note in his hand was smudged:

"It is our judgment that your son is uneducable. The impediment in his speech disrupts classroom procedure, and it is our recommendation. . . ."

"Uneducable," the teacher's note said, because he stuttered too much.

But there was in those days another teacher in Jackson, Wyoming, named Martha Marean. Her name was pronounced like "Marine," and she was-- taunting schoolboys said--built like one.

The boy's distraught mother returned the note to the log schoolhouse. Her appeal was denied. But big Martha Marean overheard and she, too, refused to accept the verdict as final. She asked permission to work with the boy after school hours. Miss Marean was convinced his stuttering could be controlled, that he could be educated.

And she did work with the boy until, one day, little Cliff was re-enrolled in school, and so began his education. The speech defect was controlled, not cured.

With patience and persistence, dedication and determination, Martha Marean continued to coach the lad. The self-confidence that his stammering had cost needed to be rebuilt. It was. Through her sympathy and understanding, the boy who had been turned away from school as "uneducable" became a superior student.

With Miss Marean's help and his mother's loving patience, the handicap grew progressively less--until one day, long after he had lost touch with his elementary school teacher, Cliff, now a man, was scheduled to make a speech in public. . .to an audience. . .of teachers.

With a little searching, he located Martha Marean. Would she come to Cheyenne to the Wyoming Education Association meeting to hear him speak?

Of course she would.

She was on her way to Cheyenne, the Wyoming Highway Patrol reported, when her car skidded on a rain-slickened curve. Martha Marean was killed.

And so, against a backdrop of tragedy, Cliff made his speech:

"Ladies and gentlemen, I did want for one particular teacher to be here today to hear me speak, because it is largely due to her efforts that I can.

"In an era when we tend to mass-produce education, I wanted to honor, in this small way, this uncommon woman so that all teachers everywhere might be reminded of the awesomeness of their responsibility, the magnitude of their opportunity."

But Martha Marean was not there--or was she?--as the Honorable Clifford Hansen, Governor of Wyoming, paid homage to her name.

--Paul Harvey

*****

THE INDISPENSABLE TIGER

A powerful old tiger, the leader of the pack, was preparing to go on a hunt. Gathering the other tigers around him, he said, "We must go out into the plains and hunt, for the winter is coming. You young fellows come with me; perhaps you will learn a thing or two."

The young tigers were pleased to hear this, for the old fellow had hitherto shown no interest in them. He usually left them behind when he went foraging, and they were tired of doing nothing but keeping order among the cubs and performing other routine tasks.

The first day out, the old tiger spotted a herd of elephants. "Here's your chance, Bernard," he said to one of the young tigers. "Look at it as a challenge."

But Bernard had no idea how to go about hunting. With a roar, he rushed at the elephants, who ran off in all directions. "It looks as though I'll have to do the job myself," said the leader philosophically. And so he did.

The next day, the tigers came upon a herd of water buffalo. "Suppose you take over now, Jerome," said the old tiger, and Jerome, reluctant to ask silly questions but determined to do his best, crept up on the grazing buffalo. He leaped straight at the largest of them, but the big buffalo tossed him to the ground, and Jerome was lucky to escape in one piece. Mortified, he crept back to the group.

"No, no, no!" said the old tiger. "What's happening to performance around here?"

"But you never taught us how to do it!" cried one of the young tigers. The old tiger was in no mood to listen. "The rest of you stay where you are," he growled, "and I will do the job myself." And so he did.

"I can see," said the old tiger, as the others gathered admiringly about him, "that none of you is yet ready to take my place." He sighed. "Much as I hate to say it, I seem to be indispenable."

Time brought little change. The old tiger sometimes took the younger ones along with him on hunts, and occasionally he let one of them try to make a kill. But having received no instruction, they were unequal to the task. And the old tiger still made no effort to teach the others his tricks; he had forgotten that he himself was a product of tiger-to-tiger coaching.

One day, when he had grown quite old, the tiger met a friend--a wise lion he had known for years. Before long, the tiger was launched on his favorite topic of conversation: the lack of initiative in the younger generation.

"Would you believe it?" he asked the lion. "Here I am, getting a bit long in the tooth, and I still have to do all the hunting for my pack. There seems to be no one of my stripes around."

"That's odd," said the lion. "I find the younger lions in my pack take well to instruction. Some of them are carrying a good bit of responsibility. In fact," he continued, "I'm thinking about retiring next year and letting the younger fellows take over."

"I envy you," said the tiger. "I'd take things easier and relax myself if I only saw a little leadership material around me." The old tiger sighed and shook his head. "You can't imagine," he said, "what a burden it is to be indispensable."

--The American Management Association

*****

NO ONE CARED

A twelfth-grade New York student, starved for attention, handed the following poem to his teacher:

He always wanted to explain things,
But no one cared,
So he drew.
Sometimes he would draw and it wasn't anything.
He wanted to carve it in stone or write it in the sky.
He would lie out on the grass and look up at the sky,
And it would be only the sky and him and the things inside him
    that needed saying.
And it was after that he drew the picture.
It was a beautiful picture.
He kept it under his pillow and would let no one see it.
And he would look at it every night and think about it.
And when it was dark, and his eyes were closed, he could still
    see it.
It was all of him.
And he loved it.
When he started school, he brought it with him.
Not to show anyone, but just to have it with him, like a friend.
It was funny about school.
He sat in a square, brown desk,
Like all the other square, brown desks,
And he thought it should be red.
And his room was a square, brown room,
Like all the other rooms.
He hated to hold the pencil and chalk
With his arm stiff and his feet flat on the floor, stiff,

With the teacher watching and watching.
The teacher came and spoke to him;
She told him to wear a tie like all the other boys.
He said he didn't like them,
And she said it didn't matter!
After that they drew.
And he drew yellow, and it was the way he felt about morning.
And it was beautiful.
The teacher smiled at him.
"What's this?" she said. "Why don't you draw something like
     Ken's drawing? Isn't that beautiful?"
After that his mother bought him a tie,
And he always drew airplanes and rocket ships like everyone else.
And he threw the old picture away.
And when he lay out alone looking at the sky, it was big and blue
     and all of everything.
But he wasn't anymore. He was square inside. And brown.
And his hands were stiff, and was like everyone else.
And the things inside him that needed saying didn't need it
     anymore.
It had stopped pushing. It was crushed. Stiff.
Like everything else.

     The teacher couldn't help but be surprised--such creativity! Such
flair! Could this twelfth-grade boy really have composed such a poem?
No one knows whether he actually wrote the poem. But they do know that,
shortly afterward, he committed suicide. You see, nothing needed saying
anymore.

                         --Carolyn Seals

                         *****

                    OUT OF THE DARK

     The most important day I remember in all my life is the one on which
my teacher, Anne Mansfield Sullivan, came to me. I am filled with wonder
when I consider the immeasurable contrast between the two lives that it
connects. It was the third of March, 1887, three months before I was
seven years old.

     On the afternoon of that eventful day, I stood on the porch, dumb,
expectant. I guessed vaguely from my mother's signs and from the
hurrying to and fro in the house that something unusual was about to
happen, so I went to the door and waited on the steps. The afternoon sun
penetrated the mass of honeysuckle that covered the porch, and fell on my
upturned face. My fingers lingered almost unconsciously on the familiar
leaves and blossoms that had just come forth to greet the sweet southern
spring. I did not know what the future held of marvel or surprise for
me. Anger and bitterness had preyed upon me continually for weeks, and
deep languor had succeeded this passionate struggle.

     Have you ever been at sea in a dense fog, when it seemed as if a
tangible white darkness shut you in, and the great ship, tense and
anxious, groped her way toward the shore with plummet and sounding line,
and you waited with beating heart for something to happen? I was like

that ship before my education began, only I was without compass or sounding line, and had no way of knowing how near the harbor was. "Light! Give me light!" was the wordless cry of my soul, and the light of love shone on me in that very hour.

I felt approaching footsteps. I stretched out my hand, as I supposed, to my mother. Someone took it, and I was caught up and held close in the arms of her who had come to reveal all things to me--and, more than all things else, to love me.

The morning after my teacher came, she led me into her room and gave me a doll. The little blind children at the Perkins Institution had sent it, and Laura Bridgman had dressed it. When I had played with it a little while, Miss Sullivan slowly spelled into my hand the word d-o-l-l. I was at once interested in this finger play, and tried to imitate it. When I finally succeeded in making the letters correctly, I was flushed with childish pleasure and pride. Running downstairs to my mother, I held up my hand and made the letters for doll. I did not know that I was spelling a word, or even that words existed; I was simply making my fingers go in monkey-like imitation. In the days that followed, I learned to spell in this uncomprehending way a great many words, among them pin, hat, cup, and a few verbs like sit, stand, and walk. But my teacher had been with me several weeks before I understood that everything has a name.

One day while I was playing with my new doll, Miss Sullivan put my big rag doll into my lap alongside my new doll, spelled d-o-l-l, and tried to make me understand that d-o-l-l applied to both. Earlier in the day we had had a tussle over the words m-u-g and w-a-t-e-r. Miss Sullivan had tried to impress upon me that m-u-g is _mug_ and that w-a-t-e-r is _water_, but I was persistent in confounding the two. In despair, she had dropped the subject for the time, only to renew it at the first opportunity.

I became impatient at her repeated attempts and, seizing the new doll, I dashed it upon the floor. I was keenly delighted when I felt the fragments of the broken doll at my feet. Neither sorrow nor regret followed my passionate outburst. I had not loved the doll. In the still, dark world in which I lived there was no strong sentiment or tenderness. I felt my teacher sweep the fragments to one side of the hearth, and I had a sense of satisfaction that the cause of my discomfort was removed. She brought me my hat, and I knew I was going out into the warm sunshine. This thought, if a wordless sensation may be called a thought, made me hop and skip with pleasure.

We walked down the path to the well house, attracted by the fragrance of the honeysuckle with which it was covered. Someone was drawing water, and my teacher placed my hand under the spout. As the cool stream gushed over one hand, she spelled into the other _water_--first slowly, then rapidly. I stood still, my whole attention fixed on the motions of her fingers. Suddenly I felt a misty consciousness as of something forgotten--a thrill of returning thought. Somehow, the mystery of language was revealed to me. I knew then that w-a-t-e-r meant the wonderful cool something that was flowing over my hand. That living word awakened my soul, gave it light, hope, joy--and set it free! There were barriers still, it is true, but barriers that could in time be swept away.

I left the well house eager to learn. Everything had a name, and each name gave birth to a new thought. As we returned to the house, every object I touched seemed to quiver with life. That was because I saw everything with the strange new light that had come to me. On entering the door, I remembered the doll I had broken. I felt my way to the hearth and picked up the pieces. I tried vainly to put them together. Then my eyes filled with tears, for I realized what I had done--and, for the first time, I felt repentance and sorrow.

I learned a great many new words that day. I do not remember what they all were, but I do know that mother, father, sister, and teacher were among them--words that were to make the world blossom for me, "like Aaron's rod, with flowers." It would have been difficult to find a happier child than I was as I lay in my crib at the close of that eventful day, living over the joys it had brought me. For the first time, I longed for a new day to come.

--Helen Keller

TIME

Nine-tenths of wisdom is being wise in time.

--Theodore Roosevelt

*****

Lose an hour in the morning, and you will be all day hunting it.

*****

You will never "find time" for anything. If you want time, you must make it.

*****

People who cannot find time for recreation are obliged, sooner or later, to find time for illness.

--John Wanamaker

*****

Your inheritance is time. It is capital more precious than any lands or stocks or houses you will ever get. Spend it foolishly, and you will bankrupt yourself. Invest it wisely, and you will bless generations to come.

--Henry B. Eyring

*****

You must give some time to your fellow man. Even if it's a little thing, do something for those who have need of help, something for which you get no pay but the privilege of doing it. For remember--you don't live in a world all your own. Your brothers are here, too.

*****

We have to live thoughtfully, to be discriminating as to everything that takes our time. We must in some measure eliminate the insignificant, the inconsequential, and not let our lives be broken into little pieces that get lost along the way. We need to live so that we can see a pattern, a plan, a purpose, and make every motion, every moment more meaningful.

--Richard L. Evans

*****

Time is one gift that is democratically distributed.

Guard your spare moments; they are like uncut diamonds. Discard them, and their value will never be known. Improve them, and they will become the brightest gems in a useful life.

--Ralph Waldo Emerson

*****

SIX STEPS TO MASTERING TIME

1. MAKE NOTES. Use a pencil and paper. Many seemingly big problems become progressively smaller when you break them down on a piece of paper. Leave a pad of notepaper at every strategic location in your home and work area. Put a pencil and paper beside your bed, or on the breakfast table, and on the sun visor of your car. Be prepared to "write it down" any time, day or night. Or, better yet, keep your planner near you at all times so that all ideas and details can be kept in one organized place.

2. REMOVE DISTRACTIONS FROM YOUR WORK AREA. Keep your desk or worktable as clean as possible. Eliminate such temptations to idleness as newspapers, personal letters, and souvenirs. And once a job is completed, get it out of sight and out of the way.

3. DISCOURAGE INTERRUPTIONS. Set up certain times in every workday when you can't be reached. Eliminate idle conversation when you're transacting business. Storytellers can wreck every deadline you set. And beware of the telephone--it can be either a time saver or a time waster. Only _you_ can control it.

4. LEARN TO SAY "NO." It's one of the most valuable and effective words in the English language. Don't let yourself be talked into commitments on things or projects in which you have no real interest. Be selective. Remember, it's _your_ time you are spending.

5. LET THE POSTMAN BE YOUR ERRAND BOY. If running around eats into your valuable time, you can hire a United States postman for just a few cents. The U.S. Postal Service is the most reliable messenger service in the world. Let him deliver magazines and books, make bank deposits, and carry the checks for payment of household bills.

6. LEARN TO LISTEN CAREFULLY. You won't have to waste time checking back to verify your understanding. Get all of the facts--who, what, when, where, and why--the first time you're exposed to them. Write them in your planner so they don't clutter your mind. Don't dash off to a dental appointment on Tuesday, when it really isn't scheduled until later in the week--all because you didn't listen carefully and make notes when the date was first arranged.

VALUES

A learned man has always wealth within him.

*****

Your possessions pass, and are forgotten. What you are, and what you help others to be, abides in the eternity of God.

--Harold Marshall

*****

Walking uplifts the spirit. Breathe out the poisons of tension, stress, and worry; breathe in the power of God. Send forth little silent prayers of goodwill toward those you meet. Walk with a sense of being a part of a vast universe. Consider the thousands of miles of earth beneath your feet; think of the limitless expanse of space above your head. Walk in awe, wonder, and humility. Walk at all times of day--in the early morning when the world is just waking up, late at night under the stars, and along a busy city street at noontime.

--Wilferd Peterson

*****

THOUGHTS ARE THINGS

I hold it true that thoughts are things;
They're endowed with bodies and breath and wings.
And we send them forth to fill
The world with good results, or ill.
That which we call our secret thought
Speeds forth to earth's remotest spot,
Leaving its blessings or its woes
Like tracks behind it as it goes.
We build our future, thought by thought,
For good or ill, yet know it not.
Yet, so the universe was wrought.
Thought is another name for fate;
Choose, then, thy destiny and wait,
For love brings love, and hate brings hate.

--Henry Van Dyke

*****

TWO SIDES

Two boys went to gather grapes. One was happy because they found grapes; the other was unhappy because the grapes had seeds in them.

Two men, convalescing, were asked how they were. One said, "I am better today." The other moaned, "I was worse yesterday."

271

When it rains, one man says, "This will make mud"; another exclaims, "This will lay the dust."
Two boys examined a bush. One observed that it had a thorn, while the other saw only the rose.

Two children looked through colored glasses. One said, "The world is blue," while the other said, "It is bright!"

Two boys had a bee. One got stung, while the other got honey; one called it a honey bee, the other a stinging bee.

"I am glad to be alive," said one man. Another reflected, "I am sad that I must die."

"I am glad," says one, "that things are no worse." "I am sorry," replies the other, "that they are no better."

One says, "Our good is mixed with evil." The other says, "Our evil is mixed with good."

--Moody

*****

DUTY, HONOR, COUNTRY

Duty, honor, country. Those three hallowed words reverently dictate what you ought to be, what you can be, what you will be. They are your rallying points: to build courage when courage seems to fail; to regain faith when there seems little cause for faith; to create hope when hope becomes forlorn. They build your basic character, they make you strong enough to know when you are weak, and brave enough to face yourself when you are afraid.

They teach you to be proud and unbending in honest failure, but humble and gentle in success; not to substitute words for actions, nor to seek the path of comfort, but to face the stress and spur of difficulty and challenge; to learn to stand up in the storm, but to have compassion on those who fall; to master yourself before you seek to master others; to have a heart that is clean, a goal that is high; to learn to laugh, yet never forget how to weep; to reach into the future, yet never neglect the past; to be serious, yet never take yourself too seriously; to be modest so that you will remember the simplicity of true greatness, the open mind of true wisdom, the meekness of true strength.

They give you a temper of the will, a quality of the imagination, a vigor of the emotions, a freshness of the deep springs of life, a temperamental predominance of courage over
timidity, an appetite for adventure over love of ease. They create in your heart the sense of wonder, the unfailing hope of what's next, and the joy and inspiration of life.

--Douglas MacArthur

CHILDREN ARE SPECIAL

Whenever we go shopping, we look for advertised specials--those things that will provide us the greatest value for the least amount of money. These are not always the things that cost less in dollars and cents, but rather those things that cost less proportionately.

In the marketplace of living, no special has ever compared to children. We are attracted in some stores to signs tht read, "Yours for only $1.98." The signs on children in the marketplace of living read, "Yours for only the time and the trouble," "Yours for only the work and the worry," or "Yours for only the patience and understanding." Children are yours--and the price is love.

Time, trouble, work, worry, patience, understanding, and love are such a small price to pay for so important a value that even those who don't fully comprehend the total worth of children desire nothing more than to have them for their own.

There are those salesmen, however, who would deceive you. They would tell you luxurious furniture is more important, that lavishly decorated homes matter much more, that freedom from responsibility and care are more to be desired, that purebred dogs and cats are more deserving of your time and trouble, your work and your worry, your patience and your understanding. Don't let such salesmen deceive you. They would have you sell your birthright for a mess of pottage.

It is people, not things, who are special. They are products of distinct and special creation. Talk about valuable antiques! Children existed long before antiques ever came into this world, as spirit children of our Heavenly Father, and they will go on living, worlds without end. They will endure long after this world and its pleasures are gone--and will add glory to your house forever and ever.

Should you seek to purchase only two such specials? Or should you get all you possibly can? The wonderful thing about this purchase is that as you spend patience and understanding, it increases. As you give love, it is returned. As you give time and trouble, work and worry, they in turn are given to you. Your purchasing power is unlimited!

WORD OF WISDOM

Take one well-rounded fool. Soak in several drinks of liquor. Mix in one high-powered car.

After fool is thoroughly soaked, put foot on gas and turn key. After due amount of time, remove from car, place in a black box, and garnish with flowers.

*****

Soon after the repeal of the Eighteenth Amendment to the Constitution, a liquor journal lamented, "The saloon fills a great social void in the community." A. C. Bane took the challenge, and wrote the following:

It is true that the saloon fills a void.
It fills men's stomachs with poison.
It fills jails with drunkards.
It fills penitentiaries with criminals.
It fills poorhouses with paupers.
It fills hospitals with sick and injured.
It fills asylums with insane.
It fills orphanages with orphans.
It fills our streets with loafers.
It fills labor's ranks with incompetents.
It fills homes with sorrow.
It fills wives and children with want.
It fills court calendars with cases.
It fills property records with mortgages.
It fills communities with disorder.
It fills politics with corruption.
It fills politicians with fear.
It fills graves with the dead.
It fills hell with the damned.
It is true, sadly true, that the saloon fills a void.

--Frankie Barlow

*****

A WALK THROUGH ETERNITY

I walked through the midst of eternity
And in the valley of life,
I found the sweetest girl of all,
And she became my wife.
We met and married here on earth,
And then I loved her more.
Through life we'd walk inseparable
Right up to death's dark door.

But when that door swings open
And one of us goes through,
Will we ever be united

As when we said, "I do"?
Could death part us so easily
And rob us of our love?
And what about our children--
Would we see them up above?

Why do you question death, my friend,
Why do you fear its power?
For wasn't death defeated
In resurrection's hour?
For Christ sweat blood and gave his life
That you might live again,
But not for you alone he came--
He died to save all men.

The only force that guides your life,
That makes you good or bad,
The only power that God has given
To make you happy or sad
Is the power of your decision--
Your right to choose each day,
Whether you will follow righteousness
Or walk a darker way.

It's not the cigarette that keeps
A man from heaven's throne;
It's not the tea or coffee that maroons
A man alone.
It's not the silver dollar that was
Stolen from the Lord,
But you, my friend, are the one
To fear--it's you who gives the word.

My wife cried out in pain one night,
No doctor could I call.
She pleaded, "Please come bless me,
My husband, straight and tall."
My hands reached out to touch her,
Her blessing she would get;
But as I gazed upon those hands
I saw a cigarette.

Oh, sure, I held the priesthood,
I received it years ago,
But how to use that power
Was the thing I didn't know.
I had to call the bishop
To come and bless my mate--
If she had had to wait for me
T'would soon have been too late.

That night I learned my lesson,
I found the man to fear.
No more would just a tiny weed

Wisdom

Part me from all that's dear.
I walk through the midst of eternity
And in the valley of life
With an eternal family--
My children and my wife.

--Arnold J. Stringham

WOMAN

WOMANHOOD

I heard the many women
Cry out for equal rights.
I pondered, then I questioned--
What is this futile fight?

We, in most every culture,
Are treated with respect.
So, why demand equality
And ask for his neglect?

Women so clearly different
By their own design,
Yet losing all distinction?
I'm holding on to mine!

Women because our maker
Planned that we should be,
And womanhood will be our role
Throughout eternity.

So, fight to keep your privileges.
Here is how you can:
Don't climb down from your pedestal
To be equal to a man!

--Sue Dean

*****

How fair is the daughter of Zion
    Whose body is unsullied.
How serene is her brow
    That houses a pure mind.
How clear is her eye,
    Shining with the light of truth.
How beautiful are her cheeks,
    Unblushed with shame.
How sweet are her lips,
    Untasting of forbidden fruit.
How lovely are her arms,
    Shaped for the nurturing of motherhood.
How sacred are her breasts,
    Life fountains for the babes, born of her flesh.
How holy is her body
    For the fashioning of her offspring,
    Begot under the covenant.
How angel-like her mind,
    The dwelling-place of righteousness.

Woman

How priceless is her soul,
    Daughter of God,
    Glorified for the eternities.

                    --J. Reuben Clark, Jr.

                    *****

                "IF" FOR GIRLS

If you can smile, and share another's gladness
    Though yours may be denied, and still rejoice;
If you can bravely face regret and sadness
    And let no bitter accent tinge your voice;
If you are free from bias and fault-finding
    And make your creed the Golden Rule;
With neither fear nor doubt your vision blinding
    Can live each day serene, and sweet, and cool--

If you can bar out envy from your spirit
    And keep the little jealousies away;
If, when some gossip starts, you do not hear it
    Unless at once you rise and ask fair play;
If you can let good sense determine pleasure,
    Can look upon yourself with honest eyes;
If you can give your friendship in full measure
    And find your life the stronger for its ties--

If you can set desire below your duty,
    And find in work and study much of joy;
If you can turn from artificial beauty
    To that real charm which never needs alloy;
If you can help where you know help is needed,
    And even make your silence sympathize;
If you can let unkindness go unheeded,
    And always see God's sunshine in the skies--

If you can fill your soul with gentle kindness,
    And hold your faith no matter what may come;
Let neither greed nor pride blight you with blindness,
    Nor self-love all your finer motives numb;
If you can love, and hope with rare believing,
    Can shun the dross, and ever seek the worth,
Then you will find life's fabric you are weaving
    Means womanhood--God's greatest gift to earth.

                    --Wilbur D. Nesbit

                    *****

            WOMANHOOD: A PARTNERSHIP WITH GOD

    Did women by their own first choice choose to be partners with God in
his creative processes? Faced with an alternative--partnership or
priesthood--did you, sister, pass up priesthood?

                    278

Did women by their own free choice choose to be the family heart rather than the family head? Scripturally, "the husband is the head of the wife" (Ephesians 5:23), and he is the family priest and spokesman. Did God, however, in this infinite wisdom, purposely make mother the family heart, blessing her with subtle power to sway his head?

God, choosing woman to be his partner in the creating process, tucked away somewhere in her bosom a spark of his divine love--which later, at the time of motherhood, glows to brilliancy in every mother's heart.

> There is a center in every home
> From which all joys must start.
> Where is that center?
> It's in the mother's heart.

*****

Lady, whence comest thou? Knowest thou not that thou art a spark of Deity, struck from the fire of his eternal blaze, and brought forth in the midst of eternal burning?

Knowest thou not that thy spirit, pure and holy, dwelt in thy Father's bosom and in his presence, and with thy mother, the queen of heaven, surrounded by thy brother and sister spirits in the spirit world, among the Gods?

Thou bade Father, Mother, and all farewell, and came to this world. The spirits thou hast chosen to come and tabernacle through their lineage had left the spirit world some years earlier, and thou came a spirit pure and holy. Thou hast chosen him you loved in the spirit world to be thy companion. Now, crowns, thrones, exaltations, and dominions are in reserve for thee in the eternal worlds, and the way is opened for thee to return to the presence of thy Heavenly Father, if thou wilt only abide by and walk in a celestial law, fulfilling the designs of thy creator and holding out to the end, that when mortality is laid in the tomb you may go down to your grave in peace, arise in glory, and receive your everlasting reward in the resurrection of the just, along with thy head and husband.

Thou wilt be permitted to pass by Gods and angels who guard the gates and onward, upward, to thy exaltation in a celestial world among the Gods, to be a priestess and queen upon thy Heavenly Father's throne. There thou wilt be a glory to thy husband and offspring, wilt bear the souls of men to people other worlds, while eternity goes and eternity comes.

And if thou wilt receive it, lady, this is eternal life.

--John Taylor

*****

I'M LIBERATED!
(With a Husband and Six Kids?)

Perhaps one of the most difficult things a person does in life is realize his or her station, so to speak.

I've listened to and read some productive--and some not so productive--articles regarding "women's liberation." So far, it seems that to be liberated means to be totally equal. Why do people have to go to such great lengths to achieve total equality? Granted, there are many facets of women's liberation that seem necessary, but does it have to be every woman's bag?

My husband and I have been married for nine and a half years. If I had to sit down and say what things are specifically his, I would probably say his shaving lather (I use half of the razor), wardrobe, and eyeglasses. The only items that are specifically mine are my clothes, electric curlers, and contact lenses. Oh, yes--I can see you saying, "Wait a minute--you own more than that!" or, "Legally, this and that and this and that belong to you, not to that male chauvenist pig!"

Wrong.

How can I claim all household items when he helps me clean, cook, and wash? Or how can he claim all of the horse equipment when we use it as a family? Or how can either of us say our home belongs to only one when we both worked on it and built a dream with all four hands--plus? How could I ever claim the children were mine when he has been beside me and counted hundreds of contractions in my labor room and watched each of our children enter this world?

Rather than being preoccupied with the idea that everything has to be designated as "his" and "hers," I like to feel that because we have been united and worked together, most things can be called "ours." We didn't have a special contract drawn up when we married stating that he uses his earnings for his needs and I use my earnings for mine. We've always pooled paychecks. I've worked six years out of the nine to take care of "our" needs.

To be liberated doesn't mean being as accomplished as your husband merely to show the world you can push and drive as hard as a man, or because you feel that women aren't accomplished if they are mere "homebodies." Being liberated does mean doing what gives you the greatest satisfaction and enjoyment in life. Granted, many career women are totally content in their world of business, and that's great for them. However, most publications indicate that we can't achieve success unless we become professional women.

What are some of the duties and responsibilities of a homemaker? She's a cook, maid, seamstress, nurse, night watchman, interior decorator, nutritionist, gardener, window washer, financial assistant (or director), beautician, carpenter, toy repairman, child psychologist, wife, and mother. How can the role of good old womanhood be considered a drag?

One of the things I've experienced that really testifies to the important role women play in the lives of other people was a recent car accident. I was home about five hours after the accident, and women had hot food on the stove for my family and my children were being cared for by loving, comforting hands. That support continued, enabling me to stay in bed at home for a week because lovely women were caring for my family.

Each of these women are truly "liberated" women, because they are able to give of themselves. They know that service to fellow human beings is vital. We can all be liberated if we involve ourselves in other people's lives. There are endless community needs, and volunteer work is always needed. Hospitals are full of people who don't have family or friends, and just a friendly smile would replace an entire bottle of medicine. Human compassion and understanding is a wonderful gift that most women possess, and giving this love away and helping others become happier allows us to become liberated.

--Beverly Martin

WORK

The work you have accomplished is the only real legacy you can leave the world.

--David Lloyd George

*****

The highest reward for a man's toil is not what he gets for it, but what he becomes by it.

*****

Only those who have the patience to do simple things perfectly will acquire the skill to do difficult things easily.

--Johann Schiller

*****

There are two things needed in these days: first, for rich men to find out how poor men live, and, second, for poor men to find out how rich men work.

--E. Atkinson

*****

NOW LET'S ALL GET TO WORK

Said the little red rooster, "Believe me, things are tough!
Seems that worms are scarcer, and I cannot find enough;
What's become of all those fat ones is a mystery to me;
There were thousands through that rainy spell, but now where can
    they be?"
Then the old black hen who heard him did not grumble or complain;
She had gone through lots of dry spells, she had lived through
    floods and rain.
So she flew upon the grindstone, and she gave her claws a whet
As she said, "I've never seen the time there were no worms to
    get."
She picked a new and undug spot, the earth was hard and firm.
The rooster jeered: "New ground! That's no place for a worm."
The old black hen just spread her feet, she dug both fast and
    free;
"I must go to the worms," she said, "the worms won't come to me."
The rooster vainly spent his day, through habit, by the ways
Where fat round worms had passed in squads back in the rainy
    days.

When nightfall found him supperless, he growled in accents rough,
"I'm hungry as a fowl can be. Conditions sure are tough!"

He turned then to the old black hen, and said, "It's worse with
   you--
For you're not only hungry, but you must be tired, too.
I rested while I watched for worms, so I feel fairly perk,
But how are you? Without worms, too, and after all your work?"
The old black hen hopped to her perch and dropped her eyes to
   sleep,
And murmured in a drowsy tone, "Young man, hear this and weep:
I'm full of worms and happy, for I've eaten like a pig.
The worms are there as always--but, boy, I had to dig."

*****

THE RESULTS OF INITIATIVE

Some years ago, three brothers left the farm to work in the city.
They were all hired by the same company at the same pay. Three years
later, Jim was being paid $500 a month, Frank was receiving $1,000, but
George was now making $1,500.

Their father decided to visit the employer and find out the basis for
the unequal pay. The employer listened to the confused father and said,
"I will let the boys explain for themselves."

Jim was summoned to the supervisor's office and told, "Jim, I
understand that Far East Importers have just brought in a large transport
plane loaded with Japanese import goods. Will you please go over to the
airport and get a cargo inventory?"

Three minutes later, Jim returned to the office. "The cargo was 1,000
bolts of Japanese silk," Jim reported. "I got the information over the
telephone from a member of the crew."

When Jim left, Frank, the $1,000-a-month brother, was called. The
supervisor repeated the instructions.

An hour later, Frank was back in the office with a list showing that
the plane carried 1,000 bolts of Japanese silk, 500 transistor radios,
and 1,000 hand-painted bamboo trays.

George, the $1,500-a-month brother, was given identical instructions.

Working hours were over when he finally returned. "The transport
plane carried 1,000 bolts of Japanese silk," he began. "It was on sale
at $60 a bolt, so I took a two-day option on the whole lot. I have wired
a designer in New York, offering the silk at $75 per bolt. I expect to
have the order tomorrow. I also found 500 transistor radios, which I
sold over the telephone at a profit of $2.30 each. There were 1,000
bamboo trays, but they were of poor quality, so I didn't try to do
anything with them."

When George left the office, the employer smiled. "You probably
noticed," he said, "that Jim doesn't do what he's told, Frank does only
what he's told, but George does without being told."

283

The moral of the story? The amount of extra effort you exert can directly affect your chances for advancement. The future is full of promise for the one who shows initiative.

SUBJECT/TITLE INDEX

This is a subject/title index identifying all entries in volumes 1, 2, 3, 4, and 5 of *Especially for Mormons*. Subjects are in roman face; titles are in italics. The number preceding the colon indicates the particular volume; the numbers following the colon indicate the page number(s) within that particular volume upon which that subject or title will be found. Semicolons separate each individual entry.